REASONING PRACTICALLY

REASONING PRACTICALLY

Edited by Edna Ullmann-Margalit

New York   Oxford
Oxford University Press
2000

Oxford University Press

Oxford   New York
Athens   Auckland   Bangkok   Bogotá   Buenos Aires   Calcutta
Cape Town   Chennai   Dar es Salaam   Delhi   Florence   Hong Kong   Istanbul
Karachi   Kuala Lumpur   Madrid   Melbourne   Mexico City   Mumbai
Nairobi   Paris   São Paulo   Singapore   Taipei   Tokyo   Toronto   Warsaw

and assoicated companies in
Berlin   Ibadan

Copyright © 2000 by Oxford University Press

Published by Oxford University Press, Inc.
198 Madison Avenue, New York, New York 10016

Oxford is a registered trademark of Oxford University Press

All rights reserved. No part of this publication may be reproduced,
stored in a retrieval system, or transmitted, in any form or by any means,
electronic, mechanical, photocopying, recording, or otherwise,
without the prior permission of Oxford University Press.

Library of Congress Cataloging-in-Publication Data
Reasoning practically / edited by Edna Ullmann-Margalit.
p.   cm.
Papers presented at the 11th Jerusalem Philosophical Encounter, 1996.
ISBN 0-19-512551-7
1. Reasoning—Congresses.   2. Practice (Philosophy)—Congresses.
I. Ullmann-Margalit, Edna.   II. Jerusalem Philosophical Encounter
(11th : 1996)
BC177.R344   1999
128'.33—dc21   98-44043

9 8 7 6 5 4 3 2 1

Printed in the United States of America
on acid free paper

ACKNOWLEDGMENTS

This volume contains papers delivered at the Eleventh Jerusalem Philosophical Encounters held in Jerusalem in January 1996 under the auspices of the S. H. Bergman Center for Philosophical Studies at the Hebrew University of Jerusalem. I am grateful to Professor Yirmiyahu Yovel, the founder and general editor of the Jerusalem Philosophical Encounters, for having entrusted me with the conference on Practical Reasoning, and to Ms. Tal Kochavi for her assistance in the organization of the conference. I also want to thank the Institute for Advanced Study in Princeton, SCASSS in Uppsala, Sweden, and the Center for Rationality and Interactive Decision Theory at the Hebrew University, who provided the environments and the facilities that helped this volume along. David Heyd, Avishai Margalit, and Cass Sunstein deserve special thanks for their special contributions to the shaping of both form and content of this volume.

Samuel Scheffler's chapter was first published in *Philosophy and Public Affairs* (Summer 1997); my gratitude goes to Princeton University Press and to the editors of the journal for their kind permission to reprint this article. Seyla Benhabib's chapter was first published in *Theoria* 90 (1997); I thank the publishers for their kind permission to reprint the article. Ariela Lazar's chapter also appears in *The Philosophy of Donald Davidson*, ed. Lewis Hahn, Library of Living Philosophers, volume 27, Open Court, 1999.

CONTENTS

List of Contributors   ix
Introduction   3
    Edna Ullmann-Margalit

Part I: *The Practical and the Theoretical*

    1. Objectivity and Practical Reason   17
        Donald Davidson
    2. Practical Reasoning   27
        Barry Stroud

Part II: *Reasoning about Practice*

    3. Akrasia and the Principle of Continence,
        or What the Tortoise Would Say to Achilles   41
        Ariela Lazar
    4. When Practical Reason Plays Dice   58
        David Heyd
    5. On Not Wanting to Know   72
        Edna Ullmann-Margalit
    6. Ordering Selves   85
        Marcia Cavell
    7. Practical Reason and Incompletely Theorized Agreements   98
        Cass R. Sunstein

Part III: The Practice Reasoned About

8. Relationships and Responsibilities   123
    Samuel Scheffler
9. Love's Dominion   138
    Yael Tamir
10. Practical Reason and Moral Certainty:
    The Case of Discrimination   151
    Janet Radcliffe Richards
11. The Embattled Public Sphere:
    Hannah Arendt, Jürgen Habermas, and Beyond   164
    Seyla Benhabib
12. Morally Speaking   182
    Gerald Dworkin

LIST OF CONTRIBUTORS

Seyla Benhabib, Department of Government, Harvard University
Marcia Cavell, Department of Philosophy, University of California at Berkeley
Donald Davidson, Department of Philosophy, University of California at Berkeley
Gerald Dworkin, Department of Philosophy, University of California at Davis
David Heyd, Department of Philosophy, The Hebrew University of Jerusalem
Ariela Lazar, Department of Philosophy, Northwestern University
Janet Radcliffe Richards, the Open University, England
Samuel Scheffler, Department of Philosophy, University of California at Berkeley
Barry Stroud, Department of Philosophy, University of California at Berkeley
Cass R. Sunstein, The Law School, University of Chicago
Yael Tamir, Department of Philosophy, Tel-Aviv University
Edna Ullmann-Margalit, Center for Rationality and Interactive Decision Theory, The Hebrew University of Jerusalem

REASONING PRACTICALLY

INTRODUCTION

Edna Ullmann-Margalit

I

Taken broadly, reasoning practically is an enquiry into the nature of reason, reasoning, and reasons—as well as of rationale, rationalization, and rationality. It is meant to ponder how we think about what to do, how we move from thinking to doing, and what may come between our thinking and our doing. All of this offers a wide scope for philosophizing. Hume said, famously, that when we act, our reason is slave to our passions. Kant said, famously, that among the four big questions a philosopher should address are What can I know, and What am I to do? Practical reason deals with the link, often elusive, between the realm of reason and the province of practice. It is concerned to find out how far can a parallel be pushed between practical reasoning, which is about what I am to do, and theoretical reasoning, which is about what I am to believe—and where this parallel breaks down.

To gain a better understanding of practical reasoning, it may be helpful to focus further on what distinguishes practical from theoretical reasoning. One approach to answering this question emphasizes the qualifier "practical," the other emphasizes the component of "reasoning." According to the first approach, the two types of reasoning differ in their *subject matter:* they are supposed to be *about* different things. According to the second approach, the two types of reasoning are supposed to differ in their *logic*.

Let us start with the first, more traditional approach. It says that theoretical reasoning is about what is, and practical reasoning is about what is to be done. The division it advocates is reflected in the disciplinary division of some Continental philosophy departments into theoretical (or speculative) philosophy on the one hand and practical philosophy on the other. Each sub-department is supposed to deal with different areas of philosophy: metaphysics, epistemology, and logic belong in the first, moral, legal, and political philosophy belong in the second.

To be sure, this is no mere bureaucratic division. The history of the division goes back to Aristotle. The modern rationale behind it is the fact-value distinction. The value-free concerns of philosophy are considered theoretical, while the value-laden concerns of philosophy are considered practical. Now an attitude of suspicion is sometimes expressed toward the fact-value distinction. One way to understand this is in terms of a suspicion that the theoretical side of the divide may not be as purely value-free as it purports to be. The charge here is that even statements that appear to be clearly observational, factual, and objective may turn out to disguise interests and evaluative biases. On the practical side of the divide, however, values certainly play a major role. It is considered to be in the nature of pronouncements about morals or politics that they are largely evaluative. In other words, legitimate doubts may be expressed as to whether theoretical reasoning can neatly be taken to be concerned with the "is" alone. There can be no doubt, however, that practical reasoning is concerned with going back and forth between the "is" and the "ought."

Denying the validity of the fact-value distinction in this vein has the effect of blurring the divide between theoretical and practical reasoning by essentially relegating the domain of the theoretical into the practical. At the same time a parallel move blurs the divide in just the opposite direction and revolves around an offshoot of the fact-value distinction, namely, the belief-desire distinction. This offshoot distinction is of course pivotal to any attempt to tell the theoretical apart from the practical. Our beliefs are about facts, in the sense that they reflect what we take to be the case, and our desires presuppose values, at the same time as they engender them. The move I refer to insists that desires play no special role in practical reasoning, since their only relevance to practical reasoning is through one's beliefs about them. There is no difference in this respect between one's future desires, the desires of others, and one's own present desires. All of these enter into one's reasoning via one's beliefs about them.[1] In this way, trying to determine the best thing to do is not really different from trying to determine what is the case. So this move assigns to beliefs the central role both in practical and in theoretical reasoning. Thus, this move has the effect of blurring the divide between theoretical and practical reasoning by essentially relegating the domain of the practical into the theoretical.

Or consider this formulation: "Practical reasoning is simply theoretical reasoning done with a view to eventual action."[2] One natural way to understand this is to take the phrase "done with a view to eventual action" as a qualifier of theoretical reasoning. But on this reading, the phrase "done with a view to eventual action" is rendered the specific difference of practical reasoning, which is thereby taken to belong, once again, within the genus of theoretical reasoning. It may be suggested, however, that what looks like a qualifying phrase does not really qualify the attribution of "theoretical reasoning," but rather that it excludes it altogether. Just as a fake diamond is not a specific sort of diamond but rather a non-diamond, so too, the suggestion goes, a theoretical reasoning done with a view to eventual action may not be a specific sort of theoretical reasoning but a non-theoretical reasoning altogether.

Still, the integrity of practical reasoning as a branch of philosophy with its own distinct subject matter may be defended on independent grounds. It is possible to argue, for example, that the separate areas of moral, legal, and political philosophy, which are supposed according to the first approach to constitute the branch of practical philosophy, share a distinct set of underlying basic concepts. Prominent among them are rights, duties, responsibilities, and justice; power and authority; reasons, rules, principles, and norms. In addition to sharing basic concepts, these practical areas may be shown to share some major basic problems, notable among them being the question of rationality in action. Alternatively, the integrity of practical reasoning as a branch of philosophy may be defended by arguing that the concern with the basic notions of values, reasons, and norms—both substantively and formally—distinguishes practical from theoretical reasoning.[3] Appropriately, within this approach the central problem of practical reasoning, if one such problem can be identified, is the justification of ultimate values. This is a fundamental epistemological question distinct from the questions of relative justification of evaluative statements with which practical reasoning is replete. The possibility of giving satisfactory answers to the latter relies on there being a satisfactory answer to the fundamental question of ultimate values.

Let us move on now to the second approach, which says that practical reasoning differs from theoretical reasoning in the way it *reasons*. This means that reasoning practically, which is concerned with what to do, is somehow different logically from reasoning theoretically, which is concerned with what to believe. But, surely, reasoning—if understood as the transition, according to some rules, from premises to conclusion—is reasoning, is reasoning. True, the conclusion in one type of case is a statement about what is the case, and in the other type of case it is a statement about what had better be done. Still, why should there be a difference in the reasoning leading up to it? Indeed, how *can* there be a difference in the reasoning leading up to it?

One suggestion that may appear to offer some solution here is Gilbert Harman's idea of distinguishing between reasoning and argument.[4] "Argument," for him, is the familiar logic-related notion that we are used to associating with "reasoning." It is argument that is concerned with the transition from premises to conclusion. It is argument that has to do with a theory of implication. The term "reasoning" he reserves for something quite different, what he refers to as "immediate modification in view" in response to new knowledge and new situations.

However, even without getting into the thick of what is meant by "view" and the ways it is supposed to be modified, we may point to one aspect of this suggestion that, for our purposes, is a disappointing snag. The snag is that, contrary to what we may have expected, "argument" is not the department of the theoretical, nor is "reasoning" the department of the practical. Rather, within the realm of reasoning itself we find a division into a theoretical component and a practical component. The theoretical component of reasoning deals with reasoned revisions of beliefs, and the practical component of reasoning deals with reasoned revisions of intentions. In other words, it is according to what the revision procedures are *about*—whether they revise one's beliefs or whether they revise one's plans of action—that the theoretical is distinguished from the practical. So we find ourselves with a new twist on the theoretical-practical divide, which is here located within the confines of Harman's idiosyncratic "reasoning." But this new twist brings us back to the first, traditional, approach, according to which the theoretical-practical divide separates different subject matters. And the question still eludes us: how can reasoning about practical matters differ, qua reasoning, from reasoning about theoretical matters?

There is a view, whose roots go back to antiquity, according to which reasoning practically must differ from reasoning theoretically because its conclusion is not a statement or a proposition at all, but an action. This view, as it stands, it too coarse and unwieldy to provide a solution. Practical reasoning is, to be sure, meant to lead to action. But the action taken—if indeed an action *is* taken after practical reasoning runs its course—is an event in time. And as such it can hardly be considered a conclusion, which is a logical construct, derived from premises, which are also logical constructs. Unless one attributes causal efficacy to the proposition that is the conclusion of practical reasoning, the rendering of action as the conclusion of practical reasoning can be taken only as metaphorical—or simply confused.

This confusion, however, has an important advantage. It underlines the need to pay much closer attention to the nature of the conclusion of a piece of practical reasoning. In particular, it underlines the need to pay much closer attention to how a conclusion might possibly be linked with—and lead to—action. Indeed, most philosophers sympathetic to this second approach with regard to what distinguishes practical from theoretical reasoning do just that: they focus on the conclusion.

Suppose we start with the assumption that practical reasoning reflects an agent's deliberation aimed at discovering what is the best thing for him or for her to do in the circumstances. And suppose the conclusion reached is something like: "So the (best; right) thing for me to do in the circumstances is A." However, if this is so, then as far as I can see there is no reason not to regard this piece of reasoning as theoretical. From the agent's various premises—both factual and evaluative in nature, recording both relevant beliefs and relevant desires—the agent draws a theoretical conclusion about what action would be best, all things considered. In other words, the agent has engaged in a piece of reasoning terminating in a conclusion that is a *belief* about what is best to do in the circumstances, all things considered. This is like solving a problem, like calculating from given data to a solution. This brings us back to David Pears's formulation, that practical reasoning is simply theoretical reasoning done with a view to eventual action.

It may be well to pause here briefly to note the following analogy. The notion that one may reason theoretically about practice is not more paradoxical than that one may reason deductively about probabilities. True, we usually associate probabilities with non-deductive (or "inductive") reasoning—when the conclusion is not necessitated by the premises, and hence cannot be detached from them, but is rather probabilized by them. But there are perfectly valid deductive arguments *about* probabilities: "This die has 6 sides; this die is fair; *therefore*, the probability that this die will fall on 6 is 1/6." Here a conclusion, which is a statement about probability, is necessitated by the premises. So the pertinent distinction is between a probabilistic argument and an argument about probabilities. In analogy, we are here talking about a distinction between practical reasoning on the one hand and reasoning about practice on the other. We seem to have established that there can be reasoning about practice, and that, qua reasoning, it can be regarded as theoretical. Moreover, practical and theoretical reasoning may actually intertwine in various other ways. They intertwine, for example, to the extent that my intending to do something involves my believing that I will do it. They may also intertwine in the opposite direction, to the extent that my theoretical reasoning may involve beliefs about what I am going to do. Even so, is there a distinct kind of reasoning that we may be justified in calling practical?

Note, also, that the conclusion in the form "So the (best; right) thing for me to do in the circumstances is A" could easily be recast as "So the (best, right) thing for *the agent* to do in the circumstances is A." That is to say, there is nothing essentially first-person in the piece of reasoning we have so far been considering. It is possible to give to a third person all the relevant data about me: my beliefs, desires, values, and my situation. This person may then proceed to calculate the best solution, so to speak, to my practical deliberation problem. Philosophers of practical reasoning still debate whether or not an analysis of practical reasoning is acceptable in which there is nothing essentially first-person.

Yet if there is to be something distinct about reasoning practically, it would seem that the conclusion of the piece of reasoning we are considering has to be reevaluated. The expectation is that a conclusion should not merely report a solution to a problem. It should somehow be linked more tightly to the ensuing action. Further, it should somehow be more intimately linked, in a first-person sort of way, to the deliberating agent.

So perhaps we can attribute to the conclusion of a piece of practical reasoning a special semantics, which will be able to fulfill a dual role: it should report what action is the solution to the agent's deliberating problem, and at the same time it should set him or her about that action. As it is sometimes put, the conclusion cannot remain in the form of "So the thing to do is —": it must rather be transformed into something like "So I shall—." This major transformation already takes the conclusion one crucial step beyond the mere spelling out of a solution. It suggests the actual adoption of the solution as one's future course of action: it expresses one's forming the appropriate intention to do it. "So I shall—" is thus to be taken as both a declarative statement and a performative. It is meant, in other words, to fulfill both a linguistic and an extra-linguistic function: the former states that A is the thing for me to do, the latter performs the act of committing my will to A-ing. When construed in this way, the conclusion of a piece of practical reasoning does indeed have an essential first-person aspect, because of the element of the formation of an intention, or the "commitment of the will," which it involves. It is in this spirit that we should understand Pears when he talks about the "reciprocal sensitivity" of the conclusion sentence, which both annunciates and self-instructs at the same time.[5] And I take something like this to be the impetus behind Donald Davidson's construal of the conclusion of practical reasoning as "an all-out evaluative judgment in favor of A-ing."

Let us pause to reflect on these attempts to figure out the nature of the conclusion of a piece of practical reasoning and to analyze its special semantics. We cannot help but feel awe in face of what looks like heroic attempts to bridge the gap between thinking and doing. These are attempts to bring thinking, or deliberating, or reasoning, about action as close as possible to the very acting itself. Recall that earlier, when considering the first approach to practical reasoning, I asked what the central problem of practical reasoning is. The answer given there was: the justification of ultimate values. We may now ask the same question within the second approach. The answer here will have to be that practical reasoning is concerned with bridging the gap between thinking and doing. This can be put, somewhat tongue-in-cheek, as follows. The central problem of practical reasoning within the first approach is strongly linked with the famous philosophical problem of the nature of the gap between "is" and "ought": can values, that is, "oughts," be justified in terms of facts, that is, in terms of how the world *is?* Now within the second approach, the central problem of practical reasoning is the nature of the gap between both "is" and "ought," taken together, and "do." This is so, because the central problem of practical reasoning within the second approach was formulated as bridging the gap between thinking and doing. The thinking part comprises both beliefs, that is, "is statements," and evaluations, or "ought statements." And the problem is the way the passage is effected from the "is"-*cum*-"ought" to "do." Behind all this lies a vision of practical reasoning whose ideal is to combine people's desires, values, intentions—and eventually actions—and to mesh them smoothly with their beliefs, so as to form a unified rational system.

Before turning to further reflections on how successful we may expect such an enterprise to be, let me add one further contribution to the enterprise itself. I would like to suggest that there is a word in the English vocabulary singularly suited to express the dual function expected of the conclusion of practical reasoning. This word is *resolution.* "To resolve" is *both* "to find a solution for," *and* "to reach a firm decision about." We may thus see the deliberating agent as concluding her practical reasoning with a resolution. This is to be construed as follows: (a) The agent arrives at a solution to the deliberating problem that confronts her. This aspect of the resolution is still in the realm of theory; it corresponds to "So the thing to do is A." (b) The agent resolves to do A: she makes up her mind, she commits her will, she forms an intention, she sets herself to act. This aspect of the resolution reaches beyond the theoretical realm: it takes a performative leap. This corresponds to "So I shall A."

This, in my view, is as far as we can go. This is as much as the gap between reasoning and acting can be bridged; no semantic sleight of hand can narrow it any further. And this is as it should be. One advantage of this approach to practical reasoning is precisely in highlighting the gap that remains. And it is in this gap that many of the interesting things—both psychologically and philosophically—happen. We can now ask meaningful questions about what may come between one's thinking and one's doing. Suppose the agent has reached a resolution, in the double sense just described, to do A. Well, *will* the agent do A? Normally, perhaps, yes. But much can come between one's resolve to do something and one's actually doing it. One may change one's mind, or break a leg, or die. Also, numerous pathologies are possible here. Prominent among them, in the philosophical interest it arouses, is the cluster of phenomena characterized as *akrasia:* succumbing to temptation, or acting against one's better judgment, or displaying weakness of will. Thus, the agent reaches the resolution not to light up another cigarette but nevertheless goes ahead and does just that. Indeed, pathologies need not all occur at the stage between the resolve to do something and actually doing it. They may occur earlier and prevent agents from successfully taking the performative leap. That is, an agent who has reached a resolution in sense (a) and has formed the belief as to what is the best (right) thing to do in the circumstances, all things considered, may nevertheless fail to make the switch to sense (b), which involves committing himself or herself to actually doing it. Self-destructive patterns of behavior, failure to desire to do what is best or right for one to do, forgetfulness and inattention, as well as the phenomenon of self-deception, are among the factors that may be at work here.[6]

So the line of investigation that tries to see where practical reasoning differs, qua reasoning, from theoretical reasoning, achieves several results. It arrives at some fine-tuning of the nature of the piece of reasoning involved. This includes the peculiar blend of belief premises, desire premises, and evaluative premises characteristic of it, and in particular the nature of the conclusion. At the same time this line of investigation enables us to face the limits of this analysis. And these limits, once confronted, open up new vistas and suggest further questions for practical reasoning to deal with. Put differently, this line of investigation leads to results that may be seen as telling a normal, or *standard,* story of how thinking leads to action. But the very notion of the normal or standard points to the varieties of *deviations* from it. That is, it points to possibilities that things might go wrong: that thinking might fail to lead to action, or, sometimes, that action might preempt thinking.

The inquiry into practical reasoning is thus, in part, an inquiry into the constraints of human deliberation. Theoretical reasoning is envisaged not only as uncontaminated by values: it is also envisaged as unfettered. It is concerned with reality but it is unconstrained by reality. Practical reasoning, in contrast, is seen as constrained. It is constrained by the realities of the deliberation situation and by bounded rationality. Reasoning practically is subject, for example, to conditions such as weakness of the will. It is subject to motivational biases, as well as to emotional limitations on the human capacity to deal with painful or stressful information. It is subject to limited information, as well as to cognitive limitations on the human capacity to possess, process, and compute complex information. All of these are further compounded when time constraints are taken into consideration. Thus, it may often happen that the time to act arrives before the appropriate reasoning could be completed. Interestingly, sometimes it is known in advance that time constraints will not allow the reasoning process to take its full course, and hence alternative short-cut devices may have to be devised ahead of time. A piece of practical reasoning may be stuck because it yields a tie, or because heterogeneity is such that no conclusion can be agreed upon.

Consider, again, the ideal mentioned before, of combining people's desires, values, intentions, and eventually actions, together with their beliefs, so as to form a unified rational system. This ideal may fail, ultimately, because people may fail to be rational. The inquiry into practical reasoning is thus, also, an inquiry into people's irrationality.

II

In the second part of the introduction I want to locate the contributions to this volume onto the grids offered in the first part. In so doing, I will retrace some of the steps of the first part. The way the volume is organized, the chapters forming its first two parts operate, broadly, within the second, reasoning-oriented, approach to practical reasoning. The more traditional, subject-matter-oriented approach is represented by the chapters forming the final part of the volume.

The first two chapters in the book elucidate some of the formal features of practical reasoning and consider to what extent reasoning practically is distinguished, qua reasoning, from theoretical reasoning. Intriguingly, both try to push the parallels between the two brands of reasoning, rather than the differences between them, as far as they possibly can.

In "Objectivity and Practical Reason" Donald Davidson offers a cognitivist approach to evaluative judgments. He argues that evaluative judgments (moral ones in particular) are objectively true or false in the same way judgments of "fact" are, thereby neutralizing the charge of subjectivity sometimes leveled at the value-based practical reasoning. He urges that Humean views err, first, in supposing it makes sense to ask whether *values* are in the world or projected by us. But it is the objects and events we value that are mostly out in the world, along with the things that are heavy, green, or elected: there are no such "things" as values, and so no particular place for them to be. Nor, second, are evaluative judgments subjective in being somehow dependent on valuers like us. To claim this is to confuse the fact that if there were no valuers, or people with eyes, no one would judge that things had values or colors, with the idea that values and colors are therefore person-dependent in a way that primary properties are not. In addition, he urges that no one has succeeded in giving a coherent account of the meaning of sentential connectives (like "'not,' "and," and "or") that does not treat them as truth-functional. Since evaluative sentences often turn up in sentences containing such connectives, we must treat the evaluative sentences as having truth values. On the positive side, he tries to show that the contents of evaluative judgments are determined in the same way as the content of other sentences: by the circumstances in which people apply evaluative predicates. We do not expect total agreement between observers of the values of things, or of their colors, or their weights. But communication depends, in values as elsewhere, on a sufficient mass of agreement and an ability to explain disagreement. Interpretation and inter-subjectivity are, Davidson tells us, the basis for objectivity; understanding depends on finding common ground.

In "Practical Reasoning" Barry Stroud takes up the question whether practical reasoning is "essentially first-personal," and concludes that it is not. Given the starting point that reasoning practically is about settling the practical question of the form "What should I do," Stroud argues that someone else, who is informed about my beliefs, desires, and values, as well as about my particular situation, may well ask—and answer—that question. Whatever is thought to be special or unique about practical reasoning is, according to Stroud, not that it contains a special kind of reasoning. Trying to determine what is the best thing to do is like trying to find out what is true or what to believe; another person's answer to the question might be right and the agent's own answer wrong. Stroud goes on to argue that the thought that others can answer questions about what a certain agent should do presents no threat to that agent's autonomy.

The chapters in the second part take seriously the idea that the inquiry into practical reasoning should investigate the constraints on human deliberation and the irrational deviations from the standard model of the route from thought to action.

In "Akrasia and the Principle of Continence" Ariela Lazar takes up the phenomenon of acting against one's better judgment. This phenomenon poses a problem for theories of practical reasoning, she says, since it focuses on the possibility that the conclusion of practical reasoning—the agent's best judgment—does not correspond to the agent's actual behavior. Normally we explain an action by reporting the agent's reasoning and its conclusion. How might we explain an action that deviates from one's better judgment? Lazar critically examines Donald Davidson's influential attempt to explain the performance of akratic actions and offers the fundamentals of an alternative solution to the puzzle. She contends that the psychological explanation of action by appeal to reason must be supplemented by appeal to psychological factors that are not reasons. In addition, she explores more generally the role of the principles of rationality in the explanation of action as well as the point of failure of the akratic agent. Lazar thus demonstrates how the study of deviant action may provide instructive lessons for the general study of action and of practical reasoning.

David Heyd, too, is concerned with exploring the limitations and possible failures of practical reasoning. In his "When Practical Reason Plays Dice" Heyd compares lotteries to akrasia on the one hand and to self-deception on the other. He sees all of these as exemplifying forms of failure of practical reason, which he further characterizes as either conative or cognitive. Focusing on lotteries, Heyd argues that they are principled responses to the failures of practical reason in that they can be rationally justified. Not doing—"just this once"—what one knows to be the right thing to do, or not wanting to know what one knows to be true, can be explained, says Heyd, but cannot be justified. In contrast, lotteries constitute responses to particular failures of practical reason to guide action that can be supported rationally. Among the grounds he offers for such rational support are pragmatic ones, and, most importantly, grounds of fairness.

Does not wanting to know, as Heyd suggests, necessarily involve self-deception? In "On Not Wanting to Know" I argue that it does not. Given the common assumption that in order to be good practical reasoners agents have to act on the basis of the totality of evidence available to them, the chapter explores various aspects of the phenomenon of not wanting to know in an attempt to find out whether it is indeed inherently unreasonable. The exploration leads to the conclusion that it is often eminently reasonable. First, the principle of total evidence is weakened by replacing it with a rebuttable presumption in favor of additional knowledge. The sustainability of this presumption is then examined in light of the large variety of circumstances in which it seems to be reasonably rebutted. The alternative that I recommend in the end is to give up any rule or presumption and to adopt instead something like a case by case cost-benefit approach where the value of additional knowledge is matched against its cost.

In "Ordering Selves" Marcia Cavell raises a somewhat parallel question, regarding the extent to which not knowledge but desires, both first order and second order, are characterized by an openness to evidence. More broadly, she is concerned with the question of what does being the author of one's actions consist of. She takes her cue from Harry Frankfurt's essays in moral philosophy, which attempt to offer an account of personhood and to articulate a relationship between autonomy and the structure of the will. Among Frankfurt's conditions for autonomy is reflexive self-consciousness, that is, the agent's ability to make his or her own desires the object of second-order desires. Cavell takes issue with Frankfurt, arguing that he makes assumptions about what a "self" is that skew his conclusions about pathologies of the will and its ideal condition. Pathologies of the will are sometimes a function of problematic interpersonal relations, and of ways in which agents may contrive, in order to protect their relations with others, to close off certain of their desires and beliefs from being known to them. This discussion, which echoes themes in both chapters 3 and 5, leads Cavell to an account of autonomy that emphasizes, first, the place of one's relations with others in constituting the self and, second, the way desires are connected with dialogical and public in reasons.

In "Practical Reason and Incompletely Theorized Agreements" Cass Sunstein addresses a question that relates to the public rather than the private domain. His concern is with the potential failure, or limitation, of collective rather than individual practical reasoning. He asks how, in reasoning practically, agents can extricate themselves in face of fundamental disagreements and heterogeneity. In a heterogenous society disagreements often involve the most important issues of social life: the distribution of wealth, the role of race and gender, the nature of free speech and private property. He argues that political and legal institutions often work through incompletely theorized agreements. Sometimes these agreements involve abstractions, accepted amidst severe disagreements on particular cases. People who disagree on pornography and hate speech can accept a general free-speech principle, and those who argue about homosexuality and disability can accept an abstract antidiscrimination principle. But sometimes incompletely theorized agreements involve concrete outcomes rather than abstractions, and this is an important source of social stability and also a way for diverse people to show each other a kind of mutual respect. Incompletely theorized agreements have an especially notable feature: they enlist silence, on certain basic questions, as a device for producing convergence despite disagreement, uncertainty, limits of time and capacity, and heterogeneity. Because such agreements bracket the largest sources of social disputes, they have special virtues in pluralistic societies, and indeed in all institutions that contain enduring disagreements.

Recall now the first approach to the question of what distinguishes practical from theoretical reasoning discussed in the first part of the introduction. According to this approach, the division of the terrain between the two types of reasoning has primarily to do with the question of subject matter: there are things about which we typically reason practically. As I pointed out, it is the areas of moral, legal, and political philosophy that are supposed in this approach to constitute the branch of practical philosophy. The chapters in the last part of this book belong here. Indeed, these chapters concern some of the prominent and distinct underlying basic concepts that were mentioned as those shared by political, moral, and legal philosophy. These concepts notably include rights, duties, responsibilities, and justice. They also invariably hark back to the notions of reasons, rules, principles, and norms.

Samuel Scheffler, in "Relationships and Responsibilities," asks how do we come to have responsibilities to some people—family, neighbors, compatriots—that we do not have to others. This question bears directly on a number of the most important debates in contemporary moral and political philosophy: for example, it bears on the debates between consequentialism and deontology, between liberalism and communitarianism, and between nationalism and cosmopolitanism. And Scheffler's answer to this question ties the notion of special responsibilities firmly with the notions of value and reasons for action. He is concerned to offer an alternative account to the powerful voluntarist tradition, which holds that all genuine "special responsibilities" must arise from consent or from other suitably voluntary acts. In his alternative account, one's relationships to other people give rise to special responsibilities to those people when they are relationships that one has reason to value. This view depends crucially on the claim that to value one's relationship to another person is just, in part, to see the relationship as a source of reasons for action of a distinctive kind, and, furthermore, that this is tantamount to seeing the relationship as a source of special responsibilities. An adequate understanding of special responsibilities requires, Scheffler argues, that we attend to the ways in which the interests of people with whom we have interpersonal relationships enter into our practical reasoning.

In a related chapter, entitled "Love's Dominion," Yael Tamir takes issue with the idea that the sole source of special responsibilities is relationships one has reason to value. The implication of Scheffler's "value-dependent" view is that no claims at all arise from relations that one considers degrading or demeaning or such that undermine rather than enhance human flourishing. Tamir argues, in contrast, that what she refers to as personal responsibilities sometimes follow from attachments that defy human growth, dignity, and respect. She discusses, as examples, such cases as ill-treated parents, exploited friends, or abused spouses and focuses especially on the story of Dora Carrington.

If the former two chapters focus on special responsibilities, the next one focuses on justice, or, more precisely, on injustice. In "Practical Reason and Moral Certainty: The Case of Discrimination" Janet Radcliffe Richards takes up the nature of the particular kind of injustice attaching to group disadvantage. She is concerned to evaluate the moral strength and legitimacy of the complaints it gives rise to and to work out how to identify forms of remedial action. Radcliffe Richards views her treatment of the particular issue of discrimination as exemplifying her general approach to practical reasoning in moral contexts. The general approach stems from the idea, discussed in the first part of the introduction, that practical reasoning is importantly constrained by time considerations. Since we cannot postpone practical decisions until philosophers have worked out the whole truth about ethics, Radcliffe Richards urges us to try starting at the other end, "with any snippets of moral certainty we can find," and see how far into other contexts that certainty can legitimately extend. Her argument results in an account that unexpectedly places discrimination in attitudes and dispositions rather than in actions and policies. This result helps underline Radcliffe Richards's methodological point, that it is possible to outline a policy direction that can be taken with confidence or agreement by people who are puzzled or otherwise disagree about wider questions of morality and politics. The latter point echoes the central theme in Cass Sunstein's contribution to this book, discussed earlier.

A different echo resonates in Seyla Benhabib's essay. She, like Sunstein, relates to practical reasoning primarily through the prism of the collective rather than the individual deliberator. In "The Embattled Public Sphere" Benhabib takes it to be a regulative ideal of democracy that we must view the major decisions of the public bodies of our polities "as if" they resulted from a deliberation among individuals considered as free and equal agents. Such processes of free and unconstrained deliberation among equals are implicit in the ideals of "government of the people, by the people, and for the people." The public sphere refers to the processes whereby the rationality, as well as legitimacy, of democratic decisions are submitted to examination. Her chapter examines various models of the public in the light of these broader normative considerations. She discusses Hannah Arendt's model of "public space," as contrasted with Jürgen Habermas's model of the "public sphere" and with John Rawls's formulations about "public reason." She also argues that a distinction must be drawn between the normative principle of the public sphere as a regulative ideal and its institutional embodiments that have varied throughout history.

Still within the framework of concern with the set of basic concepts that constitute the common denominators of politics, ethics, and law, Gerald Dworkin's chapter takes up the intriguing question of when do we consider a moral judgment hypocritical and why do we reject it as such. His hypothesis is that investigating in a systematic fashion the idea of "being in a position to" make various moral judgments is a useful way of increasing our understanding of what it is to accept a standard of conduct for oneself and what is involved in criticizing others for failing to adhere to a justified standard. An investigation of what goes into taking up a critical attitude toward others, as well as toward ourselves, is in Dworkin's view important for the study of practical reasoning qua reasoning done with a view to eventual action.

Notes

1. See Thomas Nagel, *The Possibility of Altruism*, Oxford: Oxford University Press, 1970.
2. David Pears, "Practical Reasoning," in Edna Ullmann-Margalit (ed.), *The Prism of Science*, Dordrecht: Reidel, 1986, p. 95.
3. See Joseph Raz's introduction to his *Practical Reason and Norms*, Princeton, New Jersey: Princeton University Press, [1975], 1990, p. 10.
4. Gilbert Harman, *Change in View*, Cambridge, Mass.: MIT Press, 1986.
5. Pears, "Practical Reasoning" (see n. 2), p. 102.
6. For an account of "motivational skepticism," that is, skepticism about the scope and force of reason as a motive, see Christine M. Korsgaard, "Skepticism about Practical Reason," *The Journal of Philosophy*, vol. 83, no. 1, 1986: 5–25.

Part I

The Practical and the Theoretical

1

OBJECTIVITY AND PRACTICAL REASON

Donald Davidson

One part of the brain, the amygdala, is responsible for emotional or evaluative responses to perceived facts. Another part of the brain, the hippocampus, assigns to those same facts a degree of belief or subjective probability. In other words, beliefs and desires, the main explainers of action and intention, employ quite different bits of gray matter. So striking is the effect that if the amygdala of a human adult is severely damaged, the emotive response to normally disagreeable stimuli (say a sudden loud noise) is suppressed, though the existence of the stimulus is accurately noted, while an adult whose hippocampus is damaged displays the appropriate emotion in response to the same stimulus, but fails to record its cause.[1]

It is somewhat surprising that a person can respond positively or negatively to a stimulus he or she apparently does not know to be present; it is more surprising that a person can know he or she is experiencing a normally painful stimulus and yet fail to respond appropriately. But however separable they may be as responses, the onset of belief and the onset of desire in such cases have a common cause, the stimulus itself. Furthermore, both beliefs and desires are, as we like to say, propositional, that is, they have the sort of content we attribute to declarative sentences. We desire it to be true *that* the loud sound stops (without necessarily believing there is a loud sound); we believe *that* there is a loud sound (without necessarily wanting it to stop). Or, to take a more normal example, we desire it to be true *that* we learn the meaning of the word "amygdala"; we believe *that* we will find out what "amygdala" means by looking in the OED. Given this desire and belief, we may be prompted to take the appropriate volume of the OED down from the shelf. (We will be disappointed: the word is not in the OED. Better look in Webster's Third.)

Philosophers interested in morality and action hardly need to appeal to the anatomy of the brain and ingenious experiments on subjects who have been seriously brain-damaged to be persuaded that there is a basic difference between motivational states like desires and cognitive states like beliefs. Much of the history of moral philosophy, ancient and modern, concerns the question how the distinction is to be drawn. How should it be drawn? Richard Jeffrey's ingenious version of decision theory sees it as I have just set it up: two attitudes toward items in the same set of propositions.[2] The distinction then emerges almost automatically: the natural constraints on a rational set of beliefs and desires induce quite different forms of measurement on the two attitudes: beliefs support a ratio scale, desires support an interval scale. The reason for this formal difference springs from an intuitively clear distinction. Beliefs have inherent positive and negative limits, certainty and total disbelief. Some propositions we are certain are true, some we are certain are false. All other degrees of belief fall between these end points. Zero degree of belief is fixed; tradition and convenience put certainty at one. Desire is not like this. No matter how much we want some proposition to be true, we can imagine that there may be some other proposition we would prefer were true. Similarly for those propositions we would detest to find true. The scale of better and worse has no natural limits.

But hasn't this analysis of the difference between cognitive and evaluative attitudes left something out? The contrast between the attitudes is perhaps clear enough in an elementary way, but how about the linguistic *expression* of the attitudes? Well, couldn't we say, "I want it to rain" (that is, "I want it to be the case that it rains"), or "I believe that it will rain"? We do in fact often express our attitudes by saying such things. When we talk this way, though, we are not literally expressing our attitudes, we are *describing* them. This can be appreciated by noting that if such self-describing sentences really did express our values and beliefs, there would be nothing to argue over with others, and it would be impossible to discover or decide that some judgment of our own was mistaken or wrong-headed.

Judgments have a propositional content, so if judgments are different, if they have a different subject matter, then the propositional content of those judgments must be different. Here a little care is needed. Sentences and propositions don't, strictly speaking, express attitudes. People do, for example by uttering sentences in specific circumstances. In such cases we can also say their utterances express attitudes. But there is no form of sentence reserved for any particular use. We may feel that declarative sentences are "made for" giving information or making claims or expressing beliefs or stating theories, but there is no rule of language that makes such uses "normal" and others not. There is not even a moral constraint that points in this direction, except, of course, in specific situations. Imperative sentences are not reserved for commands, nor interrogative sentences for questions. Given this independence of meaning from specific ulterior uses (this is what I have elsewhere called the autonomy of meaning), it is not hard to imagine that we could manage without the imperative and interrogative moods.

What we cannot imagine is that we might lack a way of stating our disagreements with others about the moral and other values of acts, institutions, policies, and just about everything else. It is not imaginable that we would not have words for the irreducible and various properties we ascribe to objects and events when we want to classify them as good, bad, moral, blameworthy, right, courageous, courteous, trustworthy, loyal, kind, obedient, cheerful, etc. Creatures anything like us, creatures capable of thought and action, have concepts of the evaluative properties and employ these concepts in making judgments. I belabor these thunderously obvious facts because I think many philosophers have in effect denied them, or at least have evaded their consequences.

Perhaps the simplest observation with which to start is this: predicates such as "good," "right," "honorable," and "cruel" stand for concepts. To have a concept, it is not sufficient that a creature react differentially to things that fall under the concept: the creature must be able to classify things it *believes* fall under the concept while aware that it may be making a mistake. To apply a concept is to make a judgment, and judgments may be true or false according to the creature's own understanding of the concept. If I judge that some act is immoral, I assign it to a class whose membership is determined by whatever criteria I have, but it is my criteria that determine whether the act belongs in that class, not my assignment in any particular case. Evaluative concepts no doubt differ in many ways from other concepts, but if they are concepts at all, if they are eligible for employment in judgments and can form part of the content of meaningful sentences, then they must allow the distinction between what actually falls under the concept (as understood by its user) and what the user judges in particular cases to fall under the concept.

There is a closely related consideration that conspires with these features of judgment to support the thesis that evaluative attitudes have as their objects propositions with a truth value. This is their role in practical reasoning. When we reason about what to do or try to do, or about the value or morality of the actions of others, we must combine factual judgments with our values. We *conclude* from our desire to know what the word "amygdala" means, and our belief (false as it happens) that we will find out what it means by looking in the OED, that we would do well to look there. Such reasoning, if properly laid out, is surely valid. But validity is defined as a truth-preserving mode of reasoning. If practical reasoning can be shown to be (in some cases) valid, the premises and conclusion must have truth values. Our understanding of the logical constants brings out the same point. We say, *if* it is desirable that my jet lag be cured *and* taking melatonin will cure it, *then* it is desirable that I take melatonin. But what do "and" and "if . . . then" mean here? "And" is usually defined as yielding a true sentence if and only if each conjunct is true, and "if . . . then" is similarly defined as a truth-functional connective. If we abandon these definitions, what should we put in their place?

Is there some way we can tinker with the notion of validity to avoid this outcome? It is no help to look to standard types of imperative and deontic logics. Such logics often suggest *rules* of valid inference. But it is one thing to set down intuitively attractive rules and another to show that the rules are valid, which requires a demonstration based on semantics, and this is typically lacking. Attempts have been made to supply an appropriate semantics for logics that eschew the concept of truth, but study reveals that no serious and complete semantic theory lies behind those proposals, at least those with which I am familiar.

We should then face the fact that it is difficult, if not impossible, to avoid the conclusion that evaluative judgments have truth values, that is, are objectively true or false.[3] Perhaps evaluations sometimes are neither, as may happen with ordinary declarative sentences and judgments; but even when neither, they have truth *conditions*.

Simon Blackburn has seen the power of some of these arguments, and he accepts the idea that evaluations have truth values, but he holds that accepting this idea does not commit him to the objectivity of values. He reconciles his "projectionist" view with the idea that evaluations are true or false by treating talk about truth in evaluative contexts as purely performative: when we say a judgment is true, we merely endorse it, give it the nod. He writes, "Granted that it is correct to reply to a moral utterance by saying 'That's true' or 'That's not true', the question remains of what sort of assessment is indicated by these responses," and he answers:

> But isn't the theory saying that there is really no such thing as moral truth, and nothing to be known, believed, entailed—only the appearance of such things? Not at all. It is a complete mistake to think that the notion of moral truth and the associated notions of moral attributes and propositions disappear when the realistic theory is refuted. To think that a moral proposition is true is to concur in an attitude to its subject: this is the answer to the question with which I began the essay. To identify this attitude further is a task beyond the scope of this essay, but it is the central remaining task for the metaphysic of ethics. To think, however, that the anti-realist results show that there is no such thing as moral truth is quite wrong. To think there are no moral truths is to think that nothing should be morally endorsed, that is, to endorse the endorsement of nothing, and this attitude of indifference is one that it would be wrong to recommend, and silly to practice.[4]

There is indeed an endorsing *use* of the word "true," as we should expect, given its meaning. But this use does not determine what the word means. How could it, given the word's relation to valid inference or to an orderly account of the semantics of speech generally? Truth, the serious concept we employ when we allow that what we say and what we think may or may not be true, is, by dint of this very characteristic, necessarily objective: whether an utterance or belief is true is not, in general, up to us.

Some philosophers have reasoned, from the existence of conflicting principles to the conclusion that moral judgments cannot have truth values. Thus both Bernard Williams and Phillippa Foot, in rather different ways, have argued that since we feel genuine regret when we know our action has foreclosed on a genuine value, or contravened a genuine obligation, we must admit the legitimacy of both the value or obligation served and the one foregone. But, they argue, if two obligations that are opposed are nevertheless both legitimate, then neither obligation can be called objectively valid at the expense of the other, and judgments of their validity cannot, in the logical sense, be contradictory. Thus the existence of conflicts in the personal domain becomes an argument against the idea that inter-personal or inter-cultural conflicts have an objective solution.

Taken by itself, this argument cannot withstand scrutiny. Quite apart from issues of objective truth, it is clear that we cannot hold that moral maxims (whether objective or not) are genuinely categorical and also that they may conflict in application. If, as I believe, correct moral principles sometimes (often!) conflict, this can only be because such claims are not absolute, not exceptionless, not, in Kant's word, categorical. We must be prepared to allow that though it may be an objectively correct principle that we should honor our debts, there may be cases where it would be objectively wrong to do so. It would be trivial to take this to mean only that the maxim "It is wrong not to pay one's debts" has a finite list of exceptions it is too boring to enumerate, for this would bring us back to the idea of exceptionless (but complicated) principles we are too lazy to state explicitly. There is no such list. The maxim has no exceptions; if one has a debt, the maxim applies. It can, however, be overruled by an obligation or value that, under the circumstances, is more pressing. General principles of morality, moral maxims, are conditional. They say, in effect, that *insofar as* an act is courageous or generous or a matter of keeping a promise, it is worthy, but other considerations may on occasion override this particular principle. It follows that genuine and justified regret at the course not taken cannot show that the course taken was not objectively correct.

Objectivity allows conflict; it also allows most forms of relativism, indeed, all the forms that seem intelligible. The denial that value judgments are objective, that they have truth values just as our ordinary judgments about the physical world do, is not to be confused with relativism. The relativist does not question the objective validity of value judgments; he merely insists that what is valuable or right is relative to time, place, person, culture, tribe, or legal system. We are all moral relativists to some degree; any sane person must be. Most of us hold that it is morally wrong to kill someone in order to inherit their money, but that killing may be permitted, or even obligatory, under certain other conditions. We do not blame children for actions for which we would hold an adult responsible. It may be right to hand a man beset by thieves a weapon but wrong to give the same weapon to a deranged would-be suicide. Relativism becomes progressively more plausible, but also less interesting, the more pervasive the relevant conditions are made, and the more willing we become to recognize that our judgments are valid only as relativized.

Nevertheless, the relativist cannot in consistency deny the objectivity of values. The relativist holds that an individual act has its value objectively, though an act similar in many ways might have a different, though equally objective, value. The relativist about values is no more skeptical about the objectivity of values than the linguist is skeptical about the truth of an utterance just because a sentence, true when uttered in one context, may be false in another. ("It's raining.")

A judgment is objective if it is true or false, or possibly neither, but its truth value (true, false, or neither) is fixed; its truth is independent of who makes the judgment and of the society or period in which the thinker lives (unless, of course, the judgment is *about* the thinker's thought or society). But the truth of a judgment nevertheless depends on two things: how things are, and the contents of the judgment, the proposition being judged.

If people throw rocks or shout or shoot at each other, there is not necessarily, or perhaps even often, any proposition whose truth is in dispute. A dispute requires that there be some proposition, a shared content, about which opinions differ. If one is skeptical about the clarity or usefulness of the concept of a proposition or content (and I am such a skeptic), the formulation of a dispute will need reworking. The same goes for formulations that depend on incompatible beliefs or judgments, for they depend on our understanding what it is for two people to have the same belief or to consider the same judgment. Nor will appeal to language help, since two people can agree on the truth of a sentence while not agreeing on what the sentence means. The concept of two people meaning the same thing by a sentence is exactly as vague, or open to further analysis, as the identity conditions of propositions, beliefs, or judgments. The question of the objectivity of moral judgments, or the nature of moral disputes is, then, as much a question about how the *content* of particular moral judgments is determined as it is a question about the nature and source of moral values. Here I am concerned only with the first point, with why the facts that determine the content of moral judgments give reason to suppose that such judgments are true or false.

Objectivism about values should not be confused with realism. Realism is an ontological position: it maintains that one or another sort of purported entity exists. No one doubts the existence of the acts, people, events, and institutions we call good, bad, just, or right. Nevertheless, discussions of the objectivity of value are frequently—and perennially—infected by the inherently unintelligible question *where* values are, a question that would make sense only if values were non-abstract objects of some sort. Hume famously put it this way:

> Examine the crime of *ingratitude*. . . . Enquire then where is the matter of fact which we here call *crime*; point it out; determine the time of its existence; describe its essence or nature; explain the sense or faculty to which it discovers itself . . . the crime of ingratitude is not any particular *fact*; but arises from a complication of circumstances, which, being presented to the spectator, excites the *sentiment* of blame. . . . The vice entirely escapes you . . . till you turn your reflection into your own breast.

John Mackie, in his attractively plain-spoken book *Ethics: Inventing Right and Wrong*,[5] says that for the objectivist "there is something that backs up and validates some of the subjective concern which people have for things." And he adds, "If there were something in the fabric of the world that validated certain kinds of concern, then it would be possible to acquire these merely by finding something out, by letting one's thinking be controlled by how things were." Mackie then asks:

> What is the connection between the natural fact that an action is a piece of deliberate cruelty—say, causing pain just for fun—and the moral fact that it is wrong? . . . [I]t is wrong because it is a piece of deliberate cruelty. But just what *in the world* is signified by this 'because'? It is not . . . sufficient to postulate a faculty which 'sees' the wrongness: something must be postulated which can see at once the natural features that constitute the cruelty, and the wrongness, and the mysterious consequential link between the two.

In the same vein, Blackburn writes:

> [T]he extra ingredients the realist adds [to what the projectionist assumes, namely the existence of personal reasons] (the values or obligations which, in addition to normal features of things, are cognized . . .) are pulling no explanatory weight: they just sit on top of the story which tells how our sentiments relate to the natural features of things.

I agree with Blackburn (and, as it happens, with R. M. Hare) that it adds nothing to an account of values to insist that they are real, part of the furniture of the world, something to be found or discovered. But I cannot see why this settles the issue whether the correctness of some evaluations may be independent of even our enlightened personal reasons, for I never thought values were *objects* of any sort, much less objects with a location.

Blackburn argues that if values were in the world they would explain nothing; they just "sit on top" of the natural features of the world, natural features that happen to turn us on.[6] But plenty of real features of the world just "sit on top" of others, are supervenient on them, without this counting against the objectivity of attributions of these features to objects that are certainly in the world. Being green, for example, sits on top of more fundamental properties of objects, though in a very complicated way, and so in one sense the greenness of objects explains nothing. Colors (and other so-called secondary qualities) supervene on the properties a completed physics needs. Our perceivings and thoughts supervene on the physical properties of our bodies. But of course thoughts and colors do explain things, just not in the way physics does. Colors and thoughts aren't *definable* in physical terms—that's why they can explain what physics can't. But explanatory power is not in this case related to ontology. It is true—objectively true—that some things are green and that people have certain thoughts. This doesn't require that there be objects or events in addition to physical events and objects, but it does empower and require explanations of a different order. Blackburn's argument does not, then, show that objects and events in the world may not really and truly have values.

If, instead of asking *where* values are, we turn to the problem of understanding what it is like to judge that an act or object or institution is morally desirable or ought to exist or is obligatory, we realize that such a judgment necessarily consists in assigning some property or other to an entity or group of entities. The semantic nature of such judgments, as I said, is clear: the attributor is *classifying* one or more things as having a certain property. The thing or things (assuming they exist) must either have that property or not. The acts, institutions, and objects to which values are attributed are real enough and typically exist in ordinary space and time. But to have a value is to have a property, and properties are abstract objects. They are nowhere. The question of where they are is meaningless.[7]

Hume, Bentham, Hare, Blackburn, and a host of others have emphasized the intrinsically motivational, subjective, emotive, or projective character of value judgments. They are surely right. But it is a mistake to suppose that the nature of the attitude that is revealed or expressed by evaluative judgments rules out objectivity. If we judge some act better than any other act open to us, we are motivated to perform it. If we deem an act cruel, we dislike or detest it. If we say a practice is immoral, we are (if we are sincere) expressing disapproval. Whether these connections are as simple as these remarks imply is not my present concern. My point now is simply that one can believe in these connections without questioning the objectivity of moral and other evaluative judgments.

The central issue remains: how do we tell what the content of a particular moral judgment is? This is a question of interpretation, of the understanding by one person of the utterances of another, since there is no other context in which the content of a judgment can be agreed to or disputed. One key to identifying the contents of an evaluative judgment is what W. V. Quine and I, following Niel Wilson, have called the Principle of Charity. This principle calls on us to fit our own propositions (or our own sentences) to another person's words and attitudes in such a way as to render that person's speech and other behavior intelligible. Interpretation requires us to see the mental lives of others as enough like our own in point of overall coherence and correctness to allow us to assign reasons to their acts, intentions, beliefs, and other attitudes—in other words, to understand them. It requires us to see other agents as more or less rational creatures inhabiting a shared world that they conceive much as we do.

In the case of belief, what ensures that our general picture of the world is one we share with other thinking creatures is that what we mean by our sentences, and the thoughts those sentences may be used to express are causally tied to what they are about. For in the plainest cases we can do no better than to interpret a sentence that a person is selectively caused to hold true by the presence, say, of rain as meaning that it is raining. This rule of interpretation can accommodate many exceptions, and its application is subtle and complicated, but to ignore it entirely is simply to abandon the possibility of interpretation. It follows that in the plainest and simplest matters good interpretation will generally put interpreter and interpreted in agreement. The rule also ensures that most of our plainest beliefs are true.

To what extent do these considerations apply to the evaluative attitudes? It is possible, I think, to show that the justified attribution of values to someone else provides a basis for judgments of comparisons of value, what is called the interpersonal comparison of values.[8] But the comparability of values does not in itself imply agreed-on standards, much less that we can legitimately treat value judgments as true or false. Now I want to go on to suggest that we should expect enlightened values—the reasons we would have for valuing and acting if we had all the facts straight—to converge; we should expect people who are enlightened and who fully understand one another's words to agree on many basic values. An appreciation of what makes for such convergence or agreement also shows that value judgments have truth conditions just as our so-called factual judgments do.[9]

Basic to the understanding of the utterances of another speaker is observation of the circumstances in which the speaker, sincerely as far as we can tell, applies a predicate. The application of a predicate represents a judgment and therefore is expressed by a sentence such as "This is a nose," "That is lavender," "It's warm in here." Sometimes a word does the work of a sentence: "Rain!" "Lion!" "Gavagai!" We learn to understand what is meant by evaluative expressions in the same way: "Good!" "Bad!" "That was wrong" "This is silly" "How brave." These expressions, we learn, apply to actions and objects of the sorts to which we find them applied. With time, we grasp the concept and can make our own applications. Once we have grasped a concept, we sort out for ourselves where we think others are right and where wrong in applying it, and we are in a position to appreciate that we can make mistakes. If we find that some speakers deviate wildly from our usage, it is open to us, as always, to decide they do not mean what we do by the same words.

These considerations do not, of course, show that there can be no real differences in norms among those who understand each other. There can be, as long as the differences can be seen to be real because placed within a common framework. The common framework is the area of overlap, of norms one person correctly interprets another as sharing. Putting these considerations together, the principle that emerges is: the more basic a norm is to our making sense of an agent, the less content we can give to the idea that we disagree with respect to that norm.

Good interpretation makes for convergence then, and on values in particular, and explains failure of convergence by appeal to the gap between what seems valuable and what is valuable, much as it explains disagreement in other matters. Thus, there is a basis for the claim that evaluations are correct or incorrect by interpersonal—that is, impersonal, or objective—standards. For if I am right, disputes over values can be genuine only when there are shared criteria in the light of which there is an answer to the question who is right. Of course, genuine disputes must concern the values of the very same objects, acts, or states of affairs. When we find a difference inexplicable, that is, not due to ignorance or confusion, the difference is not genuine; put from the point of view of an interpreter, finding a difference inexplicable is a sign of bad interpretation. I am not saying that values are objective because there is more agreement than meets the eye, and I certainly am not saying that what we agree on is therefore true. The importance of a background of shared beliefs and values is that such a background allows us to make sense of the idea of a common standard of right and wrong, true and false.

My emphasis on interpretation and inter-subjectivity as the basis for objectivity suggests that our words have clear application only in the areas where we use them most. Michael Dummett at one point suggests that an attribution of courage to a person who has died without ever being placed in a situation requiring courage has no truth value. Dummett's reason for saying this is that there is no way anyone will ever be able to tell whether the person was brave. I agree that such an attribution may have no truth value, but the reason is not that verification is lacking; it is that we simply haven't had to make up our minds about such cases. I think the same applies to many of the puzzles philosophers raise about split brains, multiple personalities, or, more to my point, very difficult or unusual moral problems. It is consistent with objectivity that there should be no clear answers about what is right or obligatory in such cases.

But no matter the subtleties involved, interpreting evaluative judgments rests on the same foundation as interpreting the other attitudes: understanding depends on finding common ground. Given enough common ground, we can understand and explain differences, we can criticize, compare, and persuade. The main thing is that finding the common ground is not subsequent to understanding, but a condition of it. This fact may be hidden from us because we usually more or less understand a person's language before we talk with him or her. This invites the impression that we can then, using our mutually understood language, discover whether we share his or her view of the world and basic values. This is an illusion. If we understand the words, a common ground already exists.

Notes

1. A. Bechara, et al., "Double Dissociation of Conditioning and Declarative Knowledge Relative to the Amygdala and Hippocampus in Humans," *Science*, 269 (1995): pp. 1115–1118.

2. Richard Jeffrey, *The Logic of Decision*, 2nd edition, Chicago: University of Chicago Press, 1983.

3. "Objectively true" = "true."

4. Simon Blackburn, "Moral Realism," in John Casey, ed., *Morality and Moral Reasoning*, London: Methuen, 1971, pp. 101–24. I have quoted the opening sentence and final paragraph.

5. J. L. Mackie, Harmondsworth: Penguin Books, 1977.

6. Gilbert Harmon also argues that values don't explain anything; see *The Nature of Morality*, New York: Oxford University Press, 1977.

7. Properties are abstract, that is, if they exist. About this I am agnostic. But I believe all that I have said in this chapter about properties can be said instead about predicates. Predicates are, of course, also abstract objects but are better individuated than properties.

8. See my "Judging Interpersonal Interests," in *Foundations of Social Choice Theory*, ed. J. Elster & A. Hylland, Cambridge University Press, 1986, pp. 195–211.

9. Socrates had it right: "Listen Callicles, if men had no feelings in common, some feeling one thing, some another, if each of us was affected in a way peculiar to himself and unshared by others, then it would be no easy thing to communicate what we feel to one another." *Gorgias* 481C. I owe this reference to Jeff Malpas.

2

PRACTICAL REASONING

Barry Stroud

I want to explore some basic questions about what practical reasoning is, or is supposed to be, and what is special about it. Unfortunately, I do not get beyond a few fundamental issues. Even so, I get far enough to find myself at odds with what has often been said about them. Any wider implications for the proper understanding of action, reasons for action, and even morality, must be left for other occasions.

Each of us faces practical problems. What shall I do? What shall I do now? What shall I do tomorrow? What is the best thing for me to do about this? What should I do? (understood simply as a practical question for me and not necessarily what society or morality or honor or some other such system requires). I just want to know what to do. Questions like this are asked and answered by and about particular people in determinate circumstances, at particular times and places, every day.

We settle such questions in different ways. Or perhaps there are different sorts of question. For example, I decide now to go to the movies tomorrow. After some thought, that is what I conclude is the thing to do tomorrow, and I now decide and so intend to do it. For the moment that question is settled. I can always re-open the question between now and tomorrow and settle it in a different way. And even if I don't, I still might not do tomorrow what I settled today is the best thing to do. As for what to do in the here and now, that question is settled by doing something at the time, even if that means, as we say, doing nothing. If I carry out my present decision to go to the movies at 6:00 PM tomorrow, then that is what I will do then. But if at that time tomorrow, despite my decision, I am sitting motionless nowhere near a movie theater, then that will be the way I settle the question of what to do at 6:00 PM tomorrow. Settling a practical question of what to do in the here and now is acting. Whatever an agent does at the time is what settles the question.

A philosophical interest in practical reasoning is not simply an interest in how agents come to form intentions and decisions and act on them when the time comes. It appears to be more a concern with the role of something called "reason" or reasoning in settling practical questions. But does this mean "settle" in the sense of arriving at a conclusion about what to do, or in the sense of deciding or intending to do something, or in the sense of actually doing something? Perhaps the issue is whether practical questions can be settled in any of those ways by "reason" alone. Is "reason" on its own ever practical?

That seems to be the question Hume answers negatively when he says that "reason alone can never be a motive to any action of the will."[1] He thinks "the greatest part of moral philosophy, ancient and modern," has been "founded" on the idea of a "combat" of "reason" with "passion," and on the idea that "every rational creature . . . is oblig'd to regulate his actions by reason" and to oppose any other "motive or principle" until it has been "brought to a conformity with that superior principle."[2] Hume means to reject that whole tradition of moral philosophy. He thinks reason cannot be a motive to any action, so it cannot even possibly oppose passion in what he calls "the direction of the will."[3] That is why, in his famous words, "we speak not strictly and philosophically when we talk of the combat of passion and of reason. Reason is, and ought only to be the slave of the passions, and can never pretend to any other office than to serve and obey them."[4]

As Hume thinks of "reason," it seems right to say that it alone could never produce action. What settles or resolves practical questions in the here and now, at the time of acting, is the agent's actually doing something. No action would occur at all if the putative agent were indifferent to all potential alternative courses of action. Hume thinks "reason" or "the understanding" is "cool," "indifferent," unengaged, and in itself "begets no desire or aversion."[5] It can discover relations among ideas and—in the expansive way Hume allows himself to think of it in his moral philosophy—it can discover what is so and what are the causes and effects of events. But "it can never in the least concern us to know, that such objects are causes, and such others effects, if both the causes and effects be indifferent to us."[6] If the operations of reason alone leave us always indifferent as to what we discover is so, then no operations of reason could on their own produce action. Reason alone cannot settle a practical question in the here and now.

Given Hume's understanding of the two separate faculties of "reason" and "passion," it seems equally true that "passion" alone cannot produce action either. At least not intentional action. If bodily movement occurs, something must have been sufficient to cause it. But for Hume what is at stake is not just movement but what he calls "the direction of the will." Preference, desire, or inclination is what leads to, and so is present in, intentional action: what is done is done *as* leading to the satisfaction of a certain preference or desire. And that requires that the agent have certain thoughts, in the sense that certain intentional descriptions are true of him. It must be true of an agent in an intentional sense that he is reaching out for a drink, for example, or choosing thirst-quenching over motionlessness, in order for his "will" to be involved in his action of taking a drink, and so for his desire for a drink to be relevant to the "direction" of his will. And that is a matter of how he regards what he is doing, what he sees or believes or otherwise takes to be so, at least in the sense of having certain intentional attitudes. And that involves "reason" in Hume's expansive sense: the "discovery of truth or falsehood,"[7] or the taking of certain things to be true.

If we take seriously the idea of reason and passion as two distinct faculties or departments of the mind, then, it seems that neither alone can cause intentional action; both are needed. If reason's practical insufficiency on its own were enough to render it a "slave" to passion, passion's practical insufficiency on its own would be enough to render it a slave to reason. It is probably best to drop the slavery metaphor altogether.

In any case, all this has to do with acting in the here and now, with what settles a practical question at the time of action. Hume makes action sound like an outome of certain mental dynamics: a combination of psychic forces issuing in an action. From his observations on the impotence of reason as a force in generating action, he draws the conclusion that an action cannot strictly speaking be "contrary to reason."[8] Much of modern moral philosophy has been based in one way or another on this Humean conclusion. I think the conclusion as it is usually understood does not follow.

Hume's claim that "reason alone can never be a motive to any action of the will" is a thesis about the impotence of reason in the production of action at the time of action. So when he puts the point by saying that it is "impossible, that reason and passion can ever ... dispute for the *government* of the will and actions,"[9] it must be the *executive* branch of government that he has in mind. To infer that therefore the will and its actions cannot be contrary to reason would be like inferring that since only the executive and not the legislative branch of government can carry out policy, what the executive branch cannot be contrary to what the legislature does. It is true that a legislature cannot oppose or prevent executive action by executing an action in the opposite direction, as it were. It cannot "dispute" or be in "combat" with the executive in that sense. But what the executive does can nonetheless conflict with, or fail to accord with, what the legislature legislates. Its actions can be contrary to the legislature's deliverances. And a person's action can be contrary to the deliverances of reason if it is contrary to what can be discovered by reasoning to be the thing, or the best thing, for the person to do.

This is true of reasoning in its role of settling practical questions in advance. If I come to a firm conclusion about what there is most reason, or what is the best thing, for me to do, my reasoning to that conclusion does not alone determine whether the action actually takes place or not. In that sense Hume was right. Not even my reasoning combined with my deciding or forming the intention to carry it out is enough alone to produce the action. Of course, we engage in the reasoning for the sake of action, and most of us aspire to be the sort of person who carries out what he has decided to do. Some people are better at that than others—or at least quicker. If the connection broke down in general, we would have no grounds for ascribing decisions or intentions in advance to agents. But that we have that aspiration, and that people in general live up to it, is not itself a product of reason or reasoning. If the deliverances of a legislature were never carried out, we would have no grounds for ascribing to it any legislative function; it would just be going through the motions.

Practical Reasoning 29

But the fact that its decisions are carried out is not a product of its legislative activity alone.

I do not want to press the analogy. I do not suggest that in thinking or reasoning in advance about what to do we are passing laws for ourselves, let alone for other people. The point is only a reminder of the difference between drawing a conclusion about what to do, or the best thing to do, and carrying out one's conclusions in action.

The fact that reasoning to a practical conclusion does not necessarily settle the executive question of action is revealed in another way by the fact that I can reach a practical conclusion about what is the best thing for someone else to do in a certain situation, just as others can about me. Drawing such a conclusion obviously does not lead to the action in question. Even if I continue to believe my conclusion about what someone else should do right up until the time for action, it does not lead to a decision or intention or action on my part. My thought and reasoning about other people's actions, and theirs about mine, is not *deliberation*. One can deliberate only about one's own actions, and only about one's future actions at that.

That is perhaps true of what is properly called deliberation. But we can and do engage in thought directed toward what to do, where what is in question are the actions of someone other than the person engaged in that thinking and reasoning. We do call in others to aid us in deliberating on important questions, as Aristotle pointed out.[10] There would be little point in my doing that if others could not ask and express views about what is the thing, or the best thing, for me to do. The fact that they are not themselves deliberating does not mean that they are not trying to answer the same practical question I am trying to answer.

Of course, if they are helping me, their way of putting the question is not the same as mine. My question contains the indexical expressions "I" or "me"; theirs has "you" or "he." But in the reasoning involved in answering the question, the different indexicals are in a way inessential. All of us take into account whatever we know about me and the circumstances and the alternative actions we contemplate. To draw the best practical conclusion, we have to be sure not only that we are getting things right, but that we are getting all the relevant facts. That poses a different kind of problem for me than it does for others thinking about me, especially with regard to what I want, what I would like, and what I value. But given all the facts we can discover, the question for all of us is the same: what is the thing for me to do? The fact that only I will act does not mean that in the thought and reasoning stage of the proceedings I am asking a question different from the one my advisors are asking. And for all of us, it is a practical question.

This might seem to be contradicted by Bernard Williams, who says in *Ethics and the Limits of Philosophy* that "practical thought is radically first-personal. It must ask and answer the question 'what shall *I* do?'"[11] If this means that others cannot ask and answer questions about what is the thing, or the best thing, for me to do, it doesn't seem right. They can. If it means only that the questions others can ask and answer about me are not practical questions, we have seen one way in which that is right. They are not practical questions *for them:* other people are not going to have to act on the answer to the question what I should do. The reasoning others engage in about me is not for them deliberation. Williams also puts his point that way: "Practical deliberation is in every case first-personal, and the first person is not derivative or naturally replaced by *anyone.*"[12]

I think it is right that the first-person pronoun in practical reasoning is not simply replaceable by the variable "anyone." But I do not think that means that practical thought is essentially first-personal in the sense of requiring the indexical "I." Some name or personal pronoun or other singular term is essential in the formulation of the practical conclusion; it must indicate for *whom* the thing to do is such and such. But it does not have to contain a pronoun, even a first-person pronoun. It is also true that in order to put a practical conclusion into effect, an agent must have a belief expressed in first-personal terms. He must believe that *he* is the one for whom the thing to do is such and such. But that is not required—although it might well be present—in the reasoning involved in answering the practical question in advance of action.

I can answer a question about what someone with such-and-such beliefs, desires, values, and goals should do in a certain situation, and then find that the general description is in fact true of me. My practical thought or reasoning before I make that discovery was not first-personal, but now I am in a position to draw a first-personal conclusion from it, by instantiation, as it were. I might conclude that the thing for me to do is just what I said such a person should do. I *might* draw that conclusion, but even without repudiating my earlier reasoning, I might not. To put it in the unfortunate phrase that can so bedevil this subject, "reason" does not "force" me to draw that conclusion about myself.

I may not draw it, although I find nothing wrong with the answer I gave to the completely general and impersonal practical question, because what seemed all right to say is the best thing for someone of a certain description to do does not look so good when it is applied to me, even though I fit that description. That need not be simply the arrogant insistence that I am special or above it all or not subject to the reasons that apply to everyone else. It can be the result of my knowing or believing or feeling something else about myself that was not mentioned in the original question or reasoning. Although the original description is true of me, it is not everything that is true of me. And the additional considerations can count against the reasonableness of detaching the practical conclusion of that earlier reasoning and applying it directly to me.

This is exactly parallel to "factual" or "theoretical" thought or reasoning about what to believe, or what is so. I can answer an impersonal and completely general question about what a person who has such-and-such beliefs, and is confronted with such-and-such evidence, should believe, or what such a person has most reason to believe, and then discover that that description in fact applies to me. If my answer was that the person so described should believe *p*, I might then draw that conclusion about myself, and accordingly come to believe *p*. If I do, I transmit my acceptance of the original beliefs and evidence through to the recommended proposition *p*, and so accept it too. But I need not do that, even if I continue to accept those original beliefs and evidence. I might know or believe other things that, when put together with those original beliefs and evidence, make it unreasonable for me to believe *p*, and more reasonable to believe something else. In that case, I will not conclude by direct instantiation that *I* should now believe *p*. What I find it right to say about what a person should believe, given that he has the original beliefs and evidence, does not look so good when applied to me, even though I still accept those beliefs and evidence. That is not *all* that is true of me. So I still face the epistemic question of what is best, or is most reasonable, for me to believe.

The question of what I should now believe is therefore not the same as the general impersonal question of what anyone who has such-and-such beliefs and evidence should believe, even if I have those beliefs and evidence. To answer the question about myself, I will need some general knowledge of what sorts of considerations are good reasons to believe certain things, but I cannot take the answer to any such question and automatically apply the answer to me as I am. The same holds for practical questions of what is the thing for me to do. I need some idea of what anyone who has such-and-such beliefs, desires, values, and goals should do in such-and-such circumstances, but I cannot proceed immediately and uncritically from an answer to such a question to a conclusion about what I should do, even if I have those beliefs, desires, and values. In this respect, questions of what to do and of what to believe are parallel.

So I think Williams is right that the question of what I should do is not simply the question of what anyone of such-and-such a description should do. But that is not because the question is essentially first-personal. There is nothing essentially first-personal in the recognition that a general description true of me might not be *all* that is true of me. Others who know additional considerations in my case could see the unreasonableness of drawing the practical conclusion about me that it would otherwise be most reasonable to draw from the general description alone. Williams grants that the question of what I should *believe* is not essentially first-personal. But that is not simply the question of what anyone of such-and-such a description should believe either. It is a question of what the particular, specified person should believe in the actual situation that obtains. The practical question similarly asks what the specified person should do, as things actually are. In each case it is a question that anyone can ask and try to answer.

The fact that no general, impersonal answer is directly applicable to an actual case is a consequence of an important general fact about reasons or reasoning. If P is good reason to do or believe something, it does not follow that the conjunction of P and anything else consistent with it is also good reason to do or to believe that thing. Even though certain considerations make it reasonable to do or believe something, the addition of further considerations can make it less reasonable or even unreasonable to do or to believe it. In that sense, both the practical and the epistemic questions are always open-ended, and the final verdict is always less than logically inescapable, even given extensive general knowledge of what considerations are good reasons for acting or believing in certain ways.

My question of what I should do is open-ended in that way, and so are other people's questions about what I should do in that situation. In giving an answer about ourselves or about some other person, we say more than just what is best for anyone of a certain description to do or to believe. We conclude "*a* should do F" or "the best thing for *a* to do is F," or we use the first-person pronoun to refer to *a*: "I should do F." In making that assertion we detach a categorical or unconditional conclusion about a particular person from reasoning involving facts about that person and the situation. But in detaching and stating that conclusion, we no longer mention those facts from which it is derived. If we did, and so stated only a relation between the accepted facts and a certain practical or epistemic conclusion, we would still be one step short of drawing a practical or epistemic conclusion. The question of what that particular person in that particular situation should do or believe would not have been settled. At most we would have answered a general and impersonal question of what someone of such-and-such a description should do or believe in a situation of a certain kind. Detaching a non-conditional practical or epistemic conclusion is needed to conclude the reasoning about what an actual person should do or believe, as things are.

In the epistemic case, not only might a set of beliefs and evidence support the conclusion p, while additional facts about the believer make it unreasonable for him to believe p, but those additional facts can even make it unreasonable for him to continue to accept all those original beliefs and evidence. This holds even in the rare case in which the original beliefs *logically imply* the conclusion p. Even then, reason does not force me to believe p, even if I believe the premises and I know that p follows from them. I might see right before my eyes that p. is false, or at least highly doubtful. So I should abandon or re-examine my acceptance of those original beliefs. This is equally obvious in the more typical case in which my earlier beliefs do not logically imply the conclusion p. Even if they only strongly support it, I can still find that additional considerations give me more reason to reject some of those earlier beliefs than I have to accept that conclusion.

This shows, I think, that no fixed general description of a person of a certain kind can capture the full question of what a particular person should (or has most reason to) believe or do. The question of what I should believe in the situation in which I find myself is not the same as the question of what anyone who fits a certain general description should believe, even if I fit that description and know that I do. In asking the question about myself I am in effect asking whether that description is *all* that is relevantly true of me and my situation or, if it is, whether it should continue to be true of me. Even if I grant that I now have the beliefs in question, the question is whether I should continue to believe everything I now believe. The question of what to believe is in that sense always open, whatever I believe at the moment. I do not mean that it cannot be answered, but only that the answer is never simply dictated by what I already believe. To detach the best conclusion, I have to be ready to subject even my earlier beliefs to further scrutiny or criticism.

The same is true of the practical question of what to do. Even if I have such-and-such beliefs, desires, goals, and values, and I know what it would be best for anyone who has those particular attitudes to do, I cannot conclude directly that that is what it would be best for me to do. There might be other things true of me that make it more reasonable for me to abandon or re-examine some of those beliefs or values or goals than it is to accept that practical conclusion as applied to me. Here too the question I face is in effect whether that original description is *all* that is relevantly true of me and my situation or, if it is, whether it should continue to be true of me. Should I continue to want, value, and aspire to all the things I now do? As in the epistemic case, I have to be ready to re-examine and re-evaluate all the considerations and circumstances from which the best practical conclusion is to be drawn. Nothing can be accepted as fixed and beyond scrutiny or criticism.

The epistemic question of what to believe presents itself to the believer himself as the question of what is so, or is most likely to be so. The reasons that I canvass for and against my believing *p* are other things that I believe, such as *q* and *r* and *s*, not the fact that I believe *q* or believe *r* or believe *s*. If I take the fact that it has always rained in Berkeley in January as good reason to believe that it will rain there next January, it is the past rain that I take as the reason for expecting rain, not the fact that I believe it has always rained there in the past. My *believing* that it has always rained does not amount to much of a reason for expecting rain in Berkeley in January. In trying to determine what to believe, or what there is most reason to believe, my focus is on the world, or on what is so, not on my attitudes toward what is so. I have many beliefs about how things are, and I want to find out something. And the question is settled for me, for the time being, by my coming to believe something. But my coming to believe what I do is to be based on *what* I already believe or can find out, not on my believing it or finding it out.

Another person who asks what I have most reason to believe about a particular matter must ascertain what I already believe about it, so to that extent he will attend to or take notice of the fact that I believe certain things. But again what he is interested in is the relation between *what* I now believe and *what* it is best for me to believe. He asks what those things that I believe do in fact establish or give me most reason to believe, not what my believing them establishes or gives me most reason to believe. If he wants to *explain* why I believe something that I already believe, he will perhaps cite my holding certain attitudes. But explaining why someone believes what he does is not the same as determining what he has most reason to believe.

The question of what it is best for a particular agent to do is parallel in this respect. It presents itself to the agent himself as the question of what to do, or what is best. The considerations he canvasses for and against his doing a certain thing are what he expects, wants, and values, not the fact that he expects or wants or values those things. If I take the pleasure of the sweet taste I expect to get from eating a chocolate as a reason for me to eat it right now, the expected pleasure of the sweet taste is what I take to be the reason for me to eat it, not the fact that I expect or want the pleasant sweet taste. In that sense, I consider or attend to *what* I want and expect, not to my own attitudes or to the fact that I have them. Of course, it is only *because* I have the attitudes I do that the practical problem takes the particular form for me that it does. If I didn't want the pleasure of a sweet taste, the fact that such a taste is to be expected from eating the chocolate would not for me be a good reason to eat it right now. But that does not mean that what I take to be a reason to eat it is my wanting the pleasure of a sweet taste. My having that want is what is expressed or exhibited in my taking the expected sweet taste as a reason to eat the chocolate. It is not what I take to be a reason to eat the chocolate.

Another person who asks what I have most reason to do must ascertain what I want or value, so to that extent he will attend to the fact that I want or value certain things. But again what he is interested in is the relation between *what* I want and value and the properties of certain proposed actions. His assessment rests on the relation that he thinks holds between getting a sweet taste (which is something I want) and the action of eating the chocolate, not on the relation between my wanting to get a sweet taste and the action of eating the chocolate. This latter relation is what he might appeal to in order to *explain* my action of eating the chocolate, if I do. Perhaps I ate it because I expected it would give me a sweet taste, and I wanted the pleasure of a sweet taste. Here, my holding the attitudes I do is essential to the explanation. But explaining an action that has occurred is not the same as determining what an agent faced with a practical question has most reason to do.

Another person's assessment of my position might differ from mine, so we come to different conclusions about what I should believe or do. This can happen in different ways. In the epistemic case, we might differ about what conclusion it is most reasonable to draw from what we agree are all the relevant considerations. Or we might differ in what relevant considerations we take into account. Someone who believes that a weather pattern approaching the Pacific coast in late December will bring more than a month of drought will conclude that there is not good reason to expect rain in Berkeley next January even though it has always rained there then in the past. If I have heard nothing of that weather pattern, I will continue to believe that it is going to rain then. He will perhaps grant that, given only what I believe, I have most reason to believe that it will rain, but he will think I should take into account the available information about the drought. He will think that to believe that it will rain would be contrary to what there is most reason to believe. If I have heard the story of the drought but think there is no good reason to believe it, I will disagree. There is disagreement between us, not only about the weather in Berkeley next January but also about whether the past rain we agree about is in fact good reason to expect rain next January. This looks like disagreement about what is so. If it matters, it is something we can discuss and try to settle. The same dialectical process can go on in me. If I learn of an impending drought, and so realize that there is not in fact most reason for me to expect rain, I will see that I had been wrong earlier, although I did not think so at the time. Within me, or between me and another, there can be disagreement, and then agreement, about the answer to the same question: what is there most reason for me to believe?

The practical case is parallel. You and I might agree about all the relevant considerations yet differ in what we think it is most reasonable to conclude from them. More typically, we might differ about what they are and so draw different conclusions. Someone who believes that I am allergic to chocolate will think there is not most reason for me to eat the chocolate even though it is true that I will get a sweet taste from it, which is something I want. He will think that my eating the chocolate would be contrary to what there is most reason for me to do. Someone who has heard nothing of my allergy will disagree. This again looks like disagreement as to what is so. Different judges give conflicting answers to the question "What is there most reason for me to do?"

Given that not even the person's original beliefs, desires, and values can be taken as fixed and beyond question in trying to answer an epistemic or practical question, different people's assessments of what the person should believe or do can differ in more radical and apparently more intractable ways. One person can find that, given the person's beliefs, it is reasonable for him to believe *p*, but that there is more reason for him to reject some of those beliefs and so not to believe *p* at all. Or that, given the person's present wants and values, it is reasonable for him to do so-and-so, but that there is more reason for him not to want or value all the things he now does, and so not to do so-and-so. What would be best is for him to change some of his already-accepted beliefs or evaluations. This conclusion is something with which the agent in question might disagree. If it matters, it is something they can discuss and try to settle. They might come to agree, or they might not.

Conflicting verdicts about what to believe or to do are not restricted to interpersonal disagreement. A person can reach a verdict that conflicts with an earlier conclusion he drew about himself. He will then think that if he had believed or acted in accord with that earlier conclusion it would have been contrary to what is most reasonable for him to believe or to do. That is just what another person thinks of a belief or action that goes against the conclusion he drew. Both are attempting to answer the same question: what should that person believe or do?

Bernard Williams resists the idea that what he calls "practical deliberation" and "factual deliberation" are symmetrical in these ways. Although in each case I can stand back from my current beliefs, experiences, desires, and values and reflect on them with an eye to what to do or what to believe, he thinks what he calls factual deliberation is "impersonal" or only "derivatively" first-personal, since it seeks the truth. He says the question "What should I think about this question?" could as well be "What should anyone think about this question? . . . Reflective deliberation about the truth indeed brings in a standpoint that is impartial and seeks harmony, but this is because it seeks the truth, not because it is reflective deliberation."[13] But he thinks that, in practical deliberation, I do not completely detach myself from my beliefs and desires, and I am not required to take the result of anyone else's properly conducted deliberation into account.

> The action I decide on will be mine, and . . . its being mine means not just that it will be arrived at by this deliberation, but that it will involve changes in the world of which I shall be empirically the cause, and of which these desires and this deliberation itself will be, in some part, the cause. It is true that I can stand back from my desires and reflect on them. . . . [But] The *I* that stands back in rational reflection from my desires is still the *I* that has those desires and will, empirically and concretely, act.[14]

It is true that the person who asks "What should I do about this?" is the person who will act and so will settle the question of what to do. But it is equally true that the person who asks "What should I believe about this?" is the person who, if he settles the question, will believe something. The question is not simply "What should anyone who believes, desires, and values what I do believe or do?" The reflective question in each case is what that particular person should now believe or do, where the answer might involve rejecting or ignoring or changing some of the beliefs, desires, or values that he already has. To that extent, the agent must stand back from all his current beliefs, desires, and values with an eye to altering them in the right or best way. He alone is in a position to do that precisely because they are *his* beliefs and attitudes. But the epistemic or practical reflection is directed always toward what the particular person should believe or do as things actually are. It presents itself to every inquirer, including the agent, as a question of what is so.

Aristotle held that deliberation is investigation or search—trying to find out something—even if not all investigation or search is deliberation.[15] The fact that others can ask and try to answer the same question that I ask about the best thing for me to do suggests that there is something to be found out, something for all of us to be right or wrong about, and that we are all trying to find out what it is. Even if others who try to determine what I should do are not deliberating, they could be said to be investigating or searching, just as I am. In this important respect, there is no difference between so-called practical and so-called theoretical reasoning.

That there is something to be found out is perhaps further supported by the fact that I can refuse or be reluctant to go along with a practical conclusion I have reached, even though I have found it to be the best thing, or the thing there is most reason, for me to do. Refusal or inability to do what one acknowledges one should do is often regarded in discussions of practical reason as unreasonableness, or irrationality, or "weakness of will." But one form such a refusal or reluctance can take can be a very good thing in an agent. It can be a response to feeling that the recommended action is somehow just not right, or not the thing for me, or maybe even simply out of the question for me, even though I cannot quite put my finger on why. If I could, it would be by finding some defect in what led me to that practical conclusion, or some additional considerations that point in a different direction. Identifying those additional factors would enable me to articulate my reluctance or to defend my new conclusion. But even without finding identifiable weaknesses in his earlier reasoning, or specifiable considerations in favor of a new conclusion, a sensitive, careful agent will continue to take seriously whatever reluctance he feels in the face of a practical conclusion he has reached. A more reflective agent will try to get to the bottom of it. Being capable of both reactions can be a virtue, just as a good nose or a good feel for the case can be an epistemic virtue in other kinds of investigation. An experienced detective or experimental scientist or other investigator learns to respect and pursue the feeling that something is just not right, even though all the reasons he can specify point unmistakably in a certain direction. He feels that there is definitely something more to be found out, even though he knows that so far he has not found it. The same seems true in deliberation and action.

Many people resist the idea that one person can answer the question of what another person should do. They find it offensive. They think nobody can tell anyone else what to do; it threatens or denies a person's autonomy. But it is just not true that nobody can tell anyone else what to do. They can, and at times they should. It is often just what is called for. Furthermore, someone who reaches a firm conclusion about what I should do in a particular situation is not thereby telling me what to do. For one thing, he needn't tell me anything. And even if he tells me what conclusion he has reached, he is not thereby telling me what to do in any way that threatens my autonomy. He is saying what I should do, or what is the thing, or the best thing, for me to do. Even if he is right about that, my autonomy is not thereby reduced.

I can reach a verdict myself about what to do and then act on it. If that counts as autonomy, then my *not* acting on it and doing something else instead can be acting autonomously too. So the fact that someone else reaches a verdict about what I should do does not reduce my autonomy either, even if I know about it. I might act on it and I might not. I do not mean that my autonomy cannot be reduced or threatened in any way. Of course it can, in many familiar ways, and by people with power over me who tell me what to do. But my autonomy is not threatened by other people reaching practical conclusions about what I should do. What we want in the way of autonomy, if we want it, is autonomy of action, including the actions of thinking and reasoning. The idea that our actions or thoughts accord with what we take ourselves to have the most reason to do or think is in itself no threat to autonomy. So it is no threat to autonomy if our actions accord with what someone else takes us to have most reason to do or think. Reason or reasoning, whoever engages in it is not a force, and so not a force that restricts or constrains action.[16]

Notes

1. D. Hume, *A Treatise of Human Nature* (ed. L. A. Selby-Bigge), Oxford, 1958, p. 413.
2. *Treatise*, p. 413.
3. *Treatise*, p. 413.
4. *Treatise*, p. 415.
5. D. Hume, *Enquiries Concerning the Human Understanding and Concerning the Principles of Morals* (ed. L. A. Selby-Bigge), Oxford, 1966, p. 172.
6. *Treatise*, p. 414.
7. *Treatise*, p. 458.
8. *Treatise*, p. 416.
9. *Treatise*, p. 416 (my italics).
10. *The Nicomachean Ethics of Aristotle*, (tr. W. D. Ross), Oxford, 1954, III, 3 (p. 56).
11. Bernard Williams, *Ethics and the Limits of Philosophy*, Cambridge, Mass., 1985, p. 21.
12. Williams, *Ethics and the Limits of Philosophy*, p. 68.
13. Williams, *Ethics and the Limits of Philosophy*, p. 69.
14. Williams, *Ethics and the Limits of Philosophy*, pp. 68–69.
15. Aristotle, p. 57.
16. I am grateful to Samuel Scheffler for helpful discussions of earlier drafts of this chapter.

Part II

Reasoning about Practice

3

AKRASIA AND THE PRINCIPLE OF CONTINENCE

or What the Tortoise Would Say to Achilles

Ariela Lazar

At a party, you offer me a cigarette and I consider your offer. On one hand, I reckon that smoking a cigarette now would be very enjoyable. On the other hand, I believe that smoking is detrimental to my health. Not only would smoking this cigarette be harmful in itself, I think, but it would also increase the probability of my picking up an abandoned habit of smoking. In short, accepting your offer for a cigarette decreases my chances of leading a long and healthy life. I consider this goal superior to that of enjoying the short-term pleasure from of smoking. Given my own values and goals, as well as the extent to which I believe accepting your offer would interfere with or satisfy them, I judge that I ought to decline your offer. But then I take the cigarette, muttering uncomfortably: "Just this once."

In accepting your offer for a cigarette, I act against my better judgment (or akratically). The action contrasts with my own assessment of what is dictated by my desires, goals, and values. Moreover, I am aware of this contrast. What then is the explanation of my acting in this peculiar way? Or have I really acted against my better judgment?

In a thoughtful and original series of articles, Donald Davidson has attempted to answer both these questions and has set the agenda for the discussion of practical irrationality for a long time to come. Davidson's work mainly addresses the first question—what is the psychological process that leads to akrasia. But in doing so, he also intends to say something about the second question about whether it is possible to act against one's better judgment. Davidson's discussion of akrasia, as well as that of the more general topic of irrationality, deviates from philosophical tradition in two ways. First, Davidson's discussion of akrasia is executed within a comprehensive theory of mind and action. Hence, his engagement with these questions is rooted in rather general philosophical considerations and escapes the trap of presenting obscure or ad hoc solutions (often characteristic of discussions of this topic). These considerations inform both Davidson's understanding of the problem as well as his solution. Second, Davidson's discussion of akrasia disregards altogether the moral aspects of this phenomenon. In so doing, he identifies akrasia as a tool for understanding practical reasoning and choice. This is precisely why Davidson's discussion of akrasia has significance beyond the strict scope of this problem.

This chapter will present Davidson's views on why akrasia is difficult to explain (section 2), on how the akratic action is generated (sections 3 and 4), and on the role of the principles of rationality in explaining the phenomenon of acting against one's better judgment (section 5). I will claim that, without intending to do so, Davidson offers two accounts of akrasia that are incompatible with each other in content and in spirit. The earlier account is right, I shall claim, whereas its later development should be foregone. I will also suggest what work is left to do beyond Davidson's first account (section 6). I start with a brief overview of Davison's views on practical reasoning.

I. Background: The Basics of Davidson's Theory of Action

According to Davidson, an action is an event caused by the agent's reasons for performing the action.[1] A reason for acting consists, minimally, of a pro-attitude, value, or goal of the agent, and her belief that by acting in a certain way she can promote that goal.[2] More complex reasons involve a number of different pro-attitudes and a multiplicity of beliefs. Davidson introduces the term "desire" to cover the wide range of existing pro-attitudes. Two relations between reasons and action are constitutive of the latter being explainable by the former: a logical relation and a causal relation. The logical relation makes it the case that an action explanation rationalizes the action; that is, it shows why the action is desirable in the light of the cited beliefs and desires.[3] Davidson's account of action portrays it as having a rational element at its core: the action must be rationalizable by those mental states of the agent that bring it about. An intentional action must be seen by the agent as a means towards promoting (at least) one of her goals.[4]

Davidson's account of practical reasoning is roughly this: various beliefs and desires are perceived by the agent as relevant to the action whose performance he deliberates. Some of these belief-desire sets are taken by the agent to weigh toward the performance of a certain action; some are thought to weigh against the performance of that action.[5] The fact that he has both reasons for and against an action does not involve the agent in a contradiction: the agent judges certain features of the action to count in favor of performing it and other features to count against his performing it. These small sets of beliefs and desires constitute, according to Davidson, prima facie reasons for and against the action whose performance is being deliberated. Strictly speaking, "prima facie" is to be understood in terms of a sentential connective, associating a sentence that specifies possible actions and a sentence that specifies a relevant consideration.[6] Davidson compares such judgments to probability judgments of the form pr(m_1,p), in which "m_1" represents an evidentially relevant consideration, "p" represents a state of affairs (to which m is claimed to be relevant), and "pr" represents a sentential connective (to be read "probabilizes"). The claim is that unrestricted detachment of p from an argument featuring (m_1,p) and m_1 as premises is unwarranted because there may be another consideration that probabilizes ~p (e.g., pr(m_2,~p)). A conjunction of two considerations that respectively enhance and diminish the prospects of an event's occurring does not constitute a contradiction. Similarly, says Davidson, "putting together" considerations, some of which weigh in favor of performing a certain action and some against, does not involve one in a contradiction.

In practical reasoning, the agent weighs both reasons for and against a particular course of action. She then forms a practical judgment based on the reasons surveyed. Ideally, all of the agent's relevant reasons are considered in forming the judgment concerning the practical question at hand. This, the all-things-considered judgment (ATC) is the most comprehensive judgment to arise directly out of prima facie considerations. It is a conditional judgment—conditioned by the evidence incorporated in the agent's deliberation ("Given all relevant considerations, I should do x").

The ATC judgment is followed by an additional judgment—an unconditional judgment of the form: "I ought to do x" or "x is desirable." The last judgment, an "all out," or outright, judgment is different in form from all of the previous judgments. It is not conditional, whereas the others are. The outright judgment is a necessary component of practical reasoning, according to Davidson: it corresponds to a commitment on the part of the subject to pursue the specified course of action. It is, in other words, identical with the agent's intention.[7] The justification for postulating the "all out" judgment as part of the causal history of an action concerns the possibility of deliberating—of forming a view as to what the best course of action would be (given one's reasons)—and, at the same time, failing to commit to pursuing it. Thus, a person may conclude, following a thorough deliberation, that quitting her job is best, under the circumstances. At the same time, she may have no intention of pursuing this course of action. It is this kind of independence of the intention from the relevant considerations that leads Davidson to claim that it consists of an unconditional judgment.[8]

Normally, the content of the outright judgment corresponds to that of the ATC judgment; that is, the agent forms an intention (and consequently acts) according to the outcome of her deliberation. She acts according to her better judgment. In akratic cases, however, the agent judges that the preponderance of reasons weighs against her performing the action that she eventually performs. The agent has better reasons, by her own reckoning, for opting for a course of action incompatible with the one she opts for.

II. A Conceptual Puzzle Concerning Akrasia

Davidson identifies two sources of the paradoxicality of the notion of akrasia: the notion of an action done for a reason and the holism of the mental. Only the first source—the notion of an intentional action—is directly relevant to the following discussion.[9] Within the framework of common-sense psychology, practical reasons make the performance of an action intelligible by presenting the agent's point of view, says Davidson: they show why the action makes sense in light of the agent's wants and beliefs. Davidson claims that, in akrasia, the agent's reasons do not make the action intelligible from the agent's point of view.

Davidson is right and his position should be unpacked in the following way. In deliberating, the agent reflects upon her reasons and forms a judgment as to what she ought to do in light of her reasons. In normal cases, the agent's action *reflects* the content of the judgment. In such cases, the practical judgment explains the action (the judgment itself is explained by the agent's reasons). But in cases of akrasia, the agent's action *conflicts* with her practical judgment. Take, for example, my smoking against my better judgment. A common-sense psychological explanation of this action appeals to a set of reasons (such as the desire to lead a long and healthy life, the desire not to support the tobacco companies, the desire to smoke), as well as my practical judgment based on these reasons. But even if we make this explanation as detailed as we like, we end up with something that explains my *abstaining* from smoking. If, contrary to our example, I were to act according to my best judgment and turn down your offer for a cigarette, this action would be explained by appeal to the very same explanation cited in the context of my yielding to temptation and taking you up on your offer. But if this set of reasons would explain an instance of abstaining from smoking (rather than "going for it"), it cannot explain a case of yielding to temptation (rather than abstaining from smoking). It is impossible for an explanation to explain two events that constitute each other's contrast groups. It follows that, if the explanation of an action by appeal to reasons works when the action corresponds to the agent's better judgment, it inevitably fails when the action is akratic. We must therefore wonder how we can hope to understand the occurrence of akratic actions within the framework of common-sense psychology.

III. The Definition of Akrasia and the First Account

In the case of akrasia, says Davidson, an agent x's (for a reason r) while believing that there is another course of action, y, open to him, which is incompatible with x-ing, and for which he has a reason r' "which includes r, and more, on the basis of which he judges [the] alternative y to be better than x."[10] The strongest case of akrasia is that in which the agent acts against a reason based on all of the relevant considerations (a genuine ATC judgment). In such a case, the agent judges that, according to all her relevant beliefs and desires, she should do y, and still intentionally x's, whereby x-ing is incompatible with y-ing. The idea of a genuine ATC judgment, however, ought to be understood as an ideal rather than as a descriptive notion. Most often, practical reasoning is based on a sub-set of the relevant considerations. Davidson's characterization of akrasia corresponds to this fact: it merely requires that the agent act against a more comprehensive judgment. He seems to identify a better judgment with a more comprehensive judgment, whereas a best judgment is identified with a genuine ATC judgment.[11]

In a widely discussed article ("How is Weakness of the Will Possible?") Davidson offers the following account of akrasia. The akratic agent makes the ATC judgment in favor of *x*-ing while he also forms the intention to *y*.[12] If intention and best judgment are understood in the way suggested by Davidson, the akratic agent, who makes both judgments, is not involved in a contradiction since the (conditional) ATC judgment (i.e., "In light of all my evidence, I ought to do *x*") is not inconsistent with the unconditional, "all out" judgment in favor of performing *y* (i.e., "I ought to do *y*" or "*y* is desirable").[13] This outcome is due to Davidson's construal of a best (or better) judgment as a conditional ATC judgment, and by his identifying an intention with an unconditional practical judgment. In this article, Davidson emphasizes the thesis that akrasia does not involve the agent in a contradictory frame of mind: "The *akrates* does not, as is now clear, hold logically contradictory beliefs."[14] Indeed, Davidson uses this point in order to undermine a central argument that supports skepticism with respect to akrasia. This analysis of akrasia turns on a distinction between two different features of propositional attitudes: their justificatory feature and their causal feature. A belief or a desire may constitute a weak reason in the sense that the agent takes other reasons to be better reasons. A weak reason will not be very influential in the formation of the ATC judgment. Rather, the reasons deemed weighty by the agent will mostly affect the content of this judgment. At the same time, a weak reason may be effective qua cause in determining the action, whereas a strong reason may not be too effective in determining the practical outcome.

IV. The Second Account of Akrasia

In more recent articles, particularly in "Paradoxes of Irrationality" (1982), Davidson adds a new element to his account of akrasia. This new element generates an account of akrasia that is incompatible and different in spirit from the account suggested previously in "How is Weakness of the Will Possible?" In the later articles, the agent is said to hold a second-order principle to the effect that he should act according to his ATC judgment.[15] This additional element—*the principle of continence*—is said to involve the incontinent agent in an inconsistency: "pure internal inconsistency enters if I also hold, as in fact I do, that I ought to act on my own best judgment, what I judge best or obligatory, everything considered."[16] The agent is inconsistent since in forming an outright judgment in favor of the akratic action, he goes against his own principle.

In an example offered by Davidson, a man judges that, everything considered, he should not go back to the park to restore a branch that he has previously displaced. The agent has a reason for returning to the park, namely, his wish to restore the branch and his belief that by returning to the park he will achieve this goal.[17] The internal irrationality of the man's returning to the park is described in the following way: in returning to the park the agent ignores his second-order principle. The desire to return to the park was a reason for returning to the park (a reason outweighed by other reasons), but, in addition to that, it also functioned as a reason to ignore the second-order principle: "he has a motive for ignoring the principle, namely that he wants, perhaps very strongly, to return the branch to its original position."[18]

However, "though his motive for ignoring his principle was a reason for ignoring the principle, it was not a reason against the principle itself, and so when it entered in this second way, it was irrelevant as a reason, to the principle and to the action."[19]

Davidson uses "reasons" here in two different senses that should be clearly distinguished. Reasons for an action—*practical reasons*—are, on this view, sets of beliefs and pro-attitudes that cause the action and show it to be instrumental toward satisfaction of desires. But non-practical reasons are different: they are pertinent vis-à-vis the empirical adequacy, truth value (or other features) of judgments and are not markers of instrumentality vis-à-vis the satisfaction of desires. At a certain point in his explanation, Davidson shifts the discussion from practical reasons to non-practical reasons. The following explanation is thus offered for the action depicted in the example: the action of returning to the park is caused by a practical reason (roughly, the desire to return the branch to its original position) that is not very strong qua practical reason (the agent considers the desire to return the branch to be outweighed by better reasons such as the desire to go home together with the belief that his replacing the branch in its original position will not make a great difference, etc.). However, this desire (to return the branch to its original position) is so strong that it causes the agent to decide to disregard his second-order principle. This desire, as seen from the last quotation, rationalizes the action of ignoring the principle: it serves as a practical reason for ignoring the principle, although it is not "a reason against the principle." Since the principle of continence is thus ignored, the agent is able to form an outright judgment to the effect that he should return to the park solely on the basis of the corresponding desire. It should be noted that a fuller description of the reasons that cause the agent to ignore the principle of continence must include a belief that the outcome of the act would facilitate the fulfillment of the desire of returning to the park (or some similar belief). Otherwise, the agent's desire to ignore the principle, attributed to him by Davidson, is unintelligible: the desire to return to the park cannot, in itself, explain the action of ignoring the principle of continence.

Davidson's account in "Paradoxes" has two problems. The first, more minor, concern is discussed here; the other—misrepresenting the role of the principle of continence—is discussed in the following section. It seems as though Davidson introduces two actions where it might be thought there is only one. His contention that "though [the agent's] motive for ignoring his principle was a reason for ignoring the principle, it was not a reason against the principle itself," indicates that he treats ignoring the principle of continence as an *action*. The outcome of this action, in turn, is supposed to facilitate the performance of the akratic action of returning to the park. The auxiliary action (ignoring the principle of continence) is deemed irrational since it is not justified by the reasons that cause it. More precisely, it seems to be minimally justified qua action, although the reasons that cause it do not undermine the principle of continence itself. In fact, one cannot conceive of reasons that would undermine the status of this principle.

Davidson does not seem to be aware of introducing two actions in the account offered of the park example. He seems to acknowledge a single action when he says that "in doing this [i.e., returning to the park], he ignores his principle of acting on what he thinks is best, all things considered." A sentence of this kind ("in doing A, the agent did B") implies that "A" and "B" are two different descriptions of the same event.[20] In a typical context in which such a sentence is used, the agent has an ATC judgment favoring action A and acts correspondingly. She has no such reason to do B, but as a matter of fact doing A just is doing B. Clearly, this is not the type of case described by Davidson here. The agent described in the example has a motive both for returning to the park and for ignoring the principle. In fact, the action of ignoring the principle is instrumental toward fulfilling the goal of returning to the park.[21]

Postulation of two different actions in each case of akrasia constitutes a considerable prima facie disadvantage for the offered account, even if the peculiar nature of the auxiliary action is disregarded. One would tend to think that only one action is involved when I eat a piece of cake against my ATC judgment, just as there is only one action involved when I eat the piece of cake in accordance with my better judgment. An argument is required to convince us that, unlike an individual continent action, what appears to be an individual akratic action is constituted by two separate actions.

V. The Principle of Continence

According to Davidson's more recent account, the attribution of the principle of continence to the agent makes it the case that his akratic action (as well as the corresponding intention) exemplifies internal irrationality. The agent's holding the principle of continence makes the action irrational from his point of view, it is claimed, since it shows him as acting "counter to his own conception of what is reasonable": "Only when beliefs are inconsistent with other beliefs according to principles held by the agent himself—in other words, only when there is inconsistency—that there is a clear case of irrationality."[22]

If, says Davidson, the agent does not endorse the principle of continence, his akratic action need not be irrational from his point of view—at least not in a way that poses a problem for explanation; in this kind of case, "we need only say that his desire to do what he held to be best, all things considered, was not as strong as his desire to do something else."[23]

Let us examine this point in terms of the park example. Interpreted according to Davidson's first analysis of akrasia, the agent is said to form the following judgments: given my wish to go home, I should go home; given my wish to lessen danger to walkers, I should return to the park; given the slight effect that my returning to the park will have on the safety of walkers, I should not return to the park; given all my beliefs and desires, I should not return to the park; I should return to the park. According to the second account of akrasia, in which the agent is said to hold the principle of continence, he also holds: I should act according to my ATC judgment; given my principle to act according to my ATC judgment, I should not return to the park. As can be easily detected, the set of beliefs and desires involved in the second account is inconsistent.[24]

Attributing the principles of rationality (as propositional attitudes that figure regularly in practical reasoning) to the irrational agent might be thought to have the following advantage from an explanatory point of view. Attribution of such principles (in the way specified) portrays the irrational agent as inconsistent (in the sense that her judgments imply a contradiction). In contrast, refraining from attributing the principles of rationality as propositional attitudes would not present the agent as inconsistent. It may seem, therefore, that we can ground the akratic agent's practical irrationality in logical inconsistency. In other words, it may be thought that akrasia is an instance of irrationality precisely because it involves the agent in an inconsistent frame of mind. Furthermore, it may be thought that grounding akrasia in strict logical inconsistency would account for the fact that the notion of akrasia is problematic (to the extent that some philosophers believe that it is incoherent). Attribution of such blatant inconsistency to agents who are not self-deceived is indeed puzzling.

But postulation of the principle of continence as an additional propositional attitude is not required in order to demonstrate the irrationality of ignoring one's ATC judgment. On the contrary, this approach yields a failed attempt to explain what is inherently irrational in the agent's reasoning. This may be the reasoning behind Davidson's inclusion of the principle of continence: an agent may have an ATC judgment to the effect that she should do A, and still judge ("all out") that she should do B (where A and B are incompatible) without getting involved in internal irrationality, since she may deny that she should act according to her ATC judgment. However, if she holds the principle of continence, this response is not available to her.

It may well be claimed, against Davidson, that it is questionable whether an agent may argue in this way once we attribute to her an ability for practical reasoning. Even if we disregard this concern for the moment and grant that it is possible to reason in this way, we will not salvage this account. The reason is simple: a more sophisticated agent who admits to holding the principle of continence, may deny that she believes that she should act according to the principle of continence. In other words, she may reject a third-order principle according to which she should adhere to the second-order principle. Such a strategy yields yet another version of Achilles' exasperated attempts to reason with the Tortoise.[25]

Lewis Carroll's Tortoise demonstrates that it is a misunderstanding of the notion of entailment to suppose that a premise that explicitly licenses the adoption of the conclusion in light of the other premises is always required if the adoption of the conclusion is to be rational. This is why a person's failure to grasp the relation of entailment cannot be remedied by appeal to additional, higher-order, premises that function in this way. Every such attempt must end in infinite regress. By analogy, we ought to learn from the Tortoise that the principle of continence is not a psychological state (belief or evaluative judgment), which is a required premise in practical reasoning. If we were to view the principle of continence in this way, we would not be able to explain the failure of rationality involved in akrasia. In viewing the principle of continence as a mere psychological state, we create the option of the agent's rejecting the principle (or some of its derivatives) in a seemingly rational fashion.

To clarify this point, we may distinguish between the principle of continence, on one hand, and, for example, one's strongly held principle of avoiding disorderly conduct, on the other. The heart of the difference between these two principles lies in the ways in which they respectively function in action explanations. A principle such as "I should avoid engaging in disorderly conduct," if it were to play an explanatory role vis-à-vis someone's behavior, will do so primarily by figuring in the agent's practical reasoning. A principle that functions in this way is an *action guiding principle*. A genuine action guiding principle could always fail to guide the behavior of a given agent without thereby compromising her status as an agent. An agent may be entirely indifferent as to whether or not her behavior is disorderly and so fail to hold the principle that prohibits disorderly conduct. In this frame of mind, the agent in question is no less an agent than someone who is seriously concerned with avoiding disorderly conduct. Action never guided by this concern is action nonetheless.

The principle of continence is not a genuine action guiding principle because it cannot explain behavior in the way I suggested. An agent who shows no concern for acting in accordance with her better judgment is not an agent: she does not act in the same sense that we do.[26] Such an agent does not share our concept of what it is to act for a reason. Acting for a reason implies the notion of practical reasoning, in particular, the notion of assessing and choosing among conflicting goals. Davidson agrees, of course, that the principle of continence is *constitutive* of agency. Still, he may claim that it is also a genuine action guiding principle—that it explains behavior through figuring in practical reasoning. But this cannot be the case. One cannot reason whether or not one ought to ignore a principle of rationality since the principles of rationality are constitutive of reasoning. Put differently, an agent may not choose to abide by a principle constitutive of agency. The very idea of choice presupposes that the person upholds the principle of continence as a standard. Once the idea of reasoning whether or not to abandon the principle of continence is ruled out, so is the idea that abandoning the principle is an action done for a reason. Indeed, this is Davidson's own view of the matter:

> For it is only by interpreting a creature as largely in accord with these principles that we can intelligibly attribute propositional attitudes to it, or that we can raise the question of whether it is in some respect irrational. We see then that my word "subscribe" is misleading. Agents can't decide whether or not to accept the fundamental attributes of rationality: if they are in a position to decide anything, they have those attributes.[27]

Davidson's second account of akrasia is incompatible with his own view of agency: it requires that the agent *choose* (by way of practical reasoning) to ignore the principle of continence. However, if it is to be viewed as action guiding, the principle of continence may not be viewed as constitutive of agency.[28]

Clearly, the treatment of akrasia in "Paradoxes" is incompatible with the account presented in "How Is Weakness of the Will Possible?" A major project of "Weakness" consists in showing that the akratic agent need not make judgments inconsistent with each other. In contrast, Davidson insists in "Paradoxes" that the *akrates* is characterized by a contradictory frame of mind. These accounts also differ in identifying the locus of irrationality in akrasia and, again, the earlier account is superior.

According to "Paradoxes," the akratic agent *reasons poorly* due to the presence of a strong desire: she unjustifiably ignores the principle of continence because of a strong desire to attain some practical goal and, as a consequence, forms an outright judgment that is inappropriate in light of her ATC judgment. This portrays the akratic agent as resembling the self-deceived person whose belief is undermined by the evidence at her disposal. The self-deceived person reasons poorly due to the presence of a strong desire or emotion. Thus, desires and emotions affect the formation of the belief, whereas epistemically relevant considerations are less effective in shaping it. In contrast, the earlier account portrays the akratic agent's failure as a failure to *act properly*. According to this account, akrasia does not imply flawed reasoning on the part of the agent. The *akrates* typically deliberates properly—her deliberation unbiased by the presence of strong desires—yet she does not adhere to her own reasonable judgment. The best practical reasons, in the agent's view, are inefficacious in bringing about the corresponding action.

It may be argued, against this intuitive position, and in accordance with Davidson's second account, that akrasia must involve a failure in reasoning since the akratic agent does not merely act, but also intends, against her better judgment. In support of this view, an argument may be devised along the following lines. The akratic agent *intends* poorly: she intends to do A while her better judgment indicates she ought to do B (A and B are believed to be incompatible courses of action). The formation of the intention is the final element in the sequence of practical reasoning, it may be added. If this final element is ill formed, as indeed it is in the case of akrasia, we must conclude that the agent's reasoning is flawed.

But the argument is not sound. The formation of an intention is not part of practical reasoning in a strict sense. Practical reasoning is the rational procedure by which we determine which action to perform. Once it is determined which action is best justified by one's reasons, the formation of an intention follows in the sequence of events. Once the ATC judgment is made, there is no more room for practical reasoning. The formation of the intention is not deliberated beyond the question of which action one ought to perform. Rather, the formation of the intention merely follows the formation of the ATC judgment and *indicates* that practical reasoning has concluded. The akratic agent's failure is therefore a failure to *act* according to reason, but it is not a failure in reasoning.

VI. Why Is the Better Judgment Followed by the Wrong Intention?

At the beginning of the chapter, I distinguished between two different questions that arise with respect to akrasia. The first question pertains to the possibility of acting akratically and the second concerns the psychological process that produces akrasia. It is easy to see that these two questions are tightly linked. Philosophers have often tried to answer the second question with an eye to answering the first: attempting to identify the process that brings about akrasia with the intention of meeting the skeptical challenge. In identifying the process that leads to akrasia, it is hoped, the skeptical threat according to which it is impossible to act akratically would be overcome.

This seems to be Davidson's strategy in "How Is Weakness of the Will Possible?" The response to the skeptic, which gives the essay its title, essentially consists in describing the psychological process that produces akrasia. By identifying this process, and especially by pointing out that the akratic agent does not entertain a contradiction, Davidson aims to alleviate one of the skeptic's worries: namely, that it is impossible to act akratically since such an occasion would inevitably involve the agent in a blatant contradiction.

In the first account suggested by Davidson, practical reasoning concludes normally with an ATC judgment. In the next step, an intention that does not correspond to this judgment is formed. But now it may be asked why it is that, in contrast to standard cases of action, the ATC judgment that precedes akrasia is causally inefficacious in producing a corresponding intention and action. Why is it that, in cases of akrasia, the ATC judgment is followed by the "wrong" intention? Now, in the standard case, the formation of an intention is explained merely by appeal to the formation of the ATC judgment: a person forms the intention to go fishing this summer, because she judges that, all things considered, this is the best vacation for her. But the formation of the akratic intention is obviously not explainable in this way. How then is it to be explained?

Davidson's first account does not provide a solution to this puzzle—*the puzzle of the deviant intention*; nor is it intended to do so. The account rather lays out the basic sequence of events that lead to akrasia. The psychological process that leads to this type of action, as it is depicted in this account, is identical with the process that leads to a continent action all through the formation of the ATC judgment. At that point, nothing is provided by the first account beyond the statement that, in akrasia, the ensuing intention does not correspond to the ATC judgment. But this fact in no way implies that the first account is wrong: it merely states in what direction it ought to be supplemented.

Before pointing in such a direction, it is worth noting that even though the second account may appear to provide a better answer to the puzzle of the deviant intention, it does not. The false promises of such a strategy have derailed more than one account of akrasia.[29] In this version, the second account introduces an additional step between the formation of the ATC judgment and the formation of the intention. According to both of Davidson's accounts, the "culprit" desire that causes akrasia is taken into account in the formation of the ATC judgment but is outweighed by other desires: the resulting ATC judgment is incompatible with the satisfaction of this desire. The first account concludes at this point; the second account goes further. It introduces a new problem that allegedly faces the agent: whether to adhere by the principle of continence (and act according to her better judgment), or to abandon the principle of continence (and satisfy the culprit desire). In this second stage deliberation, the culprit desire prevails.

The lure of such a solution lies in its seemingly addressing the problem of the deviant intention. It purports to explain why the ATC judgment is followed by a "mismatched" intention, by appealing to another decision problem (another ATC judgment). Essentially, the agent *chooses* to forego the principle of continence, and this results in the problematic mismatch between the initial ATC judgment and the intention. Once again, we see that Davidson's second account attempts to "rationalize" akrasia by introducing a non-akratic choice that yields the phenomenon. But we also noted that the question of whether or not to abide by the principle of continence is not a genuine practical problem: it is impossible to address by practical reasoning.

In contrast, Davidson's first account does not present akrasia as a consequence of a decision to abandon a principle of rationality in a particular instance. The framework of this account, together with Davidson's theory of action, allows, indeed invites, a solution to the puzzle of the deviant intention.[30] The "trick" lies not in showing akrasia to be a consequence of some odd decision but, as Davidson himself suggests early on, in realizing that a desire may vary its efficacy (become a stronger or weaker element in determining action) in ways that do not correspond to its role within practical reasoning. Intuitively, in akrasia, one desire (the culprit desire) is more effective in determining action than it ought to be. But how effective ought a desire to be? How dominant ought it to be in affecting an agent's behavior? In a nutshell, the role of a desire within practical reasoning is assessable only within its *role in a larger network of desires (and beliefs)*. Roughly, the status of a desire qua reason depends on how it relates to other desires: for example, which desires—if any—it is instrumental toward fulfilling, which desires would be incompatible with fulfilling it, which desires are likely to arise if it is satisfied, etc. If, for example, the desire in question is instrumental toward the fulfillment of central desires, surely its status qua reason is higher. If, on the contrary, it primarily conflicts with the fulfillment of other desires, or is instrumental toward the fulfillment of a few minor desires, it is likely to be a minor reason.[31]

The point is that the efficacy of a desire in determining action may change—increase or decrease—even if its role within the greater scheme of the agent's desires remains pretty constant. Thus, a person's desire for food or for fast cars may increase when he is presented with alluring images of such objects. When one is presented with a lavish spread, one's desire for food will increase, even though one hasn't acquired new reasons for consuming food beyond one's simply "feeling like eating." But this urge may be present and even increase when one has very good reasons for abstaining from the type of food presented (sweet foods in the case of a diabetic agent) or when one isn't hungry in the first place. Similarly, the desire for a red convertible Chevrolet may increase considerably as a consequence of one's being exposed to the appropriate commercials without a higher level of integration between this desire and others. One need not have adopted the idea that life is all about fun, or that red cars make one seem attractive to others, or that they are instrumental toward achieving long-sustained goals. Rather, one's desire to own such a car may increase significantly (to the extent that one is willing to go into serious debt) without any significant change in outlook, related goals, etc. A prominent form of advertising exploits this psychological phenomenon. Without providing the consumer with a *reason* for choosing the targeted product, some advertising merely manipulates the potential consumers' desire for it by presenting it in exotic locations, in the vicinity of attractive people, etc.[32] The consumption of the product is related to the appealing surroundings within which it is presented. But one has no reason to believe that one is more likely to visit exotic locations, meet with young models, or become as strong as the depicted driver of the car on one's television screen. Rather, the desire to own this type of car increases without changing its role qua reason merely by the establishing of strong associative links between satisfying existing goals and ownership of such a vehicle. Thus, fast cars are associated with success, sex appeal, and great adventures without being instrumental toward satisfying such goals.

Psychological causes and reasons may "part ways": factors such as physical proximity, imagination, association may affect the intensity of a desire without this being reflected in its status qua reason. Once this is recognized, the road is open for making akrasia an intelligible phenomenon from a psychological point of view. An intense desire that is a minor reason may determine action. This, in a nutshell, is Davidson's first account: it explains how weakness of the will is *possible*. It remains to take it a step further and show how weakness of the will is *plausible*.[33]

Notes

1. Davidson (1971, p. 46). The domain of actions discussed by Davidson is only that of actions done for a reason. For the purposes of this discussion, such a restriction is suitable since all akratic actions are of this kind. The essential articles in which Davidson's theory of action is presented are "Actions Reasons and Causes" (1963), "How is Weakness of the Will Possible?" (1970), "Agency" (1971), and "Intending" (1978).

2. Davidson (1963). A number of action explanations do not involve an instrumental belief but merely a belief that identifies the action at hand with the goal. Thus, a typical golf player who plays because of his desire to play golf must believe that the activity in which he now engages constitutes playing golf. If the agent lacks this belief, the desire to play golf cannot explain the agent's playing.

3. This does not mean that every action done for a reason is rational. This view merely implies that, if an action is done for a reason, some of the agent's reasons must weigh in favor of performing it.

4. This characterization of intentional action is not intended to rule out the possibility of an agent's lacking awareness of the actual reasons for which an action is done. Even in such cases, it is claimed, the agent identifies a goal that she believes (perhaps sub-consciously) may be promoted by the action in question.

5. This passage is based on Davidson (1970).

6. Prima facie judgments are comparative. In the simplest case, the comparison is made between performing a certain action and refraining from performing it.

7. The following passage is based primarily on Davidson (1978).

8. Davidson (1970, pp. 21–42). A number of objections have been raised against Davidson's identification of an "all out" judgment with an intention (e.g., Charles, 1983; Peacocke, 1985), but they are not relevant to the central concerns of my discussion. The points made here stand regardless of the status of Davidson's particular understanding of intention.

9. The second source of trouble identified by Davidson is due to his holistic view of the mental. The gist of the problem is as follows. According to Davidson, the identity of a belief or a desire is constituted by its relations to events and objects in the world, as well as its relations to other beliefs and desires. It is constitutive of the belief that it will rain, to use Davidson's example, that, together with the desire to stay dry, it causes the appropriate action (such as taking an umbrella when leaving the house). Rationality is constitutive of the mental under this view: it establishes the framework within which we understand behavior described in mental terms (i.e., in terms of beliefs, wants, actions, etc.). The identities of mental states, according to Davidson, are constituted by the ways in which they function in psychological explanations. The patterns of explanation in which these entities function are rational: we appeal to reasons in order to explain an action; we appeal to the evidence at the subject's disposal in order to explain the fact that she holds a particular belief.

If the behavior to be explained is viewed as deviant (e.g., when the agent does not act on the reasons she views as superior), holism implies that there is some measure of evidence for saying that the initial attribution of mental states to this subject was incorrect: that the agent did not opt for satisfying the desire she deemed rather minor after all. Rather, a practical judgment that corresponds to the action may be attributed to the agent. In short, holism creates a theoretical difficulty for acknowledging akrasia since, in akrasia, beliefs and desires do not function normally (i.e., rationally). And the function of beliefs and desires in psychological explanation is constitutive of their identity, according to holism. Hence, the problem of explaining an action done for a reason and yet does not correspond to the *agent's own* values, beliefs, and judgments. In light of this theory, says Davidson, the task of explaining akratic actions consists in "finding the mechanism that can be accepted as appropriate to mental processes and yet does not rationalize what is to be explained" (Davidson, 1971, p. 46). In other words, this process must meet minimal requirements of rationality (so as to constitute a psychological process in the first place) and, at the same time, yield irrationality.

Davidson's acknowledgment of irrationality in spite of holism is discussed in Lazar (1998).

10. Davidson (1970, p. 40; cf. p. 22). Davidson's requirement that the two competing courses of action be incompatible ought to be replaced with the requirement that the agent *believes* that these courses of action are incompatible. The phenomenon investigated by Davidson is that of a discrepancy between one's intention and one's better judgment. This phenomenon may occur even if the agent is mistaken in believing that the two competing courses of action are incompatible. Thus, I may deliberate between dedicating my evening to increasing my friend's motivation toward preparing for an upcoming test, on one hand, and going to the movies, on the other. I may go to the movies, against my better judgment, not realizing that the best way in which my friend's motivation may be boosted tonight is by his recognizing that no help from external sources is forthcoming. In the sense that is important to Davidson's investigation, it would be right to say that I acted akratically.

11. Davidson's notion of an ATC judgment should not be taken to imply that every case of practical reasoning results in a judgment that reflects the agent's consideration of all of the relevant reasons. It cannot be doubted that in almost all cases of deliberation, the agent fails to consider all relevant reasons. Davidson does not state explicitly that most cases of practical reasoning are based on a subset of the relevant considerations, but this interpretation seems to be in keeping with his thinking. His characterization of akrasia lends support to this interpretation. In what follows, unless otherwise specified, I use the phrase "all-things-considered judgment" ("ATC judgment") to pick out the most comprehensive conditional judgment that figures in a line of practical reasoning, even if that judgment is not based on *all* the relevant considerations. I take it that this is also the way in which Davidson understands this phrase when he distinguishes between better and best judgments: "Our 'best' judgments, I urged, could naturally be taken to be those conditioned on all the considerations deemed relevant by the agent." (Davidson, 1985b, p. 201). It is implied, I take it, that "better" judgments may be based on a subset of all of the relevant considerations.

12. According to Davidson, every instance of acting for a reason is preceded or accompanied by an intention. Hence, every akratic action involves an intention (Davidson, 1978). This view will not be assessed here.

13. Paul Grice and Judith Baker (1985) contend, contrary to Davidson, that the two judgments in question ("In light of all my evidence, I ought to do x" and "I ought to do y" whereby x and y are incompatible courses of action) are inconsistent with each other. Grice and Baker support this claim by saying that an ATC judgment, if it is genuinely based on all the relevant considerations, is conditional in name only. They claim that an ATC judgment entails the outright judgment. Grice and Baker's position is contested in Lazar (manuscript).

14. Davidson (1970, p. 41).

15. Davidson formulates the principle of continence as "perform the action judged best on the basis of all available relevant reasons"(1970, p. 41).

16. Davidson (1982, p. 297). This article is the primary locus of exposition of the new theory of akrasia. Echoes of this account may be found in more recent articles (Davidson 1985a; 1986).

17. Davidson (1982, pp. 292, 297). The example, as presented by Davidson, offers a richer description of the person's state of mind. At first, the agent believes that the branch, resting in the path, may endanger inattentive walkers and wishes to reduce danger. After removing the branch from the path, the agent comes to believe that the branch still poses danger to walkers and therefore wishes to remove the obstacle yet again. These details are not relevant to the following discussion. Davidson's example is inspired by Freud's case study of the Rat Man ("Notes Upon A Case of Obsessional Neurosis," Standard Edition, vol. 10, pp. 155–249).
18. Davidson (1982, p. 297).
19. Davidson (1982, p. 297).
20. This accords with Davidson's view. Cf. Davidson (1971, p. 53–61).
21. The phrase "in doing A, the agent did B" allows that the agent has two independent ATC judgments to perform two different types of action and that acting on these judgments happens to constitute one action token (i.e., one event). I may have an ATC judgment to attend the performance of *Aida* by the San Francisco Opera, for example, and have an additional independent ATC judgment to attend any one of the San Francisco Opera performances since I wish to see the building from within and this is the only way by which I may be admitted to the building. It may be added that, had this performance of *Aida* not taken place, I still would have attended an opera performance in order to satisfy my desire to see the building. In addition, had I been able to view the building without attending any performance, I still would have chosen to attend *Aida* tonight. It is true to say of me, when I act on the corresponding intentions, that in attending *Aida*, I also visit the Opera House.

It may be claimed that this is the relation that obtains between the action of ignoring the principle of continence and that of returning to the park. The claim would be that although Davidson's analysis of akrasia introduces two types of action, they always constitute a single token action. Therefore, it might be claimed, Davidson's analysis should not be seen as introducing two separate actions and is not counter-intuitive in this respect. Unfortunately, the respective sets of reasons that rationalize each action in the park example are not independent of each other in the way exemplified. The motivation for ignoring the principle is the desire to return to the park, which also constitutes the motivation for the action of returning to the park.

Against my view, it may be argued that an agent may acquire a reason for performing an action if she believes the action will be identical with an action for which performance she has an independent motive. Thus, say I have no interest in the architecture of the Opera House in San Francisco, but I do wish to attend the performance of *Aida* tonight. Knowing that the performance is to take place at the Opera House, I acquire a reason to visit the Opera House tonight, since I believe that this action will be identical with my attending the desired performance. The claim would be that the relation between ignoring the principle of continence and returning to the park is a relation of identity after all. Seen in this light, Davidson's account would not involve two separate actions such that the first facilitates the performance of the other. Applied to our example, this reading would suggest that the desire to return to the park serves as a motive for the agent's ignoring the principle of continence, in concert with the belief that ignoring the principle will be identical with returning to the park. Hence, Davidson's account of akrasia does not involve two separate actions in place of one.

There is a problem with this interpretation. The belief that ignoring the principle of continence will, in this case, be identical with returning to the park is rather odd. With respect to the opera example, it is clear how one may believe that visiting the Opera House tonight will be identical with attending the desired show. It is not at all clear, however, what kind of evidence the agent may have in favor of the analogous belief in the park example. How would the agent come to hold such a belief? Note also that this interpretation renders the inclusion of the principle of continence in the agent's deliberation devoid of explanatory power. According to this interpretation, it is only through believing that ignoring the principle of continence would be identical with returning to the park, that the agent acquires the motivation to perform this action: had the agent lacked this belief, he would not have had the motivation to abandon the principle of continence and the unfolding of the akratic action would have proceeded smoothly. According to the offered interpretation, a similar belief must be involved in every case of akrasia. It is rather difficult to see what grounds may be offered to support such a strong claim. This last interpretation of Davidson's account appears to rid us of the need to postulate two different actions in every case of akrasia. Unfortunately, it only does so at the high cost of introducing an unexplainable belief on the part of the akratic agent in each case of akrasia.

We must conclude, I think, that Davidson's more recent account of akrasia involves two separate actions, the first of which is of an especially strange nature. Davidson's formulation suggests that the action of abandoning the principle of continence is explained by the presence of a further goal of the agent's. The detailed analysis of the park example, the only analysis of an example in "Paradoxes," introduces two types of action that do not constitute one token action. Rather, the outcome of one action is supposed to facilitate the performance of the other.

22. Davidson (1985a, p. 348; cf. p. 346, pp. 348–349 and 1982, p. 297).

23. Davidson (1982, p. 297).

24. It is worth noting that, in his writings, Davidson is committed to an even stronger view. In some places, he suggests that if a person violates a principle of rationality that he holds (by for example, being self-deceived or acting akratically), then he must simultaneously hold a belief and its negation: "If someone has inconsistent beliefs or attitudes, as I have claimed (objective) irrationality demands, then he must at times believe some proposition p and also believe its negation." (1985a, p. 353).

This contention is not justified even in light of Davidson's more recent account of akrasia. According to this account, the akratic agent need not hold two beliefs that are negations of one another, such as p and $\sim p$. Rather, a set of the agent's beliefs is supposed to imply a contradiction. In what follows I disregard this last, stronger, claim concerning the agent's mental economy and deal with Davidson's contention that the akratic agent is inconsistent. It should be noted that Davidson no longer holds the stronger view (personal communication).

25. Carroll (1895).

26. This does not imply that an agent cannot, in her actions, violate the principle of continence. But an agent whose action violates this principle is always, in a deep sense, committed to it. The agent views such an action as defective and problematic precisely because it violates the principle of continence.

27. Davidson (1985a, p. 352).

28. It would be wrong to claim that just because an agent's behavior usually corresponds to the principle of continence we are justified in taking it as guiding her actions: one's behavior may correspond to different principles without it being guided by them.

29. Examples include Watson (1977) and Mele (1987).

30. For a more comprehensive discussion of this topic, see Lazar (manuscript).

31. Two points ought to be emphasized. First, these comments are not intended to provide a comprehensive discussion of what elements determine the status of a desire qua reason. They are merely aimed at illustrating the point that the status of a reason depends, to a significant degree, on its relations to other goals. The specification of these relations is explored elsewhere (Lazar, manuscript). Second, these remarks are also neutral on the question of whether there are other elements, outside of the relations of one desire to others, that determine its status qua reason. In other words, this discussion is silent on the status of "external" reasons.

32. The literature on this type of induction of attitude change is vast. Zajonc (1980) and Zimbardo and Leippe (1991) provide excllent overviews.

33. I received valuable comments on this chapter from Michael Della Rocca, Greg Ray, Bruce Vermazen, and Bernard Williams. Mostly, I benefitted from discussion with Donald Davidson.

References

Carroll, Lewis. (1895): "What the Tortoise Said to Achilles," *Mind* 4, pp. 278–280.
Charles, David. (1983): "Rationality and Irrationality," *Proceedings of the Aristotelian Society* 83, pp. 191–212.
Davidson, Donald. (1963): "Actions, Reasons and Causes," reprinted in Davidson (1980), pp. 3–19.
_____. (1970): "How is Weakness of the Will Possible?" reprinted in Davidson (1980), pp. 21–42.
_____. (1971): "Agency," reprinted in Davidson (1980), pp. 43–61.
_____. (1978): "Intending," reprinted in Davidson (1980), pp. 83–102.
_____. (1980): *Essays on Achons and Events* (Oxford: Oxford University Press).
_____. (1982): "Paradoxes of Irrationality," in Hopkins and Wollheim (1982), pp. 289–305.
_____. (1985a): "Incoherence and Irrationality," *Dialectica* 64, pp. 345–354.
_____. (1985b): "Reply to Paul Grice and Judith Baker," in Vermazen and Hintikka (1985).
_____. (1986): "Deception and Division," in Elster (1986), pp. 79–92.
Dupuy, Jean-Pierre (ed.). (1998): *Self-Deception and Paradoxes of Rationality* (Stanford, California: CSLI Series, Stanford University).
Elster, Jon (ed.). (1986): *The Multiple Self* (Cambridge: Cambridge University Press).
Freud, Sigmund (1981): "Notes Upon A Case of Obsessional Neuroris," in *The Standard Edition of the Complete Psychological Works of Sigmund Freud.* James Strachey translator and editor (London: Hogarth Press).
Grice, Paul, and Judith Baker. (1985): "Davidson on 'Weakness of the Will,'" in Vermazen and Hintikka (1985), pp. 27–49.
Hopkins, James, and Richard Wollheim (eds.). (1982): *Philosophical Essays on Freud* (Cambridge: Cambridge University Press).
Lazar, Ariela. (1998): "Division and Deception: Davidson on Self-Deception," in Dupuy (1998).
_____. (1999): "Deceiving Oneself or Self-Deceived: On the Formation of Beliefs 'Under the Influence.'" *Mind* 108, pp. 265–290.
_____. (manuscript): "'Just This Once': Against One's Better Judgment."
Mele, Alfred. (1987): *Irrationality: An Essay on Akrasia, Self-Deception and Self-Control* (Oxford: Oxford University Press).
Peacocke, Christopher. (1985): "Intention and Akrasia," in Vermazen and Hintikka (1985), pp. 51–73.
Vermazen, Bruce, and Merrill Hintikka (eds.). (1985): *Essays on Davidson: Actions and Events* (Oxford: Clarendon Press).
Watson, Gary. (1977): "Skepticism About Weakness of the Will," *Philosophical Review* 83, pp. 32–54.
Williams, Bernard. (1973): "Deciding to Believe," in *Problems of the Self* (New York: Cambridge University Press), pp. 67–94.
Zajonc, R. B. (1980): "Feeling and Thinking: Preferences Need No Inferences," *American Psychologist* 35, pp. 151–175.
Zimbardo Philip G., and Michael R. Leippe. (1991): *The Psychology of Attitude change and Social Influence* (Philadelphia: Temple University Press).

4

WHEN PRACTICAL REASON PLAYS DICE

David Heyd

> It related the fortuitous and the ordained into a reassuring union which we recognized as nature.
>
> — Tom Stoppard, *Rosencrantz and Guildenstern are Dead*

I. Exercising Reason under Human Limitations

God, said Einstein, does not play dice with the universe. For metaphysical reasons, one may add that he should not or even cannot engage in such activity. Being omniscient, He knows in advance the way the dice will fall; being omnipotent, He can effect whatever outcome he wills. Human beings, however, neither know all nor enjoy full control over what happens in the world. Endowed with theoretical reason, they may strive to attain as much knowledge about the world as they can; but being aware of the frequent failure of cognition, they often have rational grounds for suspending judgment. Equipped with practical reason, human beings plan their behavior in the world; yet faced with the limitations of this power, they cannot always resort to a similar move of suspension. Action is more urgent than judgment, and deferment in the exercise of practical reason is often irrational in a way that avoidance of theoretical judgment is not.

Fortunately, the so-called strategic power of practical reason compensates for its limitations by its capacity to contrive second-order solutions for first-order failures.

A classical example for the exercise of the strategic capacity of practical reason in the face of a theoretical impasse is Descartes's provisional rules of conduct. Having subjected all truths to methodical doubt, Descartes is left with the task of reconstructing human knowledge on a new basis. But this task can be undertaken only by human beings living in the world, that is, cooperating under a system of action-guiding norms. The problem is that these norms cannot derive their validity from theoretical truths of whatever kind, for these are all suspended by the skeptical principle. Reason, in its practical capacity, is consequently called to formulate temporary rules of behavior that would enable the search for theoretical truth without undermining the sincerity of this search by pre-judging its outcome.[1]

Another example of such strategic use of practical reason is casting lots. We resort to lotteries (in the sense of any process whose success is governed by chance) as a practical solution to theoretical and practical deadlocks. Tossing a coin serves us to decide an issue we do not *know* how to decide, although we have an overriding reason to *make* some decision. But the causes of our lack of knowledge, as well as the reasons for the urgency of making a decision, are varied. Thus, if we compare the strategic use of practical reason in Descartes and in casting lots, we find an interesting inversion. In Descartes the source of the theoretical impasse is an intentional move of active doubt, and the second-order rational solution to it is a passive adherence to conventional rules of socially given customs. In lotteries the source of deadlock is a given situation in which no theoretical solution seems satisfactory and the second-order rational solution to it is an active attempt to reshape the given state of affairs by manipulating the course of natural (or social) events. Descartes's use of strategic thinking is, accordingly, of a temporary and ad hoc nature, while lotteries provide what seems to be a principled solution. The temporariness of the rules of conduct in Descartes attests to the optimistic presumption that an ultimate system of truths supporting a permanent moral system will be attained; lotteries reflect a resignation of reason to its own inherent limitations in solving conflicts between equi-optimal choices or incommensurable options (limitations due either to the nature of the alternatives themselves or to the weakness of human reason).

The exercise of strategic rationality is by definition subject to rational principles. The rationality of Descartes's provisional rules of moral conduct is associated with their convenience; the rationality of casting lots is related to their fairness. But in both cases the ultimate reason for extricating oneself from the state of suspension of judgment is the urgency of action and the irrationality of not acting at all. The metaphor of getting out of a forest with no rational indication of the right direction to be followed is formative in the discussion of strategic practical thinking from Descartes to modern writings on lotteries.[2] But while in Descartes the choice of a particular direction is based on a *maxim*, that is on a kind of rule of thumb, which would enable him to lead his "life as happily as [he] could," in the case of lotteries the urgency of action is also constrained by a *principle* of achieving a fair and just solution to a problem such as the distribution of an indivisible good, like Jesus's coat found by the three guards at the tomb.[3]

Descartes's first maxim consists of a conscious attempt to avoid unnecessary "engagements by means of which we limit in some degree our liberty".[4] The idea is that the unhindered search for truth requires a freedom from commitments. This basis for the second-order rational principle is shared in a deep sense by the idea of randomly generated choice, since one of its basic aims is exactly to rid us from the dangers of *fixation* to a doubtful principle. Lotteries are often deployed in cases in which we are eager to break the monopoly of a controversial principle of distribution in an important matter. Its virtue as a rational method lies in its openness to an unstructured range of alternative outcomes in a way that leaves us unbiased toward any particular solution. The agnostic mood that characterizes the choice of random methods of selection is analogous to the skeptical attitude that secures the Cartesian construction of a reliable system of knowledge.

Both the second and the third maxims in Descartes's provisional rules of conduct commend resistance to forces outside the rational mind. The second maxim states that "those weak and vacillating creatures who allow themselves to keep changing their procedures" are never going to get out of the forest, since, as I read Descartes, they subject themselves to erratic psychological mechanisms and motives. In the third maxim Descartes chooses "to try always to conquer myself rather than fortune," which can be understood as locating the rational within that part of the decision-making process over which we have control.[5] The analogy I am trying to suggest here views both Cartesian maxims and lotteries as rejecting the "rationality" of submission to the natural course of events, to spontaneous action, to the illusion of being able to fully control the external world. Lottery, in other words, is the rational alternative to lot; artificially devised mechanisms of random selection are, as we shall see, rationally superior to resignation to the blind forces of nature, which are random in the sense that we have no grasp of their structure. In other words, the limits of knowledge are for us, human beings, a *given* fact over which in certain circumstances we have no control, and the rational way to respond to this fact is to turn to those procedures of the mind over which we do have control, such as a rationally contrived lottery. By this we follow Descartes's third maxim, which exposes the irrationality of the hopeless and illusory attempt to "change the order of the world."[6]

A final point of analogy between Descartes's rules and the casting of lots relates to responsibility. In his fourth and last rule Descartes mentions the ideal of the philosophical way of life which consists of "roaming," that is, the life of the spectator rather than the actor.[7] Lotteries achieve, albeit by a different route, as we shall see, a similar freedom, in this case from responsibility, that is, from direct accountability for the particular consequences of intentional action.

Both lotteries and Descartes's rules of conduct are interesting cases of practical reason because they address a kind of failure of reason. But unlike not wanting to do what one knows is right or not wanting to know what one knows to be true, which can be explained but not justified, lotteries and provisional rules of conduct are rationally supported responses to the failure of practical reason.

II. Randomness as Causal Separation

Randomness is a significant issue in both metaphysics and the philosophy of science. Thomas Aquinas, for instance, argues that divine providence does not necessarily preclude contingency or chance, that is, the occurrence of particular events that are not directly effected (or "predicted") by God.[8] The theory of evolution, to take a typical scientific example, assigns a major role to the random factor of mutation in its general attempt to explain the evolution of species within a lawlike scheme. However, in both cases the acceptance of "random" aspects in the theory does not necessarily imply metaphysical indeterminism or the freedom of certain phenomena from the dominion of causality.[9] Pure or absolute randomness is alien both to theological thought as well as to most scientific theory (quantum theory being an exception). The alternative concept of randomness that I am suggesting here is based on the idea of *causal separation*, that is, on the weaker assumption that even if all events are "caused," there is no unified causal theory within which every event can be explained or predicted. Accordingly, an event is said to be random only in relation to a particular causal system. Thus, mutations are random from the point of view of the laws of evolutionary biology but not from the point of view of chemistry or physics. And particular events can be explained in terms of natural causal forces though they are random or contingent from the point of view of God's design, which applies only to the general laws governing the world.[10]

Causal separation has proven a fruitful explanatory strategy, since it defines (in both the theological and the biological examples) a relevant level of abstraction of the phenomena subjected to general laws. This abstraction is a condition for any systematic explanation and prediction. But I am here interested in the way causal separation is shrewdly employed in *practical* reason, as grounds for deciding unresolvable dilemmas by lot. Aleatoric methods of decision making are based on the appeal to the outcome of a contrived mechanism, which operates on causal laws that are in a significant way *irrelevant* to the issue at hand. If I am right in characterizing lotteries in terms of causal separation, the substantive task is to articulate the relevance criteria of this separation, that is, to define and explain what is expected of the causal mechanism that is appealed to by the strategic second-order attempt to solve first-order issues by lot.

Now explanations in science and theology of the type I mentioned also appeal to causal separation in terms of irrelevance. They are based on theoretical considerations that make certain descriptions of phenomena simply irrelevant to the explanatory goal of the theory.[11] Evolutionary theory is expected to explain the survival of species but not the occurrence of a particular mutation. The explanation of the latter phenomenon must be left to other theories. Obviously these criteria of division of labor between theories (applying to different levels of description of phenomena) cannot serve practical reason. Here, the criteria must have something to do with the *acceptability* of the practical decision-making procedure and, accordingly, its outcome. And this acceptability is related to the normative value of fairness rather than to the cognitive search for the best explanation and prediction.

III. Lotteries and Epistemic Separation

Our obsession with rationality in practical (no less than in theoretical) matters means that we commonly expect choices and distributions to be guided by substantive reasons based on rules, laws, values, and norms. Consequently, we also expect these to be predictable. We also lay responsibility on the decision maker for their outcome, since we ascribe to him or her control over the way the actual outcome was effected.

A judge pronouncing sentence on the basis of random, unreasoned gut feeling is no less repugnant than a physicist deciding between two theories by instinct. However, some cases cannot be decided "rationally" in this straightforward way. The failure of reason may occur in the following cases of theoretical impasse: the total absence of reasons, the existence of competing reasons of equal weight, or the incommensurability of the competing reasons. Reason may also fail in cases of practical or normative quandary: for instance, when the decision maker is reluctant to assume the responsibility involved in a serious issue (despite having at his disposal reasons that might justify it); or a case where, despite the objective force of the reasons for one solution rather than the other, we are aware that the losing party will never be able to see this and so we assign an independent weight to the acceptability of the solution by all parties concerned.

The second-order rational strategy of practical reason in these cases is aimed at satisfying an alternative goal to the standard one of choosing on the balance of first-order reasons. The normative goal is often the respect for equality of the parties involved in the distributive choice, and when this equality cannot be achieved by dividing the benefit or the burden in question, then granting equal opportunity or chance is a second-best strategy. So whereas causal separation in scientific explanation is determined by theory-dependent considerations, causal separation in lotteries is determined by the normative goal of equality. Lotteries are thus expected to substitute an independent causal mechanism for the standard, reason-supported choice. But what does "independent" mean? What is the criterion of the separateness of the causal system that would be viewed as "random" relative to the structure of reasons and rules governing the controversial issue that stands to be solved?

My suggestion is that it is simply *ignorance*.[1][2] To secure their purpose as practically rational, lotteries must be fair, and fairness is secured by the use of a causal mechanism unknown to all the parties concerned. Thus, the coin we toss in the air is not considered to be free from the laws of physics, but we know that neither we nor our rivals can have any pre-knowledge as to how the coin will fall. The same applies to the roulette wheel or the shuffled cards, the selection of a jury by various alphabetical methods, and so on. The idea of causal separation is constituted by the lack of any correlation, or at least any known correlation, between the kind of (psychological) causality that determines how we choose "heads" or "tails" and the kind of (physical) causality that determines how the coin falls when tossed in midair.

However, it should be noted that the epistemic criterion of causal separation is by definition relative to the state of knowledge of human beings in general and of the individuals taking part in the lottery. It can by no means be characterized in an a priori manner. And, as it is hard to prove that people do not have such relevant knowledge, lotteries tend to be vulnerable above all to *suspicion*. The loser must be convinced that she was not manipulated by her rival's superior knowledge. Epistemic equi-probability is sufficient to guarantee fairness, but how do we *know* that this condition is indeed satisfied? As no foolproof guarantee can be logically provided, participants in lotteries at least want to be assured that a causal mechanism that is not known to be correlated in any way to the issue at hand is used. Thus, I know that all coins are biased to some degree, but I know that it is usually difficult to recognize the way in which they are biased and hence that my competitor cannot use such knowledge, to increase his chances. But if I suspect my rival to have such knowledge, I might insist on the use of a coin of mine. An even more efficient way of assuring causal separation will be to let one party select the coin while the other is given the first choice of "heads" or "tails."

If I am right in being satisfied with epistemic probability of this kind, it seems that there is no defect in a lottery conducted by means of a machine shown in retrospect to have been biased even in a way that gave *no* chance to one of the options chosen by the participants; of course, this is true as long as no one knew about it, or to put this more precisely, as long as the person who knew about it had no stakes in the lottery or any way of informing those who had stakes about this defect. Thus, if I choose the number 22 in a roulette game, and it is later proven that a mechanical defect made it impossible for the ball to fall into the 22 slot, I have no reason to declare the lottery unfair. Similarly, a lottery cannot be declared unfair if the choice was made *after* the coin had been tossed, as long as no player knew the way it fell. Fairness is constituted by the equal chances of people, not of numbers, that is of human subjects suffering (or enjoying, if you wish) the same degree of ignorance, rather than of abstract, objective possibilities. Indeed, the fear of cheating and manipulation calls for a more secure causal separation and lays the burden of proof of ignorance (which is hard to come by) on the agency running the lottery. But this only serves to support my general claim.

Another threat to causal separation constituted by ignorance of the relationship between different causal chains comes from what may be called "the structured outcomes of iterated lotteries." Thus, if we decide to select a jury by a random draw based on the fifth letter of surnames in a given list of eligible citizens, this might look fair. But, as has been shown,[13] a repeated application of this method can prove that members of a particular ethnic group would have a significantly higher chance of being selected. If the identity of this group is relevant to the legal case in question, the method can be challenged as unfair. But, note, the challenge can be made only after the aleatoric method is repeated and hence the outcome can be said to be *known* in advance by the selection agency. If a one-time lottery yields a jury of this same identity, no one can have cause for complaint. I should add that this structured property of a repeated decision-making mechanism is the source of a justified rejection of majority rule and its replacement by unstructured random devices. That is to say, we may decide an issue on *one* isolated occasion by majority vote, which, let us assume, is not known in advance to yield any particular outcome, but once we become aware of the structure of the distribution of opinions in the group, majority vote stops being fair in the sense of causal separation based on ignorance. I tend to agree with some political theorists from ancient Greece through today that lotteries are superior to majority rule in many such contexts, but I cannot pursue this important suggestion here.[14]

IV. Picking vs. Casting Lots

Cartesian rules of conduct and the casting of lots are not the only second-order strategies of practical reason in extricating itself from the impasse of equally attractive options. Edna Ullmann-Margalit and Sidney Morgenbesser have suggested the term "picking" to describe what Nicholas Rescher in an older article referred to as choice without preference.[15] Buridan's proverbial ass and the modern supermarket shopper selecting a particular can of soup are self-explanatory examples of picking. In a way, picking, that is, selecting with no reason, or by just "grabbing" whatever token comes first, is a sort of random selection. However, my claim is that picking is different in an interesting way from casting lots, although there is an element of picking in any lottery[16] and an element of natural lottery in every picking. The distinction can be highlighted in terms of causal separation. In picking, there is no attempt to artificially induce a causal chain selected for its alienation from the issue to be decided or from the knowledge of the parties concerned. In picking, one simply resigns oneself to whatever natural causes that could affect a selection (like extending one's hand to pick one of numerous identical cookies or "choosing" the first number that "comes to one's mind").[17] The assumption is that not only is the selection not random in the sense of not being governed by causes, but that the choice is indifferent to the possibility of the causal chain being of a kind that can be known in advance to effect a certain outcome (e.g., my hand's tendency to go right, or my stream of consciousness leading always to the number 11 for deep psychological reasons). In other words, "bias" created by a conscious or unconscious causality is no defect in picking, since selection through any causal chain is good enough to extricate us from the situation of equally rational options. On the contrary, the clearer the dominance of the causal force pushing the ass to select one of the haystacks, the greater her chances not to die of hunger.[18]

When we move from trivial cases of picking to what Edna Ullmann-Margalit has called "big decisions,"[19] the case for letting a natural, that is, an "uncontrived," process of effecting a choice becomes even stronger. In big decisions, such as whom to marry, or what career to adopt, lotteries seem not only ridiculous (as they might be in the case of choosing a particular spoon from the drawer) but outright wrong, and I dare say irrational. Why is this so? My suggestion is that our concept of the integrity of the individual implies, among other things, allowing inner psychological causal forces to effect the choice. In a serious sense, the causal separation involved in a lottery alienates the choice from the subject, the chooser, whereas a choice based on picking, gut feeling, sub-conscious or even unconscious factors *belongs* to the agent, is *his* in this deep sense of the integrity of the person. An "instinctive" choice may be "unreasoned," but it still reflects in a genuine way the personality of the agent and accordingly carries personal responsibility. The random process of drawing lots severs the link between the agent and the way the selection is actually made.

We may generalize from this contrastive discussion of lotteries and picking situations (or other cases of choice without reasoned preference): lotteries are rationally exercised in *inter*-personal contexts in which distributive choices have to be made in a fair manner and where there are no substantive reasons for making these choices; picking is a rational strategy of practical reason in *intra*-personal contexts in which constraints of fairness are relevant and no effort to counter bias or malice is required. Lotteries are rational in competitive situations in which another's gain is my loss (organ transplants or the white pieces in chess); picking is used when there is no threat of manipulation or unfair loss.[20] Furthermore, causal separation, which is a virtue of justice and fairness in the inter-personal setting, is an undesirable alienating factor in intra-personal circumstances in which the idiosyncracies of individual agency and character lend support and meaning to the choice, albeit not in providing a reasoned preference. Human beings are not in themselves random generating devices; consequently, any attempt on their part to secure randomness, at least in the relative, epistemic sense, is dependent on the degree of causal separation over which they may have some control (mainly by designing a fair lottery).

V. "Natural Lotteries"

We have distinguished between lotteries and picking as two ways of second-order choices of practical reason to break first-order deadlocks. There is, however, a third kind of solution, sometimes referred to as "let nature take its course." This is the choice of practical reason neither to pick nor to design an artificial mechanism for generating the outcome but rather to intentionally remain passive in the face of external, natural processes that would yield one outcome rather than the other. Is such resignation rational? Is it fair? And when?

On the most basic level, we should examine the widely used term "natural lottery" as referring to the way we all become what we are. Our natural endowment, in the deep sense of our genetic make-up, is considered to be our "lot," that is, the outcome of a random process rather than a morally designed and controlled choice. But to treat what we are as *our* lot is misleading, since there is no subject who gains or loses by getting ("from nature") those properties that constitute his or her identity.[21] Lotteries, in other words, cannot be applied to unidentifiable, pre-conceived "place-holders" but only to identifiable persons who may stand to win or lose from their lot in terms of their given interests and what they are.

But there is a sense of the concept of a natural lottery that is not logically incoherent; namely, what happens to us after our identity is created, that is, the share of good and bad that can be ascribed to *us*. People might turn out to be healthy or ill as a matter of random factors. But this randomness is, as I have argued, relative to a relevant causal chain. And when I say that I was lucky to escape an illness that struck others, I mean that the causes of my health have nothing to do, for instance, with my moral record, economic efforts, or, indeed, medical care. But unlike our identity, we may and do often say that we do not *deserve* what happens to us and hence that this "lot" should be changed, relieved, or redistributed. This is a moral sense of natural lottery, which on the basis of moral reasons sometimes calls for compensation. Human beings are not expected to accept whatever is bestowed on them by random natural processes. Lotteries in the primary sense are redistributive; that is, they refuse to accept the given, natural distribution.[22]

Natural lottery in both the logical and the moral sense is anyway a metaphorical concept, since it concerns a *given* state of affairs that is the outcome of a natural process rather than the *process* itself, which is random (relatively to other processes). Lotteries are intentional devices, procedures rather than processes, applied by agents or agencies as a strategy of *practical reason,* and this is exactly what is absent from natural processes.

There is, however, a third, procedural sense of natural lottery, namely, the conscious and intentional use of natural processes as the optimal procedure for deciding the issue at hand. Picking is a limiting case, since it is natural on the one hand, yet located *in* the agent on the other. Another example is the principle of "first come, first served" often used in medical ethics for deciding priority in according scarce resources.[23] The problem is that, unlike the laws governing the spinning of a coin in the air, the laws governing the accessibility to medical care are not completely alien to interests, political power, and other factors relevant to one's status. If it turns out that the first to apply for a newly discovered scarce resource are those who are rich or close to the ruling party, then the condition of causal separation and hence of fairness is not satisfied. Resigning oneself to nature's verdict may therefore be like majority vote (which I mentioned earlier), a manipulative move on the part of those who *know* in advance that they stand to gain from the allegedly randomized procedure. Fairness calls for an active intervention in the world in a way that would guarantee causal separation and "unpatterned allocation."

VI. The Rationality of Lotteries

Unlike "just this once" (akrasia) or "not wanting to know" (cognitive suppression), lotteries are not failures of practical reason but rather the rational response to particular failures of practical reason to guide action on the basis of first-order reasons. And as against both akrasia and cognitive suppression, the failure of practical reason in situations where random selection is chosen as a strategy is not blameworthy. That is, it lies in the inherent objective deadlock created by the equal weight of the competing first-order reasons rather than by a subjective defect in the psychology of the individual agent. Unlike picking, often the strategy of the lazy, and unlike letting nature take its course, often the strategy of those who shun responsibility, a lottery is a conscious and responsible effort to first admit the shortcomings of reason and then overcome them by a fair method. Lotteries are rational for they are based on refusal to act on instinct, intuition, natural chance, or any other blind force that might turn out to be biased. The rationality of lotteries consists, as was pointed out very eloquently by Otto Neurath over eighty years ago, in the conscious control over the decision-making process, that is, in the probabilities of the randomizing method or at least on its epistemic probabilities.[24]

So, in terms of my suggestion, lotteries are rational because the control over the process leading to the selection is not itself random. It is constituted by the careful and intentional construction of causal separation, thus checking bias, that is, the interference of patterned kinds of irrelevant considerations. Furthermore, unlike picking or "natural chance," lotteries are designed; they require reasoned choices concerning the scope of the participants, the timing and number of lotteries, the distribution of the probabilities ("the length of the straws"), the baseline that defines equality of opportunity, and the social and psychological costs of conducting the chance procedure.[25] All these factors of control indicate that, though there is no agent responsibility over the particular selected outcome, there is a far-reaching responsibility over the way this is achieved, and hence a better chance that the outcome will be acceptable to both winners and losers.[26]

However, once we leave the abstract level of rational justification of lotteries as such, we encounter grave problems that pertain both to practical reason, and to normative values. On the level of practical reason, we must be aware that the question *when* a situation is characterized by first-order impasse is itself highly controversial. This is often an issue of the assessment of whether the competing reasons are indeed equally weighty or incommensurable. Thus, deciding who should start with the white pieces in chess is agreed to be a question to which no first-order reasons may give an answer (at least if we are talking of a first game in a series). But whether hearts be transplanted first to young patients or rather be distributed by lot is a highly contested issue. And of course the question is not only of the theoretical judgment of the relative force of reasons but often a straightforwardly normative one. For example, the Greek choice of selecting public officials by lot rather than by majority rule (or professional expertise) is not based on the failure of practical reason to guide us through the best reasons but on the idea that these reasons are irrelevant to the social and moral value of optimal representation.

I have shown that lotteries are exercised in inter-personal contexts that call for fair decisions, mainly in hard distributive dilemmas. But beyond this formal generalization, the particular cases that call for lotteries and the way they should be conducted remains a *normative* problem that goes beyond the scope of this chapter. I will add only that our attitude to lotteries is typically ambivalent: on the one hand, our commitment to rationality and choice based on substantive reasons and direct responsibility rejects randomized choices that appear to be an easy way out of a difficult dilemma; on the other, our awareness of the limits of reason, as well as its irrelevance to deep normative commitments to the equality of human beings as such, leads us to treat lotteries as fair and even morally noble.[27]

Our ambivalence towards randomness consists of our perception of ourselves as victims both of blind natural forces and of intentional human malice and exploitation. We try to counterbalance the uncontrolled natural course of events by appealing to practical reason as a corrective measure introducing order; and we counterbalance the potential abuse of reason by appealing to the blind forces of nature, which at least make us all have an equal chance.

VII. Epilogue: The Dionysian Use of Reason

In his masterful study of lotteries, Jon Elster says that he would be surprised if he had missed any major kind of lotteries in his detailed examination.[28] Indeed, his taxonomy seems to be exhaustive. But there is one form, which I believe to be of much philosophical (though not necessarily ethical) importance, that did escape Elster's notice, and this is gambling and betting. Practical reason sometimes plays dice in a purely playful way, as a diversion or entertainment.

This sportive use of lotteries is, however, not so innocent or devoid of deeper meaning. When people take part in a national lottery (which usually involves very high monetary prizes), they seem to play a serious game, a most democratic game in which all ordinary social criteria of merit and desert give way to the absolute equality of every individual taking part in the lottery. No racial, ethnic, gender, class, or political distinction makes any difference to one's chances of winning and losing. As "a great equalizer," lotteries differ from death only in their being voluntary. This is one of the few arenas in the public sphere in which egalitarianism is exercised in a pure form. It even transcends all democratic principles of equality (e.g., before the law, in democratic participation, and so on) in which there is always a gap between the formal equality and the real differences in power that lie behind the formal equality. National lotteries give all participants real equal status.

Now the social order is always based on inequality of some sort. People are never treated as absolutely equal, even in democratic and egalitarian societies. Hard work, moral record, relevant needs—all are taken to make a difference in distributive choices. The very idea of a social *order* is conceptually linked with substantive criteria of justice and desert, that is to non-random properties and circumstances of individual members of society. But lotteries *challenge* this social order, rebuff the serious commitment to the principles of justice. In a deep sense lotteries are *subversive* of our basic political and social beliefs about who deserves what. They substitute blind chance for rational ordering of values and merit; they promote absolute formal equality of chance instead of the rationally supported fine-tuned democratic equality of rights.[29] And this subversion is paradoxically exercised by practical reason, which turns against itself, as if in an act of skeptical rebellion against the oppressive rule of reason.

There is, therefore, a Dionysian element in lotteries, a temporary suspension not only of adherence to the social order but also the deliberate rejection of responsibility and a fatalistic resignation to the effects of uncontrolled and unknown causal forces. This may explain the addictive power of gambling, as well as its entertaining element (which is associated with the temporary suspension of one's social status and responsibility in favor of a carefree subjection to formal egalitarianism). Lotteries may express defiance toward the oppressive rule of reason in its presumptuous claim to knowledge and authority. And it is, therefore, only shrewd on the part of the social order to let these anarchic tendencies express themselves but to confine them to the well-defined boundaries of institutionalized lotteries, gambling houses, and legitimate betting clubs.

Tom Stoppard's classic play *Rosencrantz and Guildenstern Are Dead* opens with the two almost indistinguishable protagonists betting on the toss of coins. Ros (as he is called in the play) wins all the coins tossed, one by one. The dramatist comments that this consecutive run of ninety-two "heads" is impossible, but the protagonists do not show any surprise though they are aware of the oddity of the situation and are bothered by its "implications." Having been coin tossing as a means of diversion (based on suspense), the two first grow bored by the single persistent outcome and are then led to suspect that there are forces intervening in the course of events that violate the laws of probability. They now have to examine the hypothesis that they live "within un-, sub- or supernatural forces." Fortunately they come out with a brilliant proof (based on self-reference) that they still live in the natural world. The whole drama is a playful, second-order challenge of rational order. Not only are all common rules and discriminations suspended in the world of the two identical twins, but the laws of probability, which seem to be the logical solution to the distribution between equally deserving parties, also fail: all the coins fall "heads." The fairest method proves to lead to the most unjust distribution. The final lesson is that human beings cannot tolerate a world of absolute order (since reason often fails) but equally that they cannot tolerate a fully randomized distribution. Only the combination of "the fortuitous and the ordained" can give us the "reassuring union which we recognized as nature".

In playing dice, practical reason goes on holiday but without completely neglecting its responsibilities.

Notes

1. R. Descartes, *Discourse on Method*, part 3 (in *The Philosophical Works of Descartes*, trs. by E. S. Haldane and G. R. T. Ross; Cambridge: Cambridge University Press, 1969; vol. 1). Descartes seeks to formulate second-order rules of practical reason "in order that I should not remain irresolute in my actions while reason obliged me to be so in my judgment" (p. 95).

2. Descartes, *Discourse*, p. 96; Otto Neurath, "The Lost Wanderers of Descartes and the Auxiliary Motive" (in *Philosophical Papers*, Dordrecht: Reidel, 1984, pp. 1–12); J. Elster, *Solomonic Judgements*, Cambridge: Cambridge University Press, 1989, pp. 121–22. While Descartes's second maxim, that of determination and resoluteness, is a practical ("auxiliary") guide, for Neurath (as well as for Elster) lotteries may serve as principles for deciding theoretical questions such as the choice between beliefs. I tend to suspect the possibility of deciding to adopt beliefs on any practical basis, lotteries included, but cannot pursue this epistemological issue here.

3. John 19:23–24; Mark 15:24.

4. Descartes, *Discourse*, pp. 95–6.

5. Descartes, *Discourse*, p. 96.

6. Descartes, *Discourse*, pp. 96–7.

7. Descartes, *Discourse*, pp. 98–9.

8. Thomas Aquinas, *Summa Contra Gentiles*, book 3, part 1, chap. 74. And cf. Aristotle, *Physics*, book 2, chaps. 6–7, where Aristotle speaks of chance in terms of "incidental cause."

9. E. Sober, *The Nature of Selection*, Cambridge, Mass.: MIT Press, 1984; chap. 4. Sober explicitly says that in the theory of evolution both mutation and natural selection are conceived as deterministic processes.

10. When lotteries are used as a means of forcing God to decide an issue, the religious believer casts lots on the assumption that God, being omnipotent, can and will control the outcome, thereby expressing his will or judgment. This assumption is challenged by Thomas Aquinas, who warns that such use of lots amounts to illegitimate "divination" and belongs to the category of magic. See Thomas Aquinas, *Summa Theologica*, 2, 2, Q. 95. But if God is described as the source of a "pre-established harmony," as in Leibniz, there cannot be any separation between different causal chains, and hence no room is left for any randomness (from a divine point of view). A Spinozistic conception of natural necessity is even a clearer case, since it allows for no contingency whatsoever, let alone randomness.

11. See Sober, *Nature*, p. 131. Sober contrasts this kind of knowledge, which is analytically associated with the assumption of randomness, with Laplaceian knowledge of a godly nature, in which everything is known in a non-probabilistic way. This distinction raises the role of *ignorance* in human scientific knowledge and hence connects, as we shall see, the role of randomness in theoretical reason to that in practical reason.

12. Cf. D. Hume, *An Inquiry Concerning Human Understanding*, the first sentence of sect. 6: "Though there be no such thing as *chance* in the world, our ignorance of the real cause of any event has the same influence on the understanding and begets a like species of belief or opinion."

13. Elster, *Judgments* p. 46, and note.

14. See Barbara Goodwin's excellent discussion in *Justice by Lottery*, Chicago: University of Chicago Press, 1992. See also Elster, *Judgments*, pp. 78–92. I should only add here that the issue of selecting public officials by lottery (versus majority vote) goes beyond our present discussion of lottery as a method of practical reason to resolve rational stalemates. In preferring lotteries to majority rule, we appeal to the *objective* superiority of the better representation of the will of the people, rather than to the fairness of the procedure based on the parties' ignorance.

15. E. Ullmann-Margalit and S. Morgenbesser, "Picking and Choosing," *Social Research* 44 (1977): 757–85. N. Rescher, "Choice without Preference," *Kant-Studien* 51 (1959/60): 145–175.

16. Rescher, "Choice," p. 168. There is no real threat of an infinite regress in the idea that picking the number for a lottery should itself be done by a further lottery: it suffices that the picking mechanism is kept causally separated from the lottery mechanism.

17. So although the first move in casting lots involves picking (e.g., deciding "heads" or "tails," or the number 11 in a roulette), this does not undermine causal separation of the sort required by lotteries, since there is no correlation whatsoever between the causality involved in the picking of the particular values of the lottery and the physical causality that effects its outcome. This is why picking cannot be fully replaced by lottery (Ullmann-Margalit and Morgenbesser, "Picking," pp. 769–70), as every lottery forces us to pick, but lotteries can be replaced by picking (though sometimes with an undesirable moral price, which is discussed later).

18. Note the difference between practical and theoretical reasons here. In scientific research, the working of the sub-conscious biases of the experimenter are detrimental to the reliability of the experiment. Consequently, the prevalent rule in medical experiments, for instance, is that they should be "double-blind," which in terms of this chapter means optimal causal separation. Natural biases in science are to be feared no less than moral biases in ethics, and both can be partly overcome by epistemic separation.

19. E. Ullmann-Margalit, "Opting: The Case of 'Big' Decisions," *Wissenschaftskolleg Jahrbuch* (1984/5): 441–54.

20. An interesting intermediate case is the proverbial "battle of the sexes" in which a married couple is debating whether to spend the evening at a restaurant or go to the movies. Although it seems that this is a typically competitive, inter-personal conflict, most couples would be reluctant to apply a lottery as a decision-making strategy. The reason seems to be that the case, after all, is not genuinely competitive or a zero-sum game, but rather closer to the intra-personal model in which the integrity of the married relation implies letting the dynamics of the relationship decide the case, thus reflecting in a more genuine way the way this relationship is constituted. I am grateful to John Landau for this example.

21. See my *Genethics: Moral Issues in the Creation of People*, Berkeley: University of California Press, 1992; chap. 6. I may be proud or ashamed of what I am, but I can only make a moral claim on the basis of what I have or have not as an individual with a fixed identity. If I am right in this, it seems that Nagel's concept of "constitutive luck," that is, the fortune of being born with a good genetic make-up, is not coherent, and that accordingly "wrongful life claims" of children suing their parents for having been born in defect cannot be logically sustained. See on this issue T. Nagel, "Moral Luck," in *Mortal Questions*; Cambridge: Cambridge University Press, 1979; p. 28; and critical examinations of the idea in S. L. Hurley, "Justice without Constitutive Luck," *Ethics* (ed. A Phillips Griffiths); Cambridge: Cambridge University Press, 1993; p. 198; and chap. 1 of my book.

22. Obviously the conditions and especially the limits of the redistributive process, typical of political and moral life, are a highly complicated issue that cannot be discussed here. Writers on lotteries have addressed the question of applying another lottery to the outcome of the first in the same way as the first lottery was applied to the outcome of the random natural process. See, for instance, the critical discussion of John Harris's

provocative suggestion in his "The Survival Lottery," *Philosophy* 50 (1975): 81–7. Harris advocates a system of a forced lottery of organs for transplantation as a fair method of redistribution; but my challenge to him concerns the limit of such redistributive moves: would we want to redistribute brain cells or genes in a way that would change people's identity? We would reach a stage in which there would be no identifiable beneficiary to the egalitarian redistribution. Borges's famous story "Lottery in Babylon" teaches the paradoxical lesson of the infinite reiteration of lotteries to whatever human beings have and do: the complete disintegration of the human person and individual identity!

23. G. Calabresi and P. Bobbitt, *Tragic Choices*, New York: Norton, 1978, pp. 43–4. Beyond this particular principle, Calabresi and Bobbitt refer to "the customary evolutionary method," which is a general method of accepting actual power relations and values in society to decide how scarce resources are allocated. This is also a case of a natural lottery in the procedural sense.

24. Neurath, "Wanderers," chap. 1. Neurath brilliantly lists in hierarchical order the strategies for resolving deadlock: instinct (which is "animal"), omens and oracles (which are religious), insight and deliberation (which in deadlock situations are pseudo-rational), and finally casting lots (which is the most rational way, since it recognizes the limits of reason). See also Elster, *Judgments*, pp. 121–22, for a discussion of Neurath.

25. One way to put these normative questions is to ask when should lotteries be practiced. The answer "never" seems to be arrogant from the point of view of reason as well as risking discrimination and bias. The answer "always" leads to the logical paradox involved in the dissolution of the identity of the subjects among whom we wish to distribute the goods and burdens by lot. But medical ethicists, political theorists, and legal scholars are debating all the options between those two extremes.

26. In some cases lotteries seem to enjoy such a high degree of acceptance due to their fairness that agencies deciding an issue on the basis of what they believe to be perfectly adequate first-order reasons might want to present the choice *as if* it were random. A classical example is Plato's method of matchmaking in his ideal republic, where partners are carefully selected by the ruling party to be married to each other on the basis of their qualities, but the partners are made to believe by an intricate manipulative method that they were matched by lot. Plato, *Republic*, St. 460a.

27. What I refer to as our obsession with rationality often makes people interpret the outcome of a fairly devised artificial lottery (satisfying the criteria of causal separation) as if it *does* nevertheless reflect some merit, moral desert, grace, or divine intention. People are rarely indifferent to the "meaning" of winning a lottery. This is natural in a worldview that consists of a belief in an ultimate causal efficacy in the world, which is not known (and hence does not interfere with causal separation) yet is reflected post hoc in the outcome of the lottery. The Israeli crowd's shouting in a basketball match "there is God" when its favorite team wins in the very last second is cynically referred to by intellectuals as another ontological proof for the existence of God! Superstition is a constant threat to the sophisticated super-rationality of practical reason since randomness is often psychologically resisted. For an illuminating study of people's attitude to lotteries, see M. Bar-Hillel and E. Neter, "Why Are People Reluctant to Exchange Lottery Tickets?" *Journal of Personality and Social Psychology* 70 (1996): 17–27.

28. Elster, *Judgments*, p. 104. In developing many of the ideas in this final section, I was inspired by insights and suggestions of John Landau.

29. This absolute formal equality obviously does not exist as a matter of social fact. In many societies one can draw the socioeconomic profile of the typical gambler; that is, not everyone is taking part in the "subversive game." Furthermore, since the lottery agencies (such as governments) take up to 50% of the money invested in the lottery and spend it on the population at large, there is a well-defined redistributive aspect in lotteries guided by social norms, moral values, and political interests. For the current rise in the gambling and lottery industry throughout the world, see *Time Magazine* (October 9, 1995).

5
ON NOT WANTING TO KNOW

Edna Ullmann-Margalit

> He that judges without informing himself to the utmost that he is capable, cannot acquit himself of *judging amiss*.
> John Locke, *Essays Concerning Human Understanding*, book 2, chapter 21, sec. 67

I. Introduction

Wanting to know seems natural and in need of no justification. Wanting not to know seems less natural and in need of some justification. But a moment's reflection reminds us that we may not want to know many types of things, perhaps justifiably so. We may wish to protect ourselves from cluttering our mind and our memory, or from boredom, or from pain; we may wish to preserve our faculties of creativity and of imagination; we may wish to avoid excessive cost or unnecessary involvements; we may wish to remain impartial or to retain an element of surprise in our lives.

Thus, you may not want to know the number of hair on your head, the telephone numbers of everyone in town, the exact details of the trip abroad your neighbor made or of the operation she has undergone. Perhaps you do not want to know certain things in advance, such as what do all the critics think about the play you intend to see, or whether or not a surprise party for your birthday is being planned, or whether the baby you are about to have is a boy or a girl. Adopted children may wish not to know who their biological parents are. It is possible that you do not want to know precisely what your spouse is up to when you are away—and many of us may not want to know the details of how prisoners are treated in Singapore.

The phenomenon of not wanting to know, then, seems secure: it exists all right. But we may want to ask ourselves whether and to what extent it can be defended. When is not wanting to know, and when is it not, inherently unreasonable or irrational? What is the relation between not wanting to know and self-deception? Is there an issue of morality here?

Theories of rationality conceive of rational action as the employment of appropriate means for achieving a desired end. Rational action is thus thought of as a product of two vectors. One is the vector of belief, or knowledge, or probability. The other is the vector of desires, or wants, or utility. I act rationally when I act to promote what I want on the basis of what I know.

Elaborate theories are constructed to account for these two constitutive elements, belief on the one hand and desire on the other. One way of looking at the present enterprise is to see what happens when we drop the assumption that these two vectors in the parallelogram of action are independent and allow them to interfere with one another. The vectors might interact in at least two ways. One would be captured by the question: do we (always) know what we want? The other would be captured by the question: do we—and should we—(always) want to know? It is the second of these two questions that I focus on here.

II. The Principle of Total Evidence

Let us consider an important component of what I have referred to as the vector of belief. It is the principle, or the requirement, of total evidence: a rational person should believe the hypothesis supported by all available relevant evidence. Addressing this issue, Rudolf Carnap distinguished the logical question of how we are to determine the degree r to which evidence E supports hypothesis H, and the practical-methodological question of what we are to *do* given r (however it is determined). The first is a question of theoretical reasoning, the second is a question of practical reasoning. From the fact that hypothesis H is supported by evidence E to the degree r, nothing follows regarding action unless a further assumption is introduced, namely, that E is the totality of evidence available to the agent. If E is indeed the totality of evidence available to the agent at time t, then, according to Carnap, the rational agent will accept the directive to believe hypothesis H at time t to the degree r and to act accordingly (e.g., to bet on H with odds not exceeding r). This Carnap calls the requirement of total evidence, tracing a distinguished historical pedigree for it, including Jacob Bernoulli (in his *Ars Conjectandi* [1713], as cited by John Maynard Keynes, *A Treatise on Probability* [1973/1921, pp. 345–6]), and C.S. Peirce.

Now when Carnap requires his rational agents to attend to the totality of evidence available to them, he means that it is irrational for them to ignore or to disregard relevant information they have. (Information is relevant insofar as it affects the degree r to which E supports H.) He discusses three types of cases meant to convince us that this is indeed so. First, we are invited to consider a judge who ignores information brought before him that is relevant to the attribution of guilt to the defendant. The second case concerns a businessman who, in evaluating a proposed deal, disregards information he has about some of the risks involved. And the third is a scientist who publishes results of experiments supporting his theory but neglects to publish—or to consider—results unfavorable to it. In all three cases, according to Carnap, the adopted procedure is not rational.

However, even a cursory reflection about these supposedly paradigmatic cases brings to the fore some problems that ought to lead to further reflection. Carnap may have been insufficiently familiar with the Anglo-American adversary legal system, in which there is of course a fundamental distinction between relevant evidence and admissible evidence. A judge (or jury) often not only may but must ignore information brought up during the trial and doubtlessly relevant but deemed inadmissible qua evidence on social-moral grounds (evidence based on hearsay, on a wife testifying against her husband, on illegal wiretapping). A similar point may be made with regard to Carnap's third case: in science too a distinction may have to be made between relevant and admissible data. Suppose scientists are presented with results from the twins experiments conducted by Mengele, the monster doctor from Auschwitz. Should we consider them irrational—as distinct from immoral—were they to refuse to look at this information or to use it in their own research, even if it may be relevant to this research?

As for the businessman, we should note that much psychological literature suggests that people as well as organizations "often expose themselves to risk because they misjudge the odds" (Kahneman and Lovallo 1993, p. 24[1])—and they misjudge the odds, sometimes, because statistical knowledge "that is known to the forecaster will not necessarily be used, or even retrieved, when a forecast is made" (p. 26).

This observation is discussed by Daniel Kahneman and Dan Lovallo in connection with the distinction they make between forecasts that draw on the "inside" and those that draw on the "outside" view: an inside view anchors predictions on the specifics of the case at hand, on detailed plans, and typically on representative scenarios; the outside view ignores the details of the case at hand and is essentially statistical and comparative. For example, consider estimates of how long it would take me to finish an academic project (a paper, a book, the development of a new curriculum). My own inside view prediction is typically based on my detailed work plan and is typically overconfident: we generally tend to exaggerate our own control over events and to underestimate the likelihood of obstacles coming our way, with the result that finishing our projects almost always takes us longer than we expected. An outside view prediction will be based on comparative statistics of how long similar projects—my own as well as other people's—took to complete.

Kahneman and Lovallo conclude that while the outside view is "much more likely to yield a realistic estimate,—the inside view is overwhelmingly preferred in intuitive forecasting" (pp. 25, 26). So in terms of our own concern, the point to be made is twofold. On the descriptive level, we have the psychologists' findings that forecasters indeed ignore relevant (statistical) information available to them. On the normative level, the question may be raised whether this is always to be condemned as unreasonable. Is it not the case that the optimistic bias, which is based on ignoring unfavorable but realistic information and which leads to unrealistic bold forecasts, may yet be beneficial? Ample evidence suggests that optimism is in fact instrumental as a causal factor that contributes to successful coping with challenges. Taking the broad view, considerations of "productive enthusiasm," entrepreneurial initiative, morale, persistence in the face of difficulty, and so on often speak for the benefits of unrealistic optimism (Seligman, *Learned Optimism*, 1991).[2]

Let us go back to Carnap's principle of total evidence and ask, what does it mean to say that evidence E is all the evidence available to agent A at time t?

Evidence "available" to A naturally means evidence in A's possession, but it might also mean evidence accessible to A, evidence that A could acquire. Carnap concentrates on the first notion: he is concerned to establish the irrationality of ignoring information that one already has. My own focus, in contrast, is on the second notion: I am questioning the rationality (or otherwise) of acquiring information that one does not yet have. But before I move on to this second notion of available evidence, let me briefly note that even for Carnap's own purposes his notion of available evidence remains problematic. The admonition not to disregard information in my possession could be variously interpreted according to whether it is meant in the narrow sense of information that I am—or happen to be—aware of at t, or whether it is meant in some broader sense that might include, for example, retrievable information that I might have, or in an even broader (and troubling) sense that includes the deductive closure of everything I know.

Consider now the idea that to act rationally one ought to act on the totality of evidence accessible to him or to her: "He that judges without informing himself to the utmost that he is capable, cannot acquit himself of *judging amiss*" (John Locke, *Essays Concerning Human Understanding*, book 2, chapter 21, sec. 67).

This idea too stands in need of further clarification. To get hold of all relevant information before I act makes sense but has its price. The acquisition of further information is likely to be costly in monetary outlay, exertion, time spent, mental or emotional burden ("He that increaseth knowledge increaseth sorrow": Ecclesiastes 1:18). So perhaps the principle of total evidence could now be recast so as to require agents, if they are to act rationally, to act on the basis of the totality of relevant information accessible to them at a price they consider acceptable, given their goals.

But here we are in danger of rendering the whole enterprise trivial. Since there will always be some price attached to the acquisition of further information, the mere fact that on some particular occasion you do not want to know something in itself attests to the fact that you judge the price of obtaining it or of knowing it unacceptable. Hence, no instance of avoiding knowledge would be considered irrational, or unreasonable.

Something like a cost-benefit approach may be useful here, in which the value of knowledge—both intrinsic value and instrumental value—is matched against its cost. The cost divides broadly into the cost of acquisition and the cost of having, and each of these can be categorized in various ways. The cost of acquiring information includes, for example, time, money, effort, boredom, unpopularity. The cost of having information is the cost of having to come to terms with it and live with it, which may include anxiety, agitation, shame, guilt, remorse, pain, injury to self-esteem, and more. Both kinds of cost may involve strategic losses as well (a point I shall return to later).

III. The Presumption in Favor of Additional Knowledge

In light of the discussion thus far, given my focus on practical rather than theoretical reasoning, I may at this point consider weakening the principle of total evidence and examining a presumption instead. The presumption to be examined establishes, for purposes of rational action, a generic bias in favor of acting on the basis of more knowledge rather than on less. To defend the adoption of the presumption in favor of being maximally informed amounts to defending the belief that following it will lead, in the long run, to better overall results, in terms of goal fulfillment, than the results of following its antithesis (i.e., a presumption establishing a generic bias in favor of acting on the basis of less knowledge rather than on more), or indeed better than the results of a case-by-case balancing (i.e., of following no rule or presumption at all).

An important feature of a presumption as distinct from a general principle or rule is that it is rebuttable in concrete instances. In any concrete instance in which we consider applying the presumption, there may be reasons, or counter-indications, that will caution us against applying it in that concrete instance. When this happens, we say that the presumption is being rebutted in that particular case. A presumption is by its nature rebuttable: it has an implicit unless-and-until clause attached to it. (Thus, the presumption of legitimacy in the Anglo-American legal system establishes a generic bias in favor of treating the mother's husband as the father of her child, unless and until there are counter-indications in a specific case.) Irrespective of being rebutted, a presumption may be revised: the generic rule itself may come to be viewed as ill motivated, or as having outlived its usefulness, or as unfitting to changed circumstances, and so on, and therefore may come to require revision. Revising a presumption may mean changing it, reversing it, or discarding it altogether.[3]

Can the presumption for additional knowledge be sustained? Is it reasonable to defend it as a presumptive principle of practical reasoning, or does it collapse under the weight of its counter-examples? The examples discussed so far suggest that in spite of the initial plausibility of the idea that acting on the basis of more knowledge better serves our interests in reaching our goals than acting on the basis of less, there is much that we do not want to know, and there are many situations when knowing less seems to serve our interests better than knowing more. Several categories of such cases emerged: cases involving useless or irrelevant knowledge, cases in which the cost of acquisition is too high, cases in which the emotional cost of having is too high, cases involving problems of impartiality, cases in which knowledge incurs hedonic losses having to do, for example, with the loss of spontaneity or surprise. In addition, in some interesting cases there are strategic problems from knowledge. Sometimes refraining from seeking knowledge may be strategically advantageous, or having more knowledge may be instrumentally dysfunctional in the sense that it may reduce the chances of success in achieving the desired goal.[4]

How are we to take all these cases when the presumption does not apply? Are we simply to view them as an accumulation of rebutting circumstances to the presumption? Or, alternatively, are we to say that the sheer volume of the types of circumstances when the presumption does not apply, as well as their sometimes systematic nature, suggests that the presumption itself needs to be reconsidered? Since the adoption of its counter-presumption (i.e., a principled bias in favor of less rather than more knowledge) is plainly irrational, perhaps the presumption ought to be revised in the sense of being localized, that is, restricted to particular contexts. Or perhaps it is to be pronounced unsustainable altogether. The latter course amounts to recommending something like a case-by-case cost-benefit approach, in which the value of additional knowledge is balanced ad hoc in every particular instance against the cost—in the broadest sense—of obtaining it (where "obtaining" is meant to cover both acquiring and having).

This recommendation is no light matter. There is something odd about taking the bias in favor of more knowledge as if it were just a putative technical principle of practical reasoning. It is, after all, well entrenched in our culture. Ever since the Enlightenment, knowledge in our culture has been contrasted with articulated ideologies, captured as dogmas, on the one hand, and with unfounded popular beliefs, captured as superstitions, on the other. Our culture treats knowledge—as it does freedom—not only as intrinsically valuable but as incrementally valuable; that is, more of it is always better than less. To be sometimes in favor of knowing less—which means to be against always knowing more—may sound like being against motherhood or friendship: it may sound like going against the grain of the culture.

In considering the question of whether the presumption for more knowledge should be sustained as a principle of practical reasoning in spite of the large number and variety of cases when it seems not to apply, or whether to abandon it altogether, one needs to look at the justification of the presumption. Broadly speaking, a presumption may be justified in instrumental terms, or it may be justified in normative terms (or, sometimes, in both kinds of terms). The first has to do with the factual question of what, in the long run, works best. The second has to do with the evaluative question, on which side we had better "err." What we have seen in the case of the presumption in favor of additional knowledge is enough, I believe, to indicate to us that an instrumental justification is shaky, at best. One would be hard pressed to show convincingly that if we adopt this presumption, then, as rational actors, our interests would ultimately be better served than if we do not adopt it and proceed on a case-by-case basis instead. As for a normative justification, it seems to me that it could only be anchored in the kind of cultural considerations outlined in the previous paragraph—that is, the intrinsic as well as incremental value our culture assigns to knowledge, and the high-minded reluctance to see knowledge as just one factor among others that enter cost-benefit calculations. Yet, given that the context in which we consider this issue is far removed from the historical context of the cultural wars of the Enlightenment against the counter-Enlightenment, it seems appropriate to consider the question of the value of additional knowledge as a question that a rational actor, engaged in practical reasoning, faces on a retail and not on a wholesale basis. (Let me muse, as an aside, that our tendency to use the term "information" rather than "knowledge" in the context of practical reasoning and rational choice theory is not unrelated to the fact that, unlike "knowledge," "information" in our culture is not put on a pedestal, so to speak, and there is consequently less aversion to think of it instrumentally.)

In what follows I shall not proceed to amass direct arguments against upholding the presumption in favor of additional knowledge. I shall instead go on to explore further aspects of the phenomenon of not wanting to know, all aimed at enriching the texture of this phenomenon, and all designed to increase our skepticism about the sustainability of the presumption. In the process I will consider several more examples and introduce several distinctions; the last section will take up the moral context.

IV. Control of Knowledge: From Third to First Person

Let us consider the formula "I don't want to know x." As our first move, let us think of it as a special case of the more general formula "I don't want A to know x." This other-person formula states my desire to prevent—or to protect—someone from knowing something; I shall be assuming here that what I do not want A to know is not some private information relating to myself. Usually when this is the case, I may be said to display paternalistic attitudes toward that person, or to engage in a manipulative power relationship with that person. If the interests I wish to promote are the other person's, then it's the former, and if the interests I wish to promote are my own, then it's the latter. What changes when we now switch from the third-person, general, formula to the special, first-person case in which the person A is myself—when I don't want *me* to know x, so to speak?

Well, to begin with, the sophist-like query may be raised: how do I know what it is that I do not want to know unless I know it already? My response to this is that while there may indeed be cases when I do not know that there is an "it" I wish I had not known until it is too late and I already know it, there are other cases when a specific question is on the table and it is the answer to this specific question ("What have you done?" "What is my test result?") that I do not want to know. And it is these cases that concern us here.

Next, the matter may be raised of the possible difference between "I do not want to know x" and "I want not to know x." While such a distinction may certainly be drawn, and in some contexts possibly even to some advantage, for my purposes I take these two formulations to be interchangeable. Both my not wanting to know and my wanting not to know imply an active attitude on my part to avoid obtaining the knowledge in question. It is not indifference to knowing that is at issue here, but aversion to knowing.

Now when the person I want not to know x is me, can I be said to want to prevent or to protect myself from knowing x? The drift of the discussion so far is that the answer to this question is yes, I can. But when this is the case, we may not wish to retain the interpretation of the formula in paternalistic or manipulative terms. To the extent that we do retain the language of paternalism or manipulation even when we talk about my not wanting me to know, I suggest that we have self-deception cases in mind.

The phenomenon of self-deception, while certainly pertaining to the field I here wish to chart, does not exhaust it. It is even possible to maintain that cases of self-deception are, strictly speaking, not cases of not wanting to know. They are, typically, cases when one does know something and at the same time is concerned to conceal this knowledge from oneself. (Or one does know the general contours of something, and at the same time prevents oneself from being informed about its details.) This phenomenon merits, and has indeed received, special expert attention. I shall set it aside and proceed to explore the remainder of the field.

Before moving on, let us briefly consider the formula: "You don't want to know x." This is a second-person formula, where another person is advising you to shield yourself from knowing something. This formula helps underline a certain ambiguity of "want," between a curiosity-sense of "want" and an interest-sense of "want." You may not want to know x in the sense that you are indifferent to x. That is, you have no particular desire or curiosity to know x, as distinct from the case where you perceive it as being harmful to you, as going against your interests, to know x. Thus, I may suspect that knowing x would make you pointlessly envious or anxious or otherwise upset you, or that it would adversely interfere with your performance of the task you face, or that it may bias you one way or another when impartiality is called for. We may think of the blindfolded Athena, the goddess of justice, as emblematic of this latter justification for not wanting to know.

Consider the following example. A defense attorney in a murder case may decide to avoid asking her client the direct question of whether he committed the crime. She will, instead, only ask him whether he wishes to plead guilty or not guilty. The attorney in such a case may say to herself, "I don't want to know the answer to the question whether my client is guilty or innocent." She assesses that she will do a better and more professional job if she does not know whether the person she is defending is innocent or not. Indeed, once she knows that the defendant did commit the crime, she is actually more restricted in her choice of defense strategies than she is when she does not know whether he committed the crime (regardless, of course, of what she happens to *believe* about him). Moreover, she may come to have ethical qualms about her job, which might further detract from her professional performance. So knowing less here implies having a larger range of options to choose from—which is in normal circumstances taken to be the preferred situation for the rational decision maker.

Thomas Schelling (in *The Strategy of Conflict*)[5] and Jon Elster (in *Ulysses and the Sirens*),[6] among others, have demonstrated some of the ways in which "tying our hands" in advance of action, that is to say, visibly blocking off some of the courses of action open to us in a decision situation, may actually further our interests and hence be rational. The attorney example suggests something similar with regard to knowledge: that there are occasions when intentionally arranging for ourselves to have less rather than more knowledge is strategically advantageous for us.

V. Control of Self-Regarding Knowledge

Next, consider the formula "I don't want to know x" when x is self-regarding knowledge.

Because the focus of this discussion is on the question of justifying my *not* wanting to know, we are exempt from discussing such issues as the freedom of and equal access to information in general, or the right of the public to know. But an assertion of my right to know that which concerns me does fall within the purview of our discussion. Let me explain. I may wish to assert my right not to be denied access to knowledge that concerns me personally, to the extent that this knowledge exists and that somebody out there has access to it. To withhold from me information about me, whether it regards my personal and family status, my health, my financial situation, my school, army, or job records is to impinge upon my autonomy. Whatever one wishes to read into the dictum that knowledge is power, it unequivocally asserts that to control knowledge is to engage in power games. To withhold such knowledge from me is paternalistic at best and manipulative otherwise. (Is information about my children considered information about me? This is a borderline case. I suppose that I have the right not to be denied access to information about my children until they reach a certain age. The other side of the same coin is that I may be denied access to certain information about me as long as I am a child under a certain age.)

To defend one's right to knowledge concerning oneself is one thing, though, and to choose to exercise this right is quite another. The question we are now asking is whether or not one has the privilege of not wanting to know such information, and what if any are the limits of this privilege. Is not an adopted child, who may have access to information about her biological parents when she reaches the age of eighteen, free not to acquire that knowledge? Does a patient, who is not denied access to the results of the medical tests performed on him, have to be informed about the results? These cases point to a conflict that may exist between autonomy and welfare, with respect to obtaining knowledge. While increasing autonomy, knowledge about oneself may at the same time hinder one's welfare.

In many types of situations, we do indeed wish to waive our right to self-regarding knowledge. In managing our lives, both externally and internally, there seems to me to be no prima facie reason why we should not have different tastes, which would express themselves in different preferences over our mental states in general, and over our states of knowledge in particular. People differ in the way they cope, say, with painful knowledge, and this will be reflected in their preferences over what they want or do not want to know about themselves.

The first headline on the front page of the *New York Times* on October 24, 1995, read: "If Tests Hint Alzheimer's, Should a Patient Be Told?" The story is about a gene, called apo E4. People with two copies of it have as high as a 90% chance of developing the disease by the age of eighty. It is, the paper goes on to tell us, "information that nobody seems to know what to do with." The fifty-one-year-old woman featured in the story is quoted as saying that in her family, two sisters and a brother went in for apo E tests after she learned that she had two apo E4 genes, but four sisters refused, saying they did not want to know. She herself never hesitated about wanting to know about her apo E result; neither did her own doctor who "found the temptation to know irresistible."

This case raises fundamental practical and ethical questions for doctors and researchers whose perspective is that of the providers of information. As for the patients' perspective, which is that of the consumers of information (as it were), this case seems to me to raise no fundamental questions. It rather helps underline the point just made that, insofar as one is dealing with knowledge that pertains to one's own vital personal affairs but that one can do nothing about, people have different tastes and preferences as to whether or not they want to possess it. What one person may find "irresistibly tempted" to know, another may be too afraid to know. And like the case with other tastes and preferences, there isn't very much more of an illuminative, normative nature to say here.

There would be something more to say about this case had we denied the assumption that there was nothing one could do with the apo E–related knowledge. Even if it is true, and remains true, that there is no way to prevent or treat Alzheimer's disease, one may well hold that there are ways to prepare for the near certainty of developing the disease. There are ways in which one, and one's family, may plan for the future. Once this point is acknowledged, the case under consideration can no longer be taken as a case exhibiting mere differences of taste preferences among people regarding their own cognitive mental states. There could then be a cogent argument for the unreasonableness of the ostrich policy of not wanting to know.

In any event, we should be clear about distinguishing cases in which I give up being informed about me when this is merely a reflection of my personal taste, from cases in which I forego being informed about me when this is supposed to be instrumental to promoting my ends. The latter cases, but not the former, may be evaluated as reasonable or unreasonable. Such cases may include those in which I give up collecting information because it is too costly to do so, others when I want to remain impartial, and still others when having the knowledge will trouble or pain me, or strategically hurt my interests.

For example, in a case such as waiving my right to read recommendation letters written on my behalf as part of my promotion procedure, my very signing of the waiver clause may causally affect the nature and quality of the procedure in a way that is ultimately more favorable to me than had I insisted on access to my file. This is a neat case when I may want to know in the curiosity sense of "want" but not in the interest sense of "want." When I participate in an experiment, it may be better for me, as well as for the experimenters, if I do not know whether I belong to the control group. A variant on this is a case when an educational experiment is conducted on my students, and I choose not to know too many details of the experimental design so as not to be biased in my own attitudes toward the students while the experiment lasts. Or think of John Rawls's veil of ignorance in the original position. One way to reconstruct this is to say that those entering the deliberation room are expected to ignore self-regarding knowledge that they have: they are to relinquish all knowledge about their own particular characteristics and position in society, so as eventually to come up with a more just—and presumably more rational—design for their societal institutions.

VI. Hindsight

"Had I known it at the time, I would not have done what I did." This is a familiar enough phrase, with various substitutions for the "it." "Had I known the real nature of the tasks and responsibilities involved in being a chairperson of this organization (board, committee), I would never have agreed to become a candidate in the first place." "Had I known what enrolling in that particular army unit really means, I would never have signed the papers." And so on. Now it is possible that when you say, "Had I known what it involved, I would never have done it," the implicature is,

"And I wish I *had* known it at the time." That is, you regret having done what you did: you acknowledge that you acted on the basis of insufficient knowledge, and as a result you judge your action to have been wrong, or suboptimal, in some sense. You reproach yourself for not having found out more, for not having been better informed.

But let us consider now the possibility that the implicature is, "And boy am I glad I had not known it at the time!" That is, you acknowledge that you acted on the basis of insufficient knowledge, and, furthermore, you realize in hindsight that on the basis of fuller knowledge the course of action you chose was not the rational one to pursue and that you would therefore not have pursued it. Yet you are happy with the result.

Of course, being a rational decision maker does not guarantee—and does not claim to guarantee—the best result on every occasion. And if you gamble against high odds without knowing them and luck out, your being happy with the result does not retrospectively make your gamble rational. But the interesting possibility to be pointed out here is the case when your not knowing contributed causally to the success of your action—whether or not it would have been the rational course of action for you to take on the basis of full knowledge. Had you known, for example, how many candidates have failed the exam you are about to take, you might either have been discouraged from even attempting it, or lost the confidence necessary for passing it. Your very ignorance of the rate of failure was thus a factor that contributed to the good result. Doubt, uncertainty, or ignorance may sometimes improve performance—as may unrealistic optimism.

VII. Morality

We come, finally, to consider the aspect of morality. There are in fact two distinct kinds of cases here, which work in opposite directions. One concerns the possibility that for reasons of morality you should forego some piece of knowledge, that is, the possibility that wanting to know is morally reprehensible. The other concerns the possibility that for reasons of morality you may not exercise your privilege not to know some piece of knowledge, that is, the possibility that not wanting to know is morally reprehensible. The existence of both kinds of cases should further strengthen us in our conclusion that the question of obtaining additional knowledge ought to be settled on the merit of each case and not on the strength of a general rule or presumption.

In the first kind of cases, recall the notion of inadmissible evidence referred to before. Our system of law recognizes that sometimes evidence, while clearly relevant to the question of guilt, should be disallowed. Knowledge gained by torturing a witness is a case in point. It is the procedure by which the information is obtained that is objected to here, not its content (albeit that the content of confessions obtained under physical torture is often tainted anyway). This procedure is judged to involve unacceptable social and moral costs. Note that the notion of cost here is not construed in terms of the price paid to obtain the knowledge, but rather in terms of the social consequences that the use of such knowledge might have for the future—as well as in terms of the intrinsic moral cost of the violation of a basic human right that torture necessarily involves.

Part of the rationale for not admitting this sort of evidence is the causal influence this ban is meant to have in discouraging torture in future cases. Similar is the case of scientific research based on unethical experiments, for which Mengele's twin experiments provide an extreme example. The information such research contains may be accessible, and it may even be of scientific value. But because its very use may be construed to condone the methods by which it was obtained, it may be best, normatively as well as prudentially, to forbid its use altogether.

As for the second kind of cases, we note our familiarity with contexts in which your saying "But I did not know" meets with the retort, "Well, you very well ought to have known." Taken as a moral admonition, when is this retort justified?[7] Are there cases when not wanting to know is morally reprehensible? In other words, are there cases where there is a moral duty to know?

The case of Nazi Germany once again provides an extreme case in point. When Germans—especially those in positions of influence—say, "But I did not know what was going on," we feel that this is no defense against charges of complicity. The general point seems to be that we have a prima facie duty to inform ourselves about what is being done by others in our own name. Insofar as one is a citizen of a democracy, one bears some sort of responsibility not just for one's own actions, but also for the actions done on one's behalf by one's representatives. How and to what extent one can be expected to discharge this responsibility is a different issue, and a very complex one. But the point remains that at the very minimum the strategic move of shutting one's eyes, of not wanting to know, may not be a morally permissible one.[8]

A related point has to do with one's obligation to those under one's care. I may shut my eyes and be negligent with regard to my own needs; I may not want to know the medical diagnosis of my condition and what the appropriate treatment should be, and—up to a certain degree of negligence—outside interference may well violate my autonomy. But when it comes to my responsibility toward my child or my aging parent, who depend on me for their care and welfare, my not wanting to know the details of their medical condition and its treatment must be morally condemned. So once again, in this situation the notion of responsibility is bound with that of knowledge in such a way that we have a prima facie duty to know.

A final observation, from a different angle: sometimes knowing something about somebody may put you under a special moral obligation to that person, even if this is not a person toward whom you have special obligations otherwise. The situation is perhaps analogous to the case when you happen to be passing by the beach where a drowning man calls for help: your mere presence there at that instant puts you under an obligation to do what you can to save him. Similarly, if a casual conversation with a stranger on a train turns into a confession in which she starts telling you all, you may well feel that the more you know, the more freedom you are losing. You realize that you are about to lose your status of a stranger with respect to this person and that the bond being created in virtue of this very conversation will make you morally obligated to her. You may well feel, then, that as long as you don't know you don't owe. I therefore offer a distinction here, between knowing and being told. And my suggestion is that in some cases the issue is my not wanting to be told rather than my not wanting to know. Moreover, some interesting cases involve neither my not wanting to know nor just my not wanting to be told, but rather my not wanting to be told *by x:* being told by *him* (or her) may bind me morally against my will to a person I do not wish to be, and would not otherwise be, morally bound to. It may also establish a power relationship between us that I want to avoid.

Notes

I wish to thank Harry Frankfurt, Avishai Margalit, and Cass R. Sunstein for valuable comments on previous drafts of this chapter.

1. Daniel Kahneman and Dan Lovallo, "Timid Choices and Bold Forecasts," *Management Science* vol. 39, no. 1, 1993: 17–31.

2. Martin E. P. Seligman, *Learned Optimism*, New York: Knopp, 1991.

3. I have drawn here on Edna Ullmann-Margalit "On Presumption," *The Journal of Philosophy* vol. 80, no. 3, 1983: 143–64; and "Revision of Norms," *Ethics* vol. 100, 1990: 756–67.

4. Known in game theory are cases, for example, where a player who wants some information may nevertheless refrain from seeking it: he may not want it to be known that he wants to know, because this in itself may be compromising information about his own position.

5. Thomas Schelling, *The Strategy of Conflict*, Cambridge Mass: Harvard University Press, 1960.

6. Jon Elster, *Ulysses and the Sirens: Studies in Rationality and Irrationality*, Cambridge: Cambridge University Press, 1979.

7. In law it is often said that it is our business to know, or at any rate that ignorance of the law does not exempt from sanction. In fact, however, this situation is conceptualized within the law in terms of a fiction, or a presumption of knowledge, rather than in terms of a duty to know.

8. A delicate balance must in fact sometimes be struck here, between the duty to inform oneself on the one hand and moral urgency on the other. The duty to be well informed is sometimes used as a pretext for doing nothing, or at least for procrastination, when it is quite clear that atrocities are being committed. There are occasions in which, even if there is some lack of clarity about the precise details of the atrocities (and there usually is), to insist on *total* evidence before taking any action against them is a total abuse of the principle and must be objected to morally.

6

ORDERING SELVES

Marcia Cavell

> I am taking off layer after layer, until at last . . . I reach the final, indivisible, firm, radiant point, and this point says: I am! like a pearl ring embedded in a shark's gory fat.
>   Vladimir Nabokov, *Invitation to a Beheading*

The concept of the self as we think of it entered modern philosophy through Descartes and epistemology: self as mind, self as consciously thinking "I"-sayer who in thinking knows for certain that he exists and knows also some of the contents of his own mind. Such knowledge is called self-reflexive: it is my knowledge that I exist that is certain; yet my knowing that Marcia Cavell exists is susceptible to doubt, for I might not after all be Marcia Cavell. And although my knowing that I am now thinking about self-knowledge is not indefeasible, it seems to enjoy a certain kind of authority.

The self also plays a central role in moral philosophy broadly conceived, where it is virtually identical with the concept of a person. We invoke the self in this second context in trying to make sense of attitudes such as self-deception and weakness of the will, authenticity, betraying and being true to oneself, and governing oneself in a way that equals autonomy. The practical context explicitly introduces the idea that the self may exist in varying degrees of internal disharmony and integration.

These two contexts, epistemology and moral philosophy, encompass issues that have sometimes been contrasted as theoretical self-consciousness versus the practical relation of oneself to oneself, one's identity as self-knowing knower versus one's identity as self-moving agent. Yet the concepts of the self at work in the two contexts are surely closely related, if not the same. If so, I assume that "the self" must refer to a creature characterized by a psychological structure. The question is how to conceive it.

Harry Frankfurt's very interesting essays on freedom of the will give a central place to reflexive self-consciousness, which I will hereafter refer to as reflexivity. The essays thus implicitly link the two sets of issues. The structure of the will, Frankfurt (1988) holds, is a self-enclosed hierarchy that depends specifically on the capacity to know what one desires, then to endorse or distance oneself from one's desires. Autonomy is a matter of the right kind of internal coherence such that the lower orders in the hierarchy are harmoniously guided by higher ones.

Frankfurt's view is subtle and attractive in many ways, but I think he has pictured the wrong sort of structure. In explaining why, I will turn toward a rather different view of the self.[1]

I. Second-Order Desires

Frankfurt's argument takes off from a claim I agree with. The claim is that while creatures other than ourselves may be conscious, reflixivity is peculiar to us and a condition for many of our attributes that we value most. Among other things, it allows us not merely to change in appropriate response to the world around us, or to be changed—rabbits too can run for the shade—but to take a peculiarly active hand in that change.

Reflexivity is hierarchical in nature in what I would call a trivial sense: when I am explicitly conscious of believing p or desiring x, that consciousness is at a higher level than the belief or desire itself. I note the triviality in order to forestall the thought that the hierarchy must be metaphysical, positing a lower self that has the status of an object and a higher self as subject. This trivial sense of hierarchy allows another, in which a desire or belief of mine is the target of a second-order desire.[2] A first-order desire has as its object the doing or the having of something, while a second-order desire takes a first-order desire as its object. The agent wants to have a desire that he does not have, or he wants an existing desire to be effective in moving him to action. A second-order desire of the latter sort is a "second-order volition," a case of wanting a first-order desire to be one's *will*. Since a first-order desire is something we merely find in ourselves, it is only our second-order desires, Frankfurt argued, that begin to define us as agents.

In his earlier essays, Frankfurt thought that the distinction between first- and second-order desires was sufficient to account for autonomy. He came to think, however, that the mere fact that one desire occupies a higher level is insufficient to give it greater authority. The ordering does not allow us to determine "where (if anywhere) the person himself stands." To fill this need, Frankfurt added the idea of a desire that is not merely second-order but also wholehearted, "resounding" throughout the other orders of desire. The hierarchical picture now is this: at the bottom are our "elementary motivational tendencies," which are "ours" only if we choose to make them so. This choice comes at a second level: "Whether a person identifies himself with these passions, or whether they occur as alien forces that remain outside his volitional identity, depend upon what he himself wants his will to be."[3] Through our volitional attitudes we structure the contour of our will, determining what we will love and care about wholeheartedly at yet a third level.

We are captive to what we love at both the first and the third levels, but there is a crucial difference between them in that our first-order desires are given, contingent, dependent on the world, while our whole-hearted volitions, originating through our second-level identifications, are authentically ours. Frankfurt thus argues against Kant that love, not only reason, can make us free; for when a person acts in ways demanded by his wholehearted love, his volitions depend wholly on the inherent nature of his will. Freedom can then consist precisely in this peculiar kind of necessity. Hence, the importance of what we care about; for if one is somehow mistaken about his own cares, or if he cares or tries to care about things that do not allow him to care wholeheartedly, he will not be able to constitute himself as an autonomous agent. Frankfurt has acknowledged that his view must countenance the Nazi storm trooper and the fanatic as wholehearted carers, along with our favorite heroes. This is not in itself an argument against him, but it should give us pause.

As a way of testing Frankfurt's view, let's look first at his analysis of an erroneous carer, the person who "cares" about not stepping on cracks in the sidewalk. I'll call him Paul. Undoubtedly Paul is committing an error. But how should we describe it? The intuitive answer, Frankfurt says, is that Paul cares about something not worth caring about. What makes something worth caring about? Frankfurt wants to answer this without appealing to anything outside the person himself. Given this constraint, he answers in perhaps the only way he can: something is worth one's caring either if it is antecedently important to him, or if the caring about it is itself important to him. The error in Paul's caring lies in the fact that "it is not important to [him] to make avoiding the cracks in the sidewalk important to himself" (p. 93).

How does Frankfurt know—how do we know—that Paul has made any kind of error? Frankfurt doesn't ask this question, but the possible answers are interesting. The first is that we know enough about our fellow creatures to know that behaviors like Paul's cannot summon into play the interests, talents, skills, and pleasures that make something worth caring about. In this respect, avoiding cracks is different, for example, from gardening, playing the violin, managing a company, climbing the Geiger—activities that one can learn to do better and better and that yield beauty and excitement as the reward. Since these are pursuits, furthermore, in which others engage, one can compete, fail, but also excel, winning the admiration of others who also appreciate gardens, music, or mountains.

Here I have implicitly invoked a different answer from Frankfurt's to the question of what makes something worth caring about. I say that it is a function of properties of the activity and of ourselves and agents and is in principle something for which we can give reasons, reasons intelligible to others by definition. This point emerges yet more clearly if we persist in trying to understand Paul. If I believe that his avoidance of cracks is genuinely an action, then I have to assume there are reasons why he cares as he does. So I might ask him to tell me more, as I sometimes ask someone who likes a painting that leaves me cold what he sees in it. We cannot argue others into liking Braque or Brahms, but we can try to get them to hear or see what we do, for example, by pointing out aspects of the object, comparing it with others, explaining some of the principles of its composition. All this I count as "giving reasons." Or I might suppose that avoiding cracks belongs to a culture that is alien to me and try, like the anthropologist, to discover the network of practices, beliefs, desires, values, and so on, that illumine it as a ritual with a communal sense. If either of these two strategies is successful, then I have no reason for thinking Paul has made an error at all.

But if these strategies fail, it should occur to me that Paul may not himself quite know what he is doing and why. In this case I try, like the psychoanalyst rather than the anthropologist, to locate the displaced or unconscious thoughts that will explain Paul's behavior. I assume a disjunction between what he is able to say about his reasons for caring as he does and what is discernible to a sensitive observer. If there is such a disjunction, then Paul's problem is not, as Frankfurt says, that he is vainly straining against some limit of caring in himself, but that he does not know what he "cares" about.

Indeed, this is likely not an instance of caring at all in the sense Frankfurt invites us to consider. He wants to distinguish caring as one kind of orientation toward the future, not to be confused with liking something or wanting it. The person who cares "*identifies* with what he cares about in the sense that he makes himself vulnerable to losses and susceptible to benefits" regarding it, Frankfurt says (p. 83). "Caring" then has the sense of to care for, to take care of, as in "take under one's wing." It would depend on the details, but typically in cases like Paul's, the motivation is not caring in this sense, but fear that something terrible will happen if one disobeys the senseless prohibition one has constructed. And although the person intends to avoid stepping on the cracks, and knows that that is what he is doing, he is not able to give the more finely grained descriptions of his behavior that would link it to his ongoing history. He knows neither what he cares about nor, in an important sense, what he is doing.

In sum, we can in principle give reasons why we care for what we do, reasons that appeal to public enterprises and "private" passions that are shareable, if not shared. Furthermore, a person's concerns are intelligible only in a network of his other beliefs, desires, valuings, and so on.

The same points are appropriate to Frankfurt's discussion of the wholehearted carer. In Frankfurt's view, Martin Luthers proclaiming "Here I stand! I can do no other" poses a puzzle, for he seems to embody not only authenticity and freedom but also a peculiar kind of necessity. It is not that of the alcoholic who wants to stop drinking but finds himself constrained by a desire he disowns, yet there is something that Luther also cannot do, if "only because he does not really want to do it." This "volitional necessity" is then both self-imposed, and involuntarily imposed, for "otherwise it will be impossible to account for the fact that [he] cannot extricate himself from it merely at will." To resolve the puzzle, Frankfurt asks us to consider the view briefly outlined before that "a person's will "may be no less truly his own when it is not by his own voluntary doing that he cares as he does" (pp. 87, 88).

What Frankfurt's account leaves out is once again the inter-relations among belief, desire, and valuing. Luther "can do no other" because, on reflection, and given everything he believes and knows and values, this action is what he most wants to do. He acts in accord with desire but also reason, for reason is among the forces that have shaped his desire. How would Luther justify his stand? Frankfurt has given us two alternatives: a person can claim that "the thing is independently important to him" or that "caring about it is itself something which is important to him" (p. 93). But these alternatives omit the most obvious way in which we justify the things we care about, by appealing simply to their importance. Luther might have justified his decision—say to his wife or his ecclesiastical subordinates—by arguing the value of his action to the life of the Church, or by repeating his reasons for thinking that the practice of indulgences, among others, was wrong. Such justifications can, in principle, stand up to public scrutiny. Luther's primary interest is not himself but the world, the world as he sees it. And he is likely to become clearer about his choice if he investigates the world, not himself, as Frankfurt suggests.

Frankfurt is right in his emphasis on the contingency of the self. Who we are is a complicated interaction between the contingent and the uncontingent, the given and the chosen, the not-I and the I. Frankfurt is right, furthermore, that an action is free to the extent that it flows from what the agent truly wants, *on the whole*. The task of philosophical analysis is then to elucidate what we mean by "truly wants." This is Frankfurt's project. But even in his revised picture, it is not clear how our contingent desires are related to the self-governing self that may—given wholehearted caring—emerge. It is not clear who the *he* is who determines his will nor how he determines it. The self who constitutes himself *as* a self is as elusive and mysterious as Descartes's thinker.

The contingency in Frankfurt's picture is not thorough enough. He seems mistakenly to think that wholehearted caring presumes an uncontingent, transcendent ego. We glimpse this ego in the contrast Frankfurt draws between human caring and the way in which, according to one theological doctrine, God cares. God's love is "entirely arbitrary and unmotivated—absolutely sovereign, and in no way conditioned by the worthiness of its objects." While it may be possible for an omnipotent being "to love altogether freely and without conditions or restrictions of any kind," such a love is not possible for us, Frankfurt continues. Yet when we care about something not because we think it is important independently of our caring about it, but just because the caring is itself important to us, then we come as close as we can to the love of God (p. 94).

The errors that I see in Frankfurt's account of autonomy come right at the start in these three inter-related ideas of his: (1) first-order desires are not "mine" but become so only by an act of endorsement; (2) it is such acts of endorsement that constitute the person; and (3) every first-order belief and desire of a person is atomic. Frankfurt writes:

> Desires and beliefs can occur in a life which consists merely of a succession of separate moments, none of which the agent recognizes as elements in his continuing history.... The moments in the life of a person who cares about something, however, are not merely linked inherently by formal relations of sequentiality. The person necessarily binds them together. (p. 83)

If desires and beliefs were linked merely "by formal relations of sequentiality," then integration would be possible only given some further capacity or faculty, perhaps the one Frankfurt calls volition. In my view, however, there is a person as soon as

Ordering Selves 89

there is first-person thinking, which necessarily includes reflexivity; such thinking can be engaged in only by a creature who recognizes some of his beliefs and desires as elements in his continuing history, and they are his whether he endorses them or not. Reflexivity by itself generates reflection, ordering, synthesis; no further faculty or ego is needed. In short, the line between persons and non-persons should be drawn not to coincide with the distinction between first- and second-order desires but between creatures who are not reflexively self-conscious and creatures who are. Distinctions among orders of desire will not yield the self-governing desires we are after. I am not going to try to give an account of autonomy. But it presumes what personhood does: a horizontal structure of mental states and attitudes in which belief is as important as desire, a holistic network interacting with the world and other agents in ways that constitute it as the mind it is. Such a structure is suggested by an analysis of reflexivity itself, to which I now turn.

II. Self-Consciousness and the Self

Lichtenberg argued that Descartes was entitled to assert only that, "p is being thought," not "I am thinking that p." As if in answer, Gareth Evans claimed, correctly, I believe, that "whenever you are in a position to assert that p, you are *ipso facto* in a position to assert 'I believe that p.'"[4] From there to my *knowing* that I believe p is not an additional step.

Evans implies that asserting is the act of a certain sort of creature, one who—in my elaboration of Evans's thought—already has the concepts of belief and of himself as a subject of beliefs and who can take a particular stance toward the world. The stance is rational and active: it makes judgments, doubts, questions the world and oneself, reflects, asks for justification and reasons, looks for evidence, is open to a change of heart and mind. Such a creature must then have, along with the concept of belief, the concepts of evidence, the true and the false. He must grasp the distinction between "objective world that I share with others" and "subjective world," or "the world as it appears uniquely from my point of view."[5] The capacity for making assertions must then also presume having learned one's place in a world one shares with others, others who, one also learns, are themselves first-person speakers. The learning must include the discoveries that every person rightly says "I" of herself, that I am "she" or "her" when I am spoken about, and "you" when you are speaking to me.[6]

Anyone who can think or speak of herself in the first person must have learned to locate herself in space and time, which entails knowing that different people cannot occupy the same place at the same time; that one person can occupy different places at different times while remaining the same person; that you are you whether you are here or there, whether it is now or then, and so with me; that nobody else traces exactly my trajectory in space and time.

Some philosophers have asked: How do I know that I am the person now speaking or thinking this thought? This question highlights yet another peculiarity of the first person, namely that such self-knowledge cannot—in the ordinary case—come by means of identifying criteria, in the way I know that the person across the street is Tom. For no matter how exhaustive the criteria, I can go on asking: "How do I know that I am the person so described?"[7]

The simple answer to the question is this: I know that I am thinking this thought because in knowing how to speak and think, I implicitly know the token-reflexive rule, that "I" refers to whoever says it. One might rightly protest, however, that this answer is teasingly insufficient. Only a creature who has the concept of a self, we want to say, can think "I am I," and knowing the token-reflexive rule presumes that concept.

Descartes was right that no identifying features of oneself as a particular person in space and time are part of the content of the thought "I am thinking that p." But Descartes did not investigate what a creature who can intelligently think such a thought would already have learned. When I say "I love you," my "I" refers to this person now speaking, me.[8] Yet for me to know what I mean in saying "I" requires a long and intricate pre-history—in the world, with other persons one has more or less loved.

We get into muddles about how I know I am "I," or the same "I" from one thought and one moment to the next, when we forget that there are background conditions for thought.[9] The form of life in which the child comes by first-person thinking has been preparing her for it in innumerable ways from the beginning, shaping habits of perception and response that eventually express themselves in belief, desire, and intention. John Campbell remarks that our concept of the first person is contingent on the particular ways the world is.[10] Were we creatures of a very different kind from what we are, creatures who, as the philosophers' puzzles imagine, continually fuse or fission, the constraints built into our concept would be lacking, or very different. Frankfurt's idea that "desires and beliefs can occur as a succession of separate moments" may fit creatures other than ourselves, but it does not fit a creature that can think in the first person. First-person thinking is necessarily accompanied by a sense of oneself as an historical continuant, one who, when he is explicitly conscious of believing p, knows that belief as his.

If reflexive self-consciousness attends the making of assertions, then achieving such consciousness does not require a perceptual act in which one spots oneself as the thinking subject. Hume's famous puzzle—that I can never catch *my very thinking self* but only various items, themselves anonymous, belonging to no one, passing across the stage that is my mind—arises in part from this false perceptual model of what self-consciousness involves.

Neither does knowing *what* I believe typically require an inward glance. In the simplest case I believe p, for example that it's raining, because I see or hear that it is. And if I am asked whether I believe that it's raining, I look at the world again. Of course if p is complicated, I may need to examine a whole network of attitudes in which p is enmeshed; in this sense I look inward. But the network itself faces the world.

That is also the reach of desire. Bishop Butler's classic refutation of Hobbes consisted in pointing out that

> the very idea of interested pursuit presupposes particular passions and appetites, since the very idea of interest or happiness consists in this, that an appetite or affection enjoys its object. Take away these affections and you leave self-love absolutely nothing at all to employ itself about.[11]

If, parallel to the question "Do I believe p" I am asked, "Do I want p" or "Do I value p," I may look to my own attitudes, seeing for example whether this desire is consistent with something else I want. But at some point I check the object of desire itself.

Unless they are unconscious in some way, both belief and desire are oriented in the first instance to the world, a world that includes of course one's own states of mind, as when I consult my memories about the past. Freud calls this openness to the world, and to the thwartings of desire it often brings, "the reality principle." It is what distinguishes "the ego"—the "I"—from the id. Freud also knew that this openness is often painful; we have various strategies, conscious and not so conscious, more and less successful but never wholly so, for sealing ourselves off from the world and for closing the world out.

Explicitly conscious belief is inherently self-conscious; so, by definition, is any explicitly conscious propositional attitude. Furthermore, one belief is connected to another, as well as to desires, emotions, intentions, memories, by ties that are not only causal and sequential, as Frankfurt says, but also logical and normative. My belief that New York is the biggest city in the United States is constituted as that belief in part by many other beliefs that I have, for example, about cities, about the United States, about what it means for one city to be bigger than another. If I consciously believe p, also that if p then q, and then decide I was wrong about q, I know I have to do something about p. If I believe that going via New York is the best way to get to Israel from San Francisco and I want to go to Israel, then I know it is reasonable to go via New York if I can; should a friend convince me otherwise, I am likely to change my plans. If I want to go to Paris this May, but also to be with my mother in Illinois, and I know where Paris and Illinois are, then I know I must choose. A person who has conscious beliefs and desires is necessarily subject to such constraints.

In sum, beliefs, desires, and all the other propositional attitudes form a holistic network in which they are related to each other and to material reality. For this reason, when I determine what to believe, I also affect desires, emotions, and values related to this belief. I potentially affect the whole web that is my mind. So also I potentially determine the person I will become. Freud had this holistic character of the mental in mind in introducing free association into psychoanalytic therapy and in describing therapy as a process of remembering, repeating, and working through.[12]

We can perhaps more easily grasp the idea of holism if we think about the identity of a psychological subject from the point of view of an observer. In order for me to understand your behavior, I must look for a synthetic unity within which what you do or say finds its sense, and I cannot do that unless I have a locus of unity to begin with. So I must assume something like this: one body, moving through space and time, one mind, one self. Something comparable must be true in my own case. I don't infer my identity through time from certain relations between identity-neutral mental states. All come at once: my ability to have conscious thoughts at all, their constitutive relations to each other, my concept of my self, and my ability to recognize a thought as something I am thinking.

For similar reasons, it cannot be, as Frankfurt says, that "the person necessarily binds [the moments of his life] together," for that would presume someone independent of any psychological states to do the binding. Achieving a new synthesis is not something one consciously does but is, usually, the natural accompaniment of any change in mental attitudes. Whether we acknowledge our beliefs and desires, and their various characteristics, can affect just how well they are integrated with our other beliefs and desires. But to some extent they are bound together from the beginning.

Creatures come to be persons—to have selves—through those complex processes that give rise to self-conscious thoughts.[13] We understand ourselves as thinking, desiring subjects only to the extent that we grasp our behavior and our thoughts as parts of a unified activity.[14] Where this breaks down to a drastic extent, so does our sense of self.

The view of the self as an organism characterized by a holistic, normative, structure, interacting causally with the world, suggests many ways in which integrity can be threatened: refusing to confront challenges to one's desires and beliefs, resisting knowing what they are, failing to acknowledge their implications and consequences, withdrawing from interpersonal dialogue, phantasizing oneself as omnipotent, retreating in certain ways from the world. When we are considering whether someone has acted autonomously, or whether his action speaks for his authentic self, we want to know whether he has reflected on his action in ways that were called for. Has he investigated, and been open to, the relevant aspects of reality? Were the values and desires that guided him genuinely his? Or were they, as it were, merely borrowed from others, or espoused by him out of fear of punishment rather than concern for the objects of his professed desires?

III. Making Up One's Mind

Jean-Paul Sartre spoke of "the vertigo of consciousness," by which he meant our uneasy awareness that the self of which we are aware, as fully conscious believers, desirers, doers, is not something knowable and fixed, but a kind of spontaneity toward the world, an endless array of possibilities.[15] In his diagnosis, we construe the self as a special kind of entity, behind and directing our various acts of consciousness, because we don't want to acknowledge that who and what we are is up to us. "Perhaps," he writes, "the essential function of the Ego is not so much theoretical as practical . . . to mask from consciousness its very spontaneity."[16]

Sartre was on to something important, that first-person thinking is a stance toward the world that only rational, desiring, agents can take. It cannot but be active and self-constituting, though the agency can be avoided or denied. Sartre was mistaken, however, in thinking that I cannot have knowledge about me of a theoretical nature, for one of the things this stance typically requires me to do is acknowledge what I am thinking, to myself, or to you.

Acknowledgment has practical implications. About belief, I assume three related different commitments: to the truth of p, to the possibility of my error, and to the relevance of evidence. About desire, I open myself to questions about whether the object of my desire is in fact desirable, given what I know about it and given also my other desires. The value in making our beliefs and desires explicitly conscious lies here, for even if they remain unchanged, I am now in a slightly different position regarding them. And that position is a newly emerging determinant of my future.

Frankfurt recognizes the peculiarity of the first person in contending that what we care about constitutes who we are. We do not in the same sense constitute others merely by having certain sorts of desires. But he overlooks the difference between first-person avowal and third-person attribution in talking about causality. He argues that the cause of an action is irrelevant to its status as an action, for if it were not, he says, then "a person who knows he is in the midst of performing an action cannot have derived this knowledge from any awareness of what is currently happening, but must have derived it instead from his understanding of how what is happening was caused to happen by earlier conditions" (pp. 70, 71). What the passage overlooks is this: you know what I am thinking by fitting my behavior into a pattern that makes the most sense of it. That is not, typically, the way I know what I am thinking. And for the same reasons, that is not typically how I know that I am engaged in an action. The causes that enter into the analysis of action are the beliefs and desires that identify the action as what it is, say *going to San Francisco* or *fighting the good fight*. If I am the agent in question, presumably those beliefs and desires are not far from my mind when I do what I do. They are its causes, but they are also my reasons.

In "The Problem of Action" Frankfurt writes:

> In asserting that the essential difference between actions and mere happenings lies in their prior causal histories, causal theories imply that actions and mere happenings do not differ in themselves at all. These theories hold that the causal sequences producing actions are necessarily of a different type than those producing mere happenings, but that the effects produced by the two types are inherently indistinguishable. (p. 69)

This is not so. Only Luther's behavior, presumably not the robot's, has a view from "inside," that is, a first-person perspective. So there is, after all, an inherent difference. It is reflected in the fact that a third-person explanation of Luther must introduce causal sequences—beliefs, desires, and intentions—unnecessary in the case of the robot. A dual-aspect view of human affairs holds that to explain some of the things we do, we need both reasons irreducible to a non-intentional language and also causes, some of which are reasons. The explanatory power of such a view is that it allows us to see an important way in which the fabric of the self can come apart and also to order itself more finely. If the reasons I give for my behavior are not in fact the ones that moved me to act as I did, or if I act under the influence of wishes and beliefs not oriented to reality, and so are relatively distant from other thoughts in the mental network, or if something prevents me in particular cases from assessing and evaluating my reasons in the appropriate ways, then I am not in control either of myself, or the world that I affect, in ways I might otherwise be.

We are familiar in religious writings with the idea that we become more our selves the less self in us there is. Frankfurt expresses it this way: "How are we to understand the paradox that a person may be enhanced and liberated through being seized, made captive, and overcome? Why is it we find ourselves to be most fully realized . . . when—through reason or love—we have lost or escaped from ourselves?" (p. 89) My answer is that desire's natural home is in the world; that is where it finds its objects. But we discover what they are only through action and interaction with them, in the process discovering—making—ourselves. Love that is relatively unambivalent explores its worldly objects with interest. It tends to establish coherent patterns of behavior, informed at once by knowledge, desire, and valuing, patterns that we identify as ourselves: "I am a pianist—an Israeli—a mother." Such love has the effect of making one's self as a thing separated by spatial boundaries from what one loves less important, so that disability, sickness, and death are less terrifying than they otherwise can be. When reason and love win out, resources that may else lie dormant emerge and liberate us from anxious self-concern.

Unfortunately, we are not all equally such lovers. Like Dickens's Miss Havisham, we have turned away from the real world when our great expectations were disappointed, preferring fantasies we author to the risks of the present. Or the fear of failure, or of success, has had a similar effect. Or like Tolstoy's Ivan Ilytch, we have mistaken a measure of esteem in the eyes of others for the pleasure that comes from embracing things outside ourselves.

There have always been liars, self-deceivers, and traitors. But the concept of authenticity as a dimension of the self is relatively modern, arriving on the scene in the sixteenth century. In Shakespeare, Montaigne, and Pascal, the authentic self is what one is in and for oneself, as distinct from what one affects for others. These writers do not question that often it is expedient, even moral, to present a false face to the world. But they worry that it may lead one to betray oneself, to become the mask one has affected.

Such worries are serious. They are among the reasons why we should be as suspicious of second-order and apparently wholehearted desires as of any others. But the line between what is authentically me and what is not cannot be drawn with the social world on the other side. Though we make the argument in different ways, depending on whether our influences are Wittgenstein or Freud, Margaret Mead or Donald Davidson or Jürgen Habermas, many of us now see the self as constituted partially out of interpersonal relations. Distinguishing the true from the false self is partly a matter of different kinds of identifications, not with our own desires, as Frankfurt has it, but with other persons, and also a matter of different ways in which these identifications are and are not integrated into the mental fabric as a whole.

Of the many ways in which we can lose ourselves, Freud is the great prophet. Freely interpreted, he also gives the best picture of the self as I see it. "The I"—"the ego"—is a structure of more or less integrated beliefs, desires, fantasies, wishes, intentions, and so on that is informed by interactions with the world and formed, in part, by the child's passionate interactions with others. As creatures who can speak in the first person, we are by nature oriented toward other persons and reality, so we cannot turn our backs entirely on either reason or love. Yet we try. We turn away, in frustration, panic, rage, or disappointment. These "negative" emotions have a rending effect, for the wheeling inward that produces private fantasy forms psychological constellations relatively separate from the psychological fabric as a whole. The result is that we can speak for only some of our psychological states, those that are most tightly meshed with the beliefs and desires that take reality into account.

As for our ideals, they bear the marks of our early relations with others, in which anger and the fear of punishment played a part at least as large as love. Even those ideals to which we give our apparently wholehearted allegiance are not necessarily either integrative in their effects or authentically ours.

Notes

1. There is a good summary of the criticisms most commonly leveled against Frankfurt in John Christman's "Constructing the Inner Citadel: Recent Work on Autonomy," *Ethics* 99 (1988), pp. 109–124. My tack in this chapter is broader than the ones Christman mentions.

2. In a note to his essay "Identification and Wholeheartedness," Frankfurt says that the notion of reflexivity is the indispensable one for dealing with the phenomena of self-division and integrity, but that he sees no way of providing for reflexivity without the notion of a hierarchical ordering (p. 165, n. 7). I wonder if he hasn't then conflated the two sorts that I am here distinguishing. All page references to Harry Frankfurt, with one exception that I note, are from the essays collected in his *The Importance of What We Care About* (New York: Cambridge University Press, 1988).

3. "Autonomy, Necessity and Love." *Vernunftbegriffe in der Moderne,* eds. Hand-Friedrich Fulda and Rolf-Peter Horstmann (Stuttgart: Klett-Cotta, 1994), p. 442.

4. Gareth Evans, *The Varieties of Reference* (Oxford: Clarendon Press, 1982), pp. 225, 226.

5. See D. Davidson, "The Myth of the Subjective," in *Relativism: Interpretation and Confrontation,* ed. M. Krausz (University of Notre Dame Press, 1989).

6. George Herbert Mead anticipated Wittgenstein, Davidson, and also Habermas, in arguing for the essentially social nature of the self. Mead holds that it is a social structure, arising only through interactions of which language is an essential aspect. Once a self has come to be, there can be solitary thought, and so on. But the processes that make for "selfhood" transform the creature's existence as an organism. Mead accepts, however, the traditional view that in self-consciousness the self is an object for itself: the child acquires the idea of "me" through the responses of others, and though the self as "I" is different from the self as "me," the two are mutually dependent. Mead may be right that as a matter of fact, experiencing oneself through the responses of others is an important piece in the development of the first-person thought.

7. The literature on this subject is enormous. Some of the most frequently cited articles are Hector-Neri Castaneda, "On the Phenomeno-Logic of the I," and John Perry, "The Problem of the Essential Indexical," both in *Self-Knowledge,* ed. Q. Cassam (Oxford: Oxford University Press, 1994). For a view very different from mine, see also Thomas Nagel, "The Objective Self," in *Knowledge and Mind: Philosophical Essays,* ed. C. Giant and S. Shoemaker (Oxford: Oxford University Press: 1983).

8. Wittgenstein and others have argued that "I" does not refer. This seems to me a mistake, but the point is not essential to my argument.

9. My use of the concept of "background" conditions is not intended as an allusion either to Martin Heidegger or John Searle. I use it because I think it captures better than "necessary conditions" the ideas that these conditions are out of sight and that without them the thing in question—in this case the self—could not appear.

10. *Space, Time, and Self* (Cambridge, Mass.: MIT Press, 1994).

11. *Five Sermons* (New York: Library of Liberal Arts, 1950), p. 14.

12. "Remembering, Repeating, and Working Through," *Standard Edition of the Complete Psychological Works of Sigmund Freud,* vol. 12.

13. This does not imply that the concept of a "person" is reducible to a collection of apersonal states. See John Campbell's *Space, Time, and Self* for an argument to this effect.

14. Jeffrey Malpas makes this argument in "The Constitution of the Mind: Synthesizing Kant and Davidson" (unpublished).

15. For some ideas in this section I am indebted to Richard Moran's "Making Up Your Mind," *Ratio (New Series)*, 12 December, 1988.

16. Jean-Paul Sartre, *La Transcendance de L'Ego* (Paris, Librairie Philosophique, 1988, my translation), p. 81.

7

PRACTICAL REASON AND INCOMPLETELY THEORIZED AGREEMENTS

Cass R. Sunstein

My central topic is the operation of practical reason in collective institutions. How might a multimember body—a legislature, a court, a club, a set of citizens composing a nation—proceed in the face of conflict and disagreement on fundamental matters? As we will see, the answer bears particularly on legal reasoning but also on the exercise of practical reason by political institutions and by individual agents.

My basic suggestion is that well-functioning multimember bodies try to solve problems through *incompletely theorized agreements.* Sometimes these agreements involve abstractions, accepted amid severe disagreements on particular cases. Thus, people who disagree on pornography and on hate speech can accept a general free speech principle, and those who argue about homosexuality and about disability can accept an abstract antidiscrimination principle. This is an important phenomenon in both law and politics. But sometimes incompletely theorized agreements involve concrete outcomes rather than abstractions, and because of the close relationship between practical reason in law and judgments about particulars, this is what I will be emphasizing here.

When people (and here we may speak of individual agents as well as of collective institutions) are uncertain about an abstraction—is equality more important than liberty? does free will exist?—they can often make progress by moving to a level of greater particularity. They attempt a *conceptual descent.* This phenomenon has an especially notable feature: it enlists silence, on certain basic questions, as a device for producing convergence despite disagreement, uncertainty, limits of time and capacity, and heterogeneity. Incompletely theorized agreements are a key to legal and political reasoning in particular and practical reason in general. They are an important source of social stability and an important way for people to demonstrate mutual respect.

Consider some examples. People may believe that it is important to protect endangered species yet have quite diverse theories about why. Some people may stress what they see as human obligations to species or nature as such; others may point to the role of endangered species in producing ecological stability; still others may emphasize the possibility that obscure species can provide resources for valuable medicines for human beings. Similarly, people may invoke many different grounds for their shared belief that the law should protect labor unions against certain kinds of employer coercion. Some people may emphasize the democratic functions of unions; others may think that unions are necessary for industrial peace; others may believe that unions protect basic rights. So, too, people may favor a rule of strict liability for certain torts from multiple diverse starting points—with some people rooting their judgments in economic efficiency, others in distributive goals, still others in conceptions of basic rights.

The agreement on particulars is incompletely theorized in the sense that the relevant participants are clear on the result without agreeing on the most general theory that accounts for it. (As we shall soon see, I understand the term "general" in a relative sense, with the thought that people try to reach agreement at a more particular level than the level at which they disagree. There is a continuum from the most ambitious theories to the simple announcement of outcomes; thus, there is no sharp discontinuity between highly theorized opinions and their opposite.) Often people can agree on a rationale offering low-level or mid-level principles. They may agree that a rule—reducing water pollution by 15%, allowing workers to unionize—makes sense without entirely agreeing on the foundations of their belief. They may accept an outcome—reaffirming the right to have an abortion, protecting sexually explicit art—without understanding or converging on an ultimate ground for that acceptance. What accounts for the outcome, in terms of a full-scale theory of the right or the good, is left unexplained.

There is a limiting case of incomplete theorization: *full particularity*. This phenomenon occurs when people agree on a result without agreeing on any kind of supporting rationale. Any rationale—any reason—is by definition more abstract than the result that it supports. Sometimes people do not offer any reasons at all, because they do not know what those reasons are, or because they cannot agree on reasons, or because they fear that their reasons would turn out, on reflection, to be inadequate and hence might be misused in the future. This is an important phenomenon in law. Juries usually do not offer reasons for outcomes, and negotiators sometimes conclude that something should happen without concluding why it should happen. I will not emphasize this limiting case here; instead, I will focus on outcomes accompanied by low-level or mid-level principles.

My emphasis on incompletely theorized agreements is intended partly as descriptive. These agreements are a pervasive phenomenon in ordinary human reasoning and in both law and politics. But my goal is not simply descriptive. There are special virtues in avoiding large-scale theoretical conflicts. Incompletely theorized agreements can operate as foundations for both rules and analogies, and such agreements are especially well suited to the institutional limits of many collective institutions, including courts.

Enthusiasm for incompletely theorized agreements should not be seen as a form of antitheory, and even less as a form of general skepticism or relativism about reason in law. Those who endorse incompletely theorized agreements base their judgments on norms appropriate to the particular culture of law. In social life, people reason in ways that grow out of the particular role in which they find themselves. They know what actions are permissible, and what actions are off-limits, only because of their role. As practical reasoners, people take their roles for granted and live accordingly. Consider the close relationship between reasoning and role for such diverse figures as parents, students, waiters, doctors, employees, consumers, and automobile drivers. Any particular role is accompanied by a set of relevant and irrelevant considerations. The particular social role of judges fits especially well with incompletely theorized agreements.

I. How People Converge

It seems clear that people may agree on a *correct* outcome even though they do not have a theory to account for their judgments. Jones may know that dropped objects fall, that bee stings hurt, that hot air rises, and that snow melts, without knowing exactly why these facts are true. The same is true for morality. Johnson may know that slavery is wrong, that government may not stop political protests, that every person should have just one vote, and that it is bad for government to take property unless it pays for it, without knowing exactly or entirely why these things are so. Moral judgments may be right or true even if they are reached by people who lack a full account of those judgments (though moral reasoners may well do better if they try to offer such an account, a point to which I will return). The same is very much true for law. Judge Thompson may know that if you steal someone's property, you must return it, without having a full account of why this principle has been enacted into law. We may thus offer an epistemological point: people can know *that* X is true without entirely knowing *why* X is true.

There is a political point as well. Sometimes people can agree on individual judgments even if they disagree on general theory. In American law, for example, diverse judges may agree that *Roe v. Wade*,[1] protecting the right to choose abortion, should not be overruled, though the reasons that lead each of them to that conclusion sharply diverge. Some people think that the Court should respect its own precedents; others think that *Roe* was rightly decided as a way of protecting women's equality; others think that the case was rightly decided as a way of protecting privacy; others think that the decision reflects an appropriate judgment about the social role of religion; still others think that restrictions on abortion are unlikely to protect fetuses in the world, and so the decision is good for pragmatic reasons. We can find incompletely theorized political agreements on particular outcomes in many areas of law and politics—on both sides of racial discrimination controversies, both sides of disputes over criminal justice, both sides of disputes over health care.

II. Rules and Analogies

Rules and analogies are the two most important methods for resolving disputes without obtaining agreement on first principles. Both of these devices attempt to use practical reason to promote a major goal of a heterogeneous society: *to make it possible to obtain agreement where agreement is necessary, and to make it unnecessary to obtain agreement where agreement is impossible.* People can often agree on what rules mean even when they agree on very little else. And in the face of persistent disagreement or uncertainty about what morality requires, people can reason about particular cases by reference to analogies. They point to cases in which their judgments are firm. They proceed from those firm judgments to the more difficult ones. This is how ordinary people tend to think.

We might consider in this regard American Supreme Court justice Stephen Breyer's discussion of one of the key compromises reached by the seven members of the United States Sentencing Commission.[2] As Breyer describes it, a central issue was how to proceed in the face of highly disparate philosophical premises about the goals of criminal punishment. Some people asked the commission to follow an approach to punishment based on "just deserts"—an approach that would rank criminal conduct in terms of severity. But different commissioners had very different views about how different crimes should be ranked. In these circumstances, there could be an odd form of deliberation in which criminal punishments became ever more, and more irrationally, severe, because some commissioners would insist that the crime under consideration was worse than the previously ranked crimes. In any case, agreement on a rational system would not likely follow from efforts by the seven commissioners to rank crimes in terms of severity.

Other people urged the commission to use a model of deterrence. There were, however, major problems with this approach. We lack empirical evidence that could link detailed variations in punishment to prevention of crime, and the seven members of the commission were highly unlikely to agree that deterrence provides a full account of the aims of criminal sentencing. An approach based on deterrence seemed no better than an approach based on just deserts.

In these circumstances, what route did the commission follow? In fact, the commission abandoned large theories altogether. It adopted no general view about the appropriate aims of criminal sentencing. Instead, the commission abandoned high theory and adopted a rule founded on precedent: "It decided to base the Guidelines primarily upon typical, or average, actual past practice." Consciously articulated explanations, not based on high theory, were used to support particular departures from the past.

Justice Breyer sees this effort as a necessary means of obtaining agreement and rationality within a multimember body charged with avoiding unjustifiably wide variations in sentencing. Thus, in his more colorful oral presentation he says:

> Why didn't the Commission sit down and really go and rationalize this thing and not just take history? The short answer to that is: we couldn't. We couldn't because there are such good arguments all over the place pointing in opposite directions. . . . Try listing all the crimes that there are in rank order of punishable merit. . . . Then collect results from your friends and see if they all match. I will tell you they don't.[3]

The example suggests a more general point. Through both analogies and rules, it is often possible for practical reasoners to converge on particular outcomes without resolving large-scale issues of the right or the good. People can decide what to do when they disagree on exactly how to think.

III. Agreements and Justice

The fact that people can obtain an agreement of this sort—about the value and meaning of a rule or about the existence of a sound analogy—is no guarantee of a good outcome, whatever our criteria for deciding whether an outcome is good. Perhaps the sentencing commission incorporated judgments based on ignorance, confusion, or prejudice. Some of the same points can be made about analogies. People in positions of authority may agree that a ban on same-sex marriages is acceptable, because it is analogous to a ban on marriages between uncles and nieces; but the analogy may be misconceived, because there are relevant differences between the two cases, and because the similarities are far from decisive. The fact that people agree that case A is analogous to case B does not mean that case A *or* case B is rightly decided. Perhaps case A should not be taken for granted. Perhaps case A should not be selected as the relevant foundation for analogical thinking; perhaps case Z is more pertinent. Perhaps case B is not really like case A. Problems with analogies and low-level thinking might lead us to be more ambitious. We may well be pushed in the direction of general theory—and toward broader and perhaps more controversial claims—precisely because analogical reasoners offer an inadequate and incompletely theorized account of relevant similarities or relevant differences.

All this should be sufficient to show that the virtues of decisions by rule and by analogy are partial. But no system of politics and law is likely to be either just or efficient if it dispenses with rules and analogies. In fact, it is not likely even to be feasible.

IV. Constitutions, Cases, and Incompletely Theorized Agreements

Incompletely theorized agreements play a pervasive role in law and society. It is quite rare for a person or group to theorize any subject completely, that is, to accept both a general theory and a series of steps connecting that theory to concrete conclusions. Thus, we often have an *incompletely theorized agreement on a general principle*—incompletely theorized in the sense that people who accept the principle need not agree on what it entails in particular cases. This is the sense emphasized by American Supreme Court justice Oliver Wendell Holmes in his great aphorism, "General principles do not decide concrete cases."[4] The agreement is incompletely theorized in the sense that it is *incompletely specified.* Much of the key work must be done by others, often through casuistical judgments, specifying the abstraction at the point of application.

Consider the political domain. Sometimes constitution making itself becomes possible only through this form of incompletely theorized agreement. Many constitutions contain incompletely specified standards and avoid rules, at least when it comes to the description of basic rights. Consider the cases of Eastern Europe and South Africa, where constitutional provisons include many abstract provisions whose concrete specification has engendered sharp dispute. Abstract provisions protect "freedom of speech," "religious liberty," and "equality under the law," and citizens agree on those abstractions in the midst of sharp dispute about what these provisions really entail. Much lawmaking also becomes possible only because of this phenomenon, as when a multimember legislature uses such terms as reasonable, fair, feasible, and public interest.

Let us turn to a second phenomenon. Sometimes people agree on a mid-level principle but disagree about both more general theory and particular cases. People may believe, for example, that government cannot discriminate on the basis of race, without having a large-scale theory of equality, and also without agreeing whether government may enact affirmative action programs or segregate prisons when racial tensions are severe. People may think that government may not regulate speech unless it can show a clear and present danger—but disagree about whether this principle is founded in utilitarian or Kantian considerations, and disagree too about whether the principle allows government to regulate a particular speech by members of the Ku Klux Klan.

My particular interest here is in a third kind of phenomenon, of special interest for practical reason in politics and law: incompletely theorized agreements on particular outcomes, accompanied by agreements on the narrow or low-level principles that account for them. There is no algorithm by which to distinguish between a high-level theory and one that operates at an intermediate or lower level. We might consider, as conspicuous examples of high-level theories, Kantianism and utilitarianism and see illustrations in the many distinguished (academic) efforts to understand such areas as tort law, contract law, free speech, and the law of equality as undergirded by highly abstract theories of the right or the good. By contrast, we might think of low-level principles as including most of the ordinary material of low-level justification, often the material of daily conversation among ordinary people and legal "doctrine" in courts—the general class of principles and justifications that are not said to derive from any particular large theories of the right or the good, that have ambiguous relations to large theories, and that are compatible with more than one such theory.

By the term low-level principles, I refer to something relative, not absolute; I mean to do the same thing by the terms theories and abstractions (which I use interchangeably). In this setting, "low-level," "high," and "abstract" are best understood in comparative terms, like the terms "big" and "old" and "unusual." Thus, the "clear and present danger" standard for regulation of speech is a relative abstraction when compared with the claim that members of the Nazi Party may march in Skokie, Illinois. But the "clear and present danger" idea is relatively particular when compared with the claim that nations should adopt the constitutional abstraction "freedom of speech." The term freedom of speech is a relative abstraction when measured against the claim that campaign finance laws are acceptable, but the same term is less abstract than the grounds that justify free speech, as in, for example, the principle of personal autonomy. What I am emphasizing here is that even when people diverge on some (relatively) high-level proposition, they might be able to agree when they lower the level of abstraction.

In analogical reasoning, this phenomenon occurs all the time. People might think that A is like B, and covered by the same low-level principle, without agreeing on a deep theory to explain why the low-level principle is sound. They agree on the matter of similarity, without agreeing on a large-scale account of what makes the two things similar. In the law of discrimination, for example, many people think that sex discrimination is "like" race discrimination and should be treated similarly, even if they lack, or cannot agree on, a general theory of when discrimination is unacceptable. In the law of free speech, many people agree that a ban on speech by a Communist is "like" a ban on speech by a member of the Ku Klux Klan and should be treated similarly—even if they lack, or cannot agree on, a general theory about the foundations of the free speech principle.

V. Incomplete Theorization and the Constructive Uses of Silence

What might be said on behalf of incompletely theorized agreements, or incompletely theorized judgments, about particular cases? Some people think of incomplete theorization as quite unfortunate—as embarrassing or reflective of some important problem or defect. When people theorize, by raising the level of abstraction, they do so to reveal bias, or confusion, or inconsistency. Surely participants in politics and law should not abandon this effort.

There is a some truth in these usual thoughts. But they are not the whole story. On the contrary, incompletely theorized judgments are an important and valuable part of both private and public life. They help make politics and law possible; they even help make life possible. Most of their virtues involve *the constructive uses of silence,* an exceedingly important social and legal phenomenon. Silence—on something that may prove false, obtuse, or excessively contentious—can help minimize conflict, allow the present to learn from the future, and save much time and expense. What is said and resolved is no more important than what is left out.

My principal concern in this section is the question of how judges on a multimember body should justify their opinions in public; the argument, therefore, concerns the problem of collective choice. But some of the relevant points bear on other issues as well. They have implications for the question of how an individual judge not faced with the problem of producing a majority opinion—a judge on trial court, for example—might write; they bear on the question of how a single judge, whether or not a member of a collective body, might think in private; and they relate to appropriate methods of both thought and justification wholly outside of the adjudication and even outside of law. Thus, we might understand the term "judge" to refer not only to those who are technically judges, but also to many other agents attempting to use practical reason to settle their problems.

Begin with the special problem of public justification on a multimember body. The first and most obvious point is that incompletely theorized agreements are well suited to a world—and especially a legal world—containing social dissensus on large-scale issues. By definition, such agreements have the great advantage of allowing a convergence on particular outcomes by people unable to reach anything like an accord on general principles. This advantage is associated not only with the simple need to decide cases but also with social stability, which could not exist if fundamental disagreements broke out in every case of public or private dispute.

Second, incompletely theorized agreements can promote two goals of a liberal democracy and a liberal legal system: to enable people to live together and to permit them to show each other a degree of reciprocity and mutual respect. The use of low-level principles or rules allows judges on multimember bodies, and hence citizens generally, to find commonality and thus a common way of life without producing unnecessary antagonism. Both rules and low-level principles make it unnecessary to reach areas in which disagreement is fundamental.

Perhaps even more important, incompletely theorized agreements allow people to show each other a high degree of mutual respect, or civility, or reciprocity. Frequently ordinary people disagree in some deep way on an issue—what to do in the Middle East, about pornography, about homosexual marriages—and sometimes they agree not to discuss that issue much, as a way of deferring to each other's strong convictions and showing a measure of reciprocity and respect (even if they do not at all respect the particular conviction at stake). If reciprocity and mutual respect are desirable, it follows that public officials or judges, perhaps even more than ordinary people, should not challenge their fellow citizens' deepest and most defining commitments, at least if those commitments are reasonable and if there is no need for them to do so.

To be sure, some fundamental commitments might appropriately be challenged in the legal system or within other multimember bodies. Some such commitments are ruled off-limits by the authoritative legal materials. Many provisions involving basic rights have this function. Of course, it is not always disrespectful to disagree with someone in a fundamental way; on the contrary, such disagreements may sometimes reflect profound respect. When defining commitments are based on demonstrable errors of fact or logic, it is appropriate to contest them. So too when those commitments are rooted in a rejection of the basic dignity of all human beings, or when it is necessary to undertake the contest to resolve a genuine problem. But many cases can be resolved in an incompletely theorized way, and that is all I am suggesting here.

Turn now to reasons that call for incompletely theorized agreements that may or may not concern a multimember body. The first consideration here is that for arbiters of social controversies, incompletely theorized agreements have the crucial function of reducing the political cost of enduring disagreements. If judges disavow large-scale theories, then losers in particular cases lose much less. They lose a decision, but not the world. They may win on another occasion. Their own theory has not been rejected or ruled inadmissible. When the authoritative rationale for the result is disconnected from abstract theories of the good or the right, the losers can submit to legal obligations, even if reluctantly, without being forced to renounce their most fundamental ideals.

The second point is that incompletely theorized agreements are valuable when we seek to allow moral evolution over time. Consider the area of equality, where considerable change has occurred in the past and will inevitably occur in the future. A completely theorized judgment would be unable to accommodate changes in facts or values. If a culture really did attain a theoretical end-state, it would become too rigid and calcified; we would know what we thought about everything. This would disserve posterity. Hence, incompletely theorized agreements are a key to debates over equality, with issues raised for example, about whether gender, sexual orientation, age, and disability are analogous to race; such agreements have the important advantage of allowing a large degree of openness to new facts and perspectives. At one point, we might think that homosexual relations are akin to incest; at another point, we might find the analogy bizarre. Of course, a completely theorized judgment would have many virtues if it is correct. But at any particular time, this is an unlikely prospect for human beings, not excluding judges.

Compare practical reasoning in ordinary life. At a certain time, you may well refuse to make decisions that seem foundational in character—about, for example, whether to get married within the next year; or whether to have two, three, or four children; or whether to live in San Francisco or New York. Part of the reason for this refusal is knowledge that your understandings of both facts and values may well change. Indeed, your identity may itself change in important and relevant ways, and for this reason a set of commitments in advance—something like a fully theorized conception of your life course—would make no sense. Legal systems and nations are not very different.

The third point is practical. Incompletely theorized agreements may be the best approach available for people of limited time and capacities. A single judge (or ordinary agent) faces this problem as much as a member of a multimember panel. Here too, the rule of precedent is crucial; attention to precedent is liberating, not merely confining, since it frees busy people to deal with a restricted range of problems. Incompletely theorized agreements have the related advantage, for ordinary lawyers and judges, of humility and modesty. To engage in analogical reasoning, for example, one ordinarily need not take a stand on contested issues of social life, some of which can be resolved only on what will seem to many a sectarian basis.

Fourth, incompletely theorized agreements are well adapted to a system that should or must take precedents as fixed points. This is a significant advantage over more ambitious methods, for ambitious thinkers, in order to reach horizontal and vertical coherence, will likely have to disregard many decided cases. In light of the sheer number of decided cases and adjudicative officials, law, for example, cannot speak with one voice; full coherence in principle is extremely unlikely.

We can find many analogies in ordinary life. A parent's practices with his children may not fully cohere. Precedents with respect to bedtime, eating, homework, and much else are unlikely to be susceptible to systematization under a single principle. Of course, parents do not seek to be inconsistent; of course, a child may justly feel aggrieved if a sibling is permitted to watch more hours of television for no apparent reason; but full coherence would be a lot to ask. The problem of reaching full consistency is all the more crucial in politics and law, where so many people have decided so many things, and where disagreements on basic principles lurk in the background.

VI. Overlapping Consensus and Incomplete Theorization

There is a relationship between the notion of incompletely theorized agreements and the well-known idea of an "overlapping consensus," set out by John Rawls.[5] Rawls suggests that a society might seek a reasonable overlapping consensus on certain basic political principles, allowing people, from their own diverse foundations, to agree on those principles. The idea of an overlapping consensus, like the notion of incompletely theorized agreement, attempts to bring about stability and social agreement in the face of diverse "comprehensive views."

But the two ideas are not the same. I have said that when we disagree on the relatively abstract, we can often find agreement by moving to lower levels of generality. Rawls is more interested in the opposite possibility—that people who disagree on much else can agree on political abstractions and use that agreement for political purposes. Rawls says that when we find disagreement or confusion, or when "our shared political understandings... break down," we move toward political philosophy and become more abstract.[6] Thus, Rawls writes that abstraction "is a way of continuing public discussion when shared understandings of lesser generality have broken down. We should be prepared to find that the deeper the conflict, the higher the level of abstraction to which we must ascend to get a clear and uncluttered view of its roots."[7] Of course, what Rawls says may be true: people can be moved toward greater abstraction by their disagreement on particulars. But people may have trouble with abstraction. A special goal of the incompletely theorized agreement on particulars is to obtain a consensus on a concrete outcome among people who do not want to decide questions in political philosophy. They may be uncertain about how to choose among different forms of liberalism, or about whether to select liberalism or a certain alternative.

One of the basic aspirations of Rawls's approach is to avoid certain abstract debates in philosophy generally. Rawls wants to enable people to agree on political principles when they are uncertain how to think about many questions of philosophy or metaphysics. Thus, Rawls seeks to ensure a political approach that "leaves philosophy as it is."[8] But if what I have said is right, judgments in law and politics sometimes bear the same relation to political philosophy as (on Rawls's view) do judgments in political philosophy to questions in general philosophy and metaphysics. The political philosopher may attempt not to take a stand on important philosophical or metaphysical questions; so too the lawyer, the judge, or the political participant may urge outcomes that make it unnecessary to solve such questions in political philosophy. Because of their limited role, judges, legislators, and citizens may very much want to leave political philosophy "as it is."

Of course, some background abstractions should limit the permissible set of incompletely theorized agreements. Otherwise there is no assurance that an incompletely theorized agreement is just, and we should design our legal and political systems so as to counteract the risk of unjust agreement. If we want to limit the category of incompletely theorized agreements, to ensure that they are defensible and not mere accident, we may have to move toward more ambitious ways of thinking. But if an incompletely theorized judgment does command agreement—and if at least one good account of justice calls for it—nothing should be amiss.[9]

VII. Analogies in General

I turn now to analogical thinking, an important mechanism by which people reach incompletely theorized agreements. For present purposes, we can put to one side the formal dimensions of analogical reasoning[10] and suggest more simply that, as I understand it here, analogical reasoning has four different but overlapping features: *principled consistency, a focus on particulars, incompletely theorized judgments, and principles operating at a low or intermediate level of abstraction.* In concert, these features produce both the virtues and the vices of analogical reasoning in law. Here are some brief remarks on each of these features.

First, and most obviously, judgments about specific cases must be made consistent with one another. A requirement of principled consistency is a hallmark of analogical reasoning (as it is of practical reasoning of almost all sorts). It follows that in producing the necessary consistency, some principle, harmonizing seemingly disparate outcomes, will be invoked to explain the cases. The principle must of course be more general than the outcome for which it is designed.

Second, analogical reasoning focuses on particulars, and it develops from concrete controversies. The great American Supreme Court justice Oliver Wendell Holmes put the point in this suggestive if somewhat misleading way: a common law court "decides the case first and determines the principle afterwards."[11] Holmes's suggestion is misleading, for in order to decide the case at all, one has to have the principle in some sense in mind; there can be no sequential operation of quite the kind Holmes describes. But Holmes is right to say that ideas are developed with close reference to the details, rather than imposed on them from above. In this sense, analogical reasoning, as a species of casuistry, is a form of "bottom-up" thinking.

Despite the analogizer's focus on particulars, any description of a particular holding inevitably has more general components. We cannot know anything about case X if we do not know something about the reasons that count in its favor. We cannot say whether case X has anything to do with case Y unless we are able to abstract, a bit, from the facts and holding of case X. In this sense, the form of thinking I am describing rejects the understanding, rooted in Aristotle, that practical reasoners can move "from particular to particular." There is no such movement; principles must be developed to unite the particulars. The key point is that analogical reasoning involves a process in which principles are developed from, and with constant reference to, particular cases.

Third, analogical reasoning in law operates with no deep or comprehensive theory that would account for the particular outcomes it yields. The judgments that underlie convictions about the relevant case are incompletely theorized. Of course, there is a continuum from the most particularistic and low-level principles to the deepest and most general. I suggest only that analogizers avoid those approaches that come close to the deeply theorized or the foundational. In this way, analogical thinkers do not attempt to reach reflective equilibrium. Their way of proceeding involves little in the way of width or breadth. They do not compare cases with all possible cases; they do not try to develop deep theories. Along these dimensions, analogical reasoners are far less ambitious than those who seek reflective equilibrium.

There is another, related difference between analogical thinking and the search for reflective equilibrium. In that search, all judgments are, in principle, subject to revision if they conflict with some other judgment that is general, particular, or somewhere in between. But in many domains, analogical reasoners must take certain particular judgments as rigidly fixed points. Certainly this is true for practical reason in law. It is often true for practical reason in politics as well. The fact that some particular points are fixed makes it unlikely that analogical reasoners can reach reflective equilibrium, since several of those particular points might seem to those reasoners to be wrong. Hence, analogical reasoners aspire only to local and partial coherence.

Fourth, and finally, analogical reasoning produces principles that operate at a low or intermediate level of abstraction. If we say that an employer may not fire an employee for accepting jury duty, we might mean (for example) that an employer cannot require an employee to commit a crime. This is a standard, perhaps even a rule, and it does involve a degree of abstraction from the particular case, but it does not entail any high-level theory about labor markets, or about the appropriate relationship between employers and employees. If we say that a Communist march cannot be banned, we might mean that political speech cannot be stopped without a showing of clear and immediate harm, but in so saying, we do not invoke any general theory about the purposes of the free speech guarantee, or about the relation between the citizen and the state. People can converge on the low-level principle from various foundations, or without well-understood foundations at all.

VIII. The Common Law, the Constitution, and Rules

Common law judges decide particular controversies by exploring how previous cases have been resolved. This is a familiar point; participants in common law are insistently analogical and tend to avoid abstractions. It is less often emphasized that analogical reasoning is crucial in constitutional cases. This is so in a wide range of nations, including the United States, Israel, Germany, Canada, Australia, and Hungary. Indeed, American constitutional law is often constructed from analogies—not from text or history, not from moral theory, and not from existing social consensus. Much of the meaning of the American Constitution comes through analogies.

In cases decided *under rules*, people also engage, much of the time, in a form of analogical reasoning. This is a counterintuitive claim. Interpretation of rules is often said to be at an opposite pole from analogical reasoning. But the opposition is far too simple. Often interpretation of rules involves analogy too.[12] In so saying we can vindicate justice Holmes's striking suggestion that rules should be interpreted through examination of "the picture" that the words "evoke in the common mind."[13]

Some intriguing work in cognitive science and psychology supports Holmes's view. Because of how human beings think, rules and categories are defined by reference to characteristic instances. Suppose, for example, that we are investigating a single class of things—birds, or vehicles, or nations, or works of art, or mammals. How do we know whether members of any such class are alike or different? It turns out that people have a mental picture of a model or typical example of the category, and they reason analogically, asking whether a member of the class is "like" or "unlike" that typical example. Thus, people tend to think that a canary is more "bird" than a penguin, though both are birds; a truck is more "vehicle" than an elevator; an apple is more "fruit" than a coconut.[14] Experiments show "the robust psychological reality of the typicality of a single exemplar of a given class.... The typicality of an exemplar is then routinely measured by the distance between the exemplar and the class as a whole."[15]

These experiments reveal that categories receive their meaning by reference to typical instances. When we are asked whether a particular thing falls within a general category, we examine whether that thing is like or unlike the typical or defining instances. Very much the same is true in the interpretation of rules.

Consider these cases:

1. A statute enacted in 1920 forbids people to "sell babies." In 1993, Mr. and Ms. Jones hire Ms. Andrea Smith to be a surrogate mother. Does the contract violate the statute?[16]
2. A statute makes it a crime, with a thirty-year mandatory minimum, for someone to "use a firearm in connection with a sale of an unlawful substance." Smith sells a firearm in return for cocaine, an unlawful substance. Has Smith violated the statute?[17]
3. In 1964, Congress enacted a law forbidding any employer from "discriminating on the basis of race." Bennett Industries has an affirmative action program, offering preferential treatment to African-American applicants. Does Bennett Industries discriminate on the basis of race, in violation of the 1964 statute?[18]

Here we have three cases involving the meaning of rules. All of them produced divided courts. It would be especially desirable to be able to decide such cases without invoking large-scale theories of the good or the right. If judges, to decide such cases, must develop a deep account of what lies behind the ban on discrimination, or the prohibition on baby selling, or the ban on the use of guns in connection with drug transactions, things will become very difficult very quickly. But there is a feasible alternative, and it is roughly the same for all three cases, which should therefore be seen as variations on a single theme.

For the dissenting judge, the first case was especially easy. The statute forbids "baby selling." Smith sold her baby to the Jones couple. No controversial claim is necessary in order for us to see that a baby has been sold. We do not need analogies at all. Much less do we need deep theories of any kind. Here is a simple case of rule-following.

But things cannot proceed so quickly. Has Smith really sold "her" baby? How do we know whether it was ever hers? Mr. and Ms. Jones say that they are simply purchasing what might be called gestational services, and not a baby at all. In this way, they say, the case is quite different from one in which a parent sells a born child who is unquestionably hers. To be sure, it may seem natural to think that Smith's biological connection to the baby gives her ownership rights—whether whole or partial—in the child she has brought to term. But property rights do not come from the sky or even from nature; property rights as we understand them have legal sources. The claim that "X has a property right" means that X has a *legal* right of some sort to the interest in question. The problem for the court is that when the case arose, the legal system had made no antecedent decision at all on the subject of ownership of the baby. The legal system had not allocated the child to Smith, or for that matter to Mr. and Ms. Jones. It follows that we do not really know whether we have a sale of a baby. Staring at the language of the statute will not be enough.

In deciding the case, the majority of the court acknowledged that the text was not simple as applied to the situation of surrogacy. Instead, the court asked whether a surrogacy arrangement is relevantly similar to or relevantly different from the sale of a baby. The court therefore reasoned analogically. It held that the surrogacy arrangement was lawful. Its argument took the following form. There is at least a plausible difference between a surrogacy arrangement and the sale of a born child. In the former case, the child would not exist but for the arrangement. A ban on the sale of an existing child causes special risks for the child and for poor parents in general, who might be put under particular pressure to sell their children. The surrogacy situation is factually different on both of these counts. The child would not exist without the arrangement and may face lower risks from any deal, and the surrogate mother is in a quite different situation from parents who sell a born child. (Despite the bow in the direction of literalism, the dissenting judges used a similar method. They reasoned analogically and found the analogy apposite.)

In any case, the legislature that outlawed baby selling made no specific, considered judgment to ban surrogacy. The court thought that it ought not to take the language of the statute to foreclose a voluntary arrangement for which the legislature had made no considered judgment, at least where there is a plausible difference between that situation and the obvious or defining cases.

Does this approach take a theoretical stand? Does it offer an account of why baby selling is banned? In a sense, the answer to both questions is yes. To reason analogically, the court had to decide whether the sale of a baby is relevantly similar to or relevantly different from a surrogacy arrangement, and to make that decision, it had to come up with an account of why the sale of a baby is banned. But notice the special form of the argument. There was no deep theoretical claim about the limits of the marketplace or about the sale of human beings. The court described the justification behind the ban at a relatively low, commonsensical level of abstraction. Moreover, the court did not say that a surrogacy arrangement was, in terms of basic principle, really different from a ban on baby selling. It said only that there were differences that might be thought relevant.

Much of the court's decision involved the use of *default rules*,[19] motivated by the goal of easing decision and obtaining an appropriate allocation of authority between courts and legislatures. In the court's view, a broadly worded criminal statute should not be applied to a controversial situation not within the contemplation of the enacting legislature, and plausibly different from the "picture" that inspired the legislation—unless and until there has been democratic deliberation on that question.

The use of the resulting default rule much simplified the exercise of practical reason in the case. In this way the decision can be seen as one of a large class of cases in which a default rule operates to simplify and constrain the operation of practical reason. This is an especially important and underanalyzed phenomenon. It occurs when agents identify a principle (itself likely to be incompletely theorized) by which to settle cases that are otherwise close to equipoise. Default rules are a standard part of practical reason, whether or not they are visible to the relevant agents.[20]

Now turn to the second case. In one understanding of the word "use," Smith has certainly "used" a firearm in connection with the sale of drugs. The gun was part of the transaction. But there is another linguistically possible conception of the word "use," one suggesting that if we read the law in its context, Smith has not really violated the statute. Perhaps someone "uses" a gun only if he uses it as a weapon. Smith did no such thing.

The Supreme Court held that Smith violated the statute. The Court did not really pretend that the words of the statute were clear. Instead it reasoned partly in this way: we know that a gun may not be used as a weapon in connection with the sale of drugs. Is the use of a gun as an object of barter relevantly similar? The Court said that it was. It said that Smith's own use of a gun, as an item of barter, poses serious risks to life and limb, since that very use puts a gun into the stream of commerce with people engaged in unlawful activity. Notice here that the Court did generate an account of what lay behind the ban on use of guns, but the account was quite commonsensical and low-level, and it worked by analogy.

Writing in dissent, Justice Scalia was incredulous. In part he relied on what he took to be the ordinary meaning of the word "use." But in part he too relied on an argument from analogy. In his view, Smith's conduct was different from that contemplated by the statute. Smith did not threaten to shoot anyone. He should therefore be treated differently from people whom Congress sought specifically to punish.

Now let us go to the third case. The antidiscrimination law prohibits "discrimination on the basis of race." But is an affirmative action program "discrimination on the basis of race"? If we consult any good dictionary, we will find that "discrimination" is ambiguous on the point, and in any case there are real hazards in relying on dictionaries. "Discrimination" could be interpreted so as to forbid any form of differentiation and hence any racial differentiation, but it could also be interpreted to include invidious discrimination, or distinctions based on prejudice and hostility, in which case affirmative action programs might be unobjectionable.

Seeing the case like the majority in the surrogacy dispute and like Justice Scalia in *Smith*, the majority of the Supreme Court treated the words of the civil rights statute as ambiguous in their context. Instead of relying on a "plain" text, it proceeded roughly in the following way. We know that discrimination against members of racial minorities is unlawful. Is discrimination against whites similar or different? The Court said that it could be seen as relevantly different. The purpose and effect of the antidiscrimination law were to eliminate second-class citizenship for blacks, not to perpetuate it. The Court appeared to be arguing that the controversial issue of affirmative action should not be resolved through the broad interpretation of an ambiguous term, if that issue had never been squarely faced by the enacting legislature.

The three cases are hard, and they could be analyzed in many different ways. I believe that in each of them, the statutory barrier should have been found inapplicable. This is not for deeply theoretical reasons, but because of institutional concerns justifying a default rule: if it is reasonable to see a relevant difference between the obvious instances covered by the statute and the case at hand, if application to the case at hand would outlaw a voluntary social practice, and if there is good reason to doubt that the case at hand was or would have been within the contemplation of the enacting legislature, courts should not apply the statutory term.

Whether or not we think these cases were rightly decided, they support a simple point. Sometimes a rule is ambiguous. For the practical reasoner, the unambiguous applications serve as fixed points. The judge cannot question those applications. The applications operate very much like holdings in decided cases, or like precedents. But on the question at hand, there is no rule at all. This is a pervasive phenomenon in the interpretation of rules. It is pervasive not only in law, but in everyday life when the meaning of rules becomes unclear.

IX. Conceptual Ascent?

Borrowing from Henry Sidgwick's writings on ethical method,[21] an enthusiast for ambitious thinking might respond to analogical argument and for incompletely theorized agreements in the following way. There is often good reason for practical reasoners to raise the level of abstraction and ultimately to resort to large-scale theory. As a practical matter, concrete judgments about particular cases will prove inadequate for morality or law. Sometimes people do not have clear intuitions about how cases should come out. Sometimes seemingly similar cases provoke different reactions, and it is necessary to raise the level of theoretical ambition to explain whether those different reactions are justified, or to show that the seemingly similar cases are different after all. Sometimes people simply disagree. By looking at broader principles, we may be able to mediate the disagreement. In any case, there is a problem of explaining our considered judgments about particular cases, in order to see whether they are not just a product of accident, and at some point it is important to offer that explanation. When our modest judge joins an opinion that is incompletely theorized, he has to rely on a reason or a principle, justifying one outcome rather than another. The opinion must itself refer to a reason or principle; it cannot just announce a victor. Perhaps the low-level principle is wrong, because it fails to fit with other cases, or because it is not defensible as a matter of (legally relevant) political morality.

In short, the incompletely theorized agreement may be nothing to celebrate. It may be wrong or unreliable. Thus, if a judge is reasoning well, he should have before him a range of other cases, C through Z, in which the principle is tested against others and refined. At least if he is a distinguished judge, he will experience a kind of "conceptual ascent," in which the more or less isolated and small low-level principle is finally made part of a more general theory. Perhaps this would be a paralyzing task, and perhaps our judge need not often attempt it. But it is an appropriate model for understanding law and an appropriate aspiration for evaluating judicial and political outcomes.

There is some truth in this response. At least if they have time, moral reasoners should try to achieve vertical and horizontal consistency, not just the local pockets of coherence offered by incompletely theorized agreements. In democratic processes, it is appropriate and sometimes indispensable to challenge existing practice in abstract terms. But the response ignores some of the distinctive characteristics of the arena in which real-world judges must do their work. Some of these limits involve bounded rationality and thus what should happen in a world in which all of us face various constraints. But some of them involve limits of role morality in a world in which judges (now using the term technically) are mere actors in a complex system, and in which people legitimately disagree on first principles. In light of these limits, incompletely theorized agreements have the many virtues I described, including the facilitation of convergence, the reduction of costs of disagreement, and the demonstration of humility and mutual respect.

As I have noted, incompletely theorized agreements are especially well adapted to a system that must take precedents as fixed points; practical reasoners could not try to reach reflective equilibrium without severely compromising the system of precedent. Usually local coherence is the most to which lawyers and judges may aspire. Just as legislation cannot be understood as if it came from a single mind, so precedents, compiled by many people responding to different problems in many different periods, will not reflect a single authorial voice.

There are many lurking questions. How we do know whether moral or political judgments are right? What is the relation between provisional or considered judgments about particulars and corresponding judgments about abstractions?[22] Sometimes people interested in practical reason write as if abstract theoretical judgments, or abstract theories, have a kind of reality and hardness that particular judgments lack, or if as abstract theories provide the answers to examination questions that particular judgments, frail as they are, may pass or fail. On this view, theories are searchlights that illuminate particular judgments and show them for what they really are. But we might think instead that there is no special magic in theories or abstractions and that theories are simply the (humanly constructed) means by which people make sense of the judgments that constitute their ethical and political worlds. The abstract deserves no priority over the particular; neither should be treated as foundational. A (poor or crude) abstract theory may simply be a confused way of trying to make sense of our considered judgments about particular cases, which may be much better than the theory. In fact, it is possible that moral judgments are best described not as an emanation of a broad theory but instead as a reflection of prototypical cases, or "precedents," from which moral thinkers—ordinary citizens and experts—work.

X. Is Incomplete Theorizing Conservative?

A separate challenge, traceable to Jeremy Bentham, is that the method of analogy and incompletely theorized agreement is insufficiently scientific, unduly tied to existing intuitions, and partly for these reasons is static or celebrates of existing social practice. In this view, analogical reasoning is particularly problematic, because it works so modestly from existing holdings and convictions. It needs to be replaced by something like a general theory. For the critics, analogizers are Burkeans, and their approach suffers from all the flaws associated with Edmund Burke's celebration of the English common law. It is too insistently backward-looking, too skeptical of theory, too lacking in criteria by which to assess legal practices critically.

At first glance, the claim seems mysterious. Analogical reasoning cannot work without criteria. Whether analogical reasoning calls for the continuation of existing practice turns on the convictions or holdings from which analogical reasoning takes place. Without identifying those convictions or holdings, we cannot say whether existing practices will be celebrated. The process of testing initial judgments by reference to analogies can produce sharp criticism of many social practices and, eventually, can yield reform. Judgments or holdings that are critical of some social practices can turn out, through analogy, to be critical of other practices as well.

In fact, analogical thinking has often produced large-scale change. In American law, *Brown v. Board of Education* invalidated racial segregation in education. By analogy to *Brown*, American courts invalidated racial segregation elsewhere too.

Even more than that, they reformed prisons and mental institutions; struck down many racial classifications, including affirmative action programs; invalidated sex discrimination; and prevented states from discriminating on the basis of alienage and legitimacy. The analogical process has hardly run its course. Whether analogical reasoning is conservative or not depends not on the fact that it is analogical, but on the nature of the principles brought to bear on disputed cases.[23]

Of course, a full theory of practical reasoning should explain which holdings are wrong and which particular judgments or "holdings" should be rejected because they are wrong. Analogical reasoning, at least as thus far described, is not helpful here. But sometimes reasoning by analogy does help to reveal mistakes. Reference to other cases helps show us that our initial judgments are inconsistent with what we actually think. Certainly, every system must make many decisions on how to weigh the interest in stability against the interest in getting things right (with the acknowledgment that current thinking about right might not in fact be right).

XI. Judges, Theory, and the Rule of Law

At this point we might distinguish between the role of high theory within the courtroom and within the political branches of government. To be sure, incompletely theorized agreements play a role in democratic arenas; consider laws protecting endangered species or granting unions a right to organize. But in democratic arenas, there is no general taboo, presumptive or otherwise, on invoking high-level theories of the good or the right. On the contrary, such theories have played a key role in many social movements with defining effects on American constitutionalism, including the Civil War, the New Deal, the women's movement, and the environmental movement. Abstract, high-level ideas are an important part of democratic discussion, and sometimes they are ratified publicly and placed in a constitution.

By contrast, development of large-scale theories by ordinary courts is problematic and usually understood as such within the judiciary. The skepticism about large-scale theories results partly from the fact that such theories may require large-scale social reforms, and courts have enormous difficulties in implementing such reforms.[24] When courts invoke a large-scale theory as a reason for social change, they may well fail, simply because they lack the tools to bring about change on their own. An important reason for judicial incapacity is that courts must decide on the legitimacy of rules that are aspects of complex systems. In invalidating or changing a single rule, courts may not do what they seek to do. They may produce unfortunate systemic effects, with unanticipated bad consequences not visible to them at the time of decision and perhaps impossible to correct thereafter.[25] Legislatures are in a much better position on this score. Judge-initiated changes are not always bad, but the piecemeal quality of such changes is a reason for caution.

More fundamentally, in the absence of a democratic pedigree, the system of precedent, analogy, and incompletely theorized agreement assumes a crucial role. The need to discipline judicial judgment arises from the courts' complex and modest place in any well-functioning constitutional system. To be sure, judges have, in some societies, a duty to interpret the Constitution, and sometimes that duty authorizes them to invoke relatively large-scale principles, seen as part and parcel of the Constitution as democratically ratified. Many people think that judicial activity is best characterized by reference to use of such principles. Certainly an some occasions this practice is legitimate and even glorious.

To identify those occasions, it would be necessary to develop a full theory of legal interpretation. For present purposes we can say something more modest. Most judicial activity does not involve constitutional interpretation, and the ordinary work of common law decision and statutory interpretation calls for low-level principles on which agreements are possible. Indeed, constitutional argument is itself based largely on low-level principles, not on high theory, except on those rare occasions when more ambitious thinking becomes necessary to resolve a case, or when the case for the ambitious theory is so insistent that a range of judges converge on it. And there are good reasons for the presumption in favor of low-level principles: the limited capacities of judges, the need to develop principles over time, the failure of monistic theories of the law, and the other considerations I have traced.

XII. Incompletely Theorized Agreements and Disagreement, Democratic and Otherwise

Incompletely theorized agreements have virtues; but their virtues are partial. Stability, for example, is maintained by such agreements, and stability is usually desirable. But a stable and unjust system should probably be made less stable. In this section I offer some qualifications. Some cases cannot be decided *at all* without introducing a fair amount in the way of theory. Some cases cannot be decided *well* without introducing theory. If a good theory is available, and if judges can be persuaded that the theory is good, there should be no taboo on its judicial acceptance. The claims on behalf of incompletely theorized agreements are presumptive rather than conclusive.

What of disagreement? The discussion thus far has focused on the need for convergence. There is indeed such a need, but it is only part of the picture. In law, politics, and private life, disagreement can be a productive and creative force, revealing error, showing gaps, moving discussion and results in good directions. The American political order has placed a high premium on "government by discussion," and when the process is working well, this is true for the judiciary as well as for other institutions. Agreements may be a product of coercion, subtle or not, or of a failure of imagination.

Legal disagreements have many legitimate sources, two of which are especially important. First, people may share general commitments but disagree on particular outcomes. Second, people's disagreements on general principles may produce disagreement over particular outcomes and low-level propositions as well. People who think that an autonomy principle accounts for freedom of speech may also think that the government cannot regulate truthful, nondeceptive commercial advertising—whereas people who think that freedom of speech is basically a democratic idea, and is focused on political speech, may have no interest in protecting commercial advertising at all. Academic theorizing can have a salutary function in part because it tests low-level principles by reference to more ambitious claims. Disagreements can be productive by virtue of this process of testing.

Certainly if everyone having a reasonable general view converges on a particular (by hypothesis reasonable) judgment, nothing is amiss. But if an agreement is incompletely theorized, there is a risk that everyone who participates in the agreement is mistaken, and hence that the outcome is mistaken. There is also a risk that someone who is reasonable has not participated, and that if that person were included, the agreement would break down. Over time, incompletely theorized agreements should be subject to scrutiny and critique. That process may result in more ambitious thinking than law ordinarily entails.

Nor is social consensus a consideration that outweighs everything else. Usually it would be much better to have a just outcome, rejected by many people, than an unjust outcome with which all or most agree. Consensus or agreement is important largely because of its connection with stability, itself a valuable but far from overriding social goal. As Thomas Jefferson wrote, a degree of turbulence is productive in a democracy.[26] We have seen that incompletely theorized agreements, even if stable and broadly supported, may conceal or reflect injustice. Certainly, agreements should be more fully theorized when the relevant theory is plainly right and people can be shown that it is right, or when the invocation of the theory is necessary to decide cases. None of this is inconsistent with what I have claimed here.

It would be foolish to say that no general theory can produce agreement, even more foolish to deny that some general theories deserve support, and most foolish of all to say that incompletely theorized agreements warrant respect whatever their content. What seems plausible is something more modest: except in unusual situations, and for multiple reasons, general theories are an unlikely foundation for law and politics, and caution and humility about general theory are appropriate at least when multiple theories can lead in the same direction. This more modest set of claims helps us to characterize incompletely theorized agreements as important phenomena with their own special virtues, both public and private. The argument on behalf of incompletely theorized agreements is ultimately part of a theory of just institutions in general and deliberative democracy in particular, with a claim that basic social principles are best developed politically rather than judicially. And whether or not this is so, incompletely theorized agreements play a fundamental role in practical reasoning, especially, but not only, in the public domain.

Notes

Some aspects of this chapter, designed for a legal audience, appear in "Incompletely Theorized Agreements," 108 *Harv. L. Rev.* 1733 (1995); a general treatment appears in Cass R. Sunstein, *Legal Reasoning and Political Conflict* (Oxford University Press, 1996). The earlier discussions focus on legal reasoning; although I draw on those discussions, I deal here with the quite different topic of practical reason in general.

1. 410 U.S. 113 (1973). On the refusal to overrule Roe, see *Planned Parenthood v. Casey*, 112 S Ct 2791 (1992).
2. Breyer, "The Federal Sentencing Guidelines and the Key Compromises upon Which They Rest," 17 *Hofstra L. Rev.* 1, 14–19 (1988).
3. As quoted in *The New Republic*, June 6, 1994, p. 12.

4. *Lochner v. New York*, 198 U.S. 48, 69 (1908) (Holmes, J., dissenting).

5. *Political Liberalism*, pp. 133–72. See also John Rawls, "Reply to Habermas," 92 *Journal of Philosophy* 132 (1995).

6. See *Political Liberalism*, pp. 43–45.

7. *Political Liberalism*, pp. 46.

8. "Reply to Habermas" p. 134.

9. I am grateful to Yael Tamir for helpful discussion of the points in this paragraph.

10. These are discussed in *Legal Reasoning and Political Conflicy*, chapter 3.

11. Holmes, "Codes and the Arrangements of Law," 44 *Harv. L. Rev.* 725 (1931) (reprinted from 5 *Am. L. Rev.* 11 (1870).

12. Cf. Ludwig Wittgenstein, *Philosophical Investigations* 83 (New York: MacMillan, 1953): "But if a person has not yet got the concepts, I shall teach him to use the words by means of examples and by practice.—And when I do this I do not communicate less to him than I know myself." See also Paul Churchland, *The Engine of Reason, the Seat of the Soul* (Cambridge: MIT Press, 1995), which uses cognitive science to suggest the same result.

13. *McBoyle v. U.S.*, 283 U.S. 25, 28 (1931).

14. See Churchland, *Engine of Reason*; Massimo Piattelli-Palmarini, Inevitable Illusions: How Mistakes of Reason Rule Our Minds, (New York: Wiley, 1994).

15. Churchland, *Engine of Reason* p. 152.

16. *Surrogate Parenting Assn. v. Kentucky*, 704 SW2d 209 (1986).

17. *Smith v. U.S.*, 113 S Ct 2050 (1993).

18. *United Steelworkers v. Kaiser Aluminum*, 443 U.S. 193 (1979).

19. See Edna Ullmann-Margalit, "On Presumption," 80 *Journal of Philosophy* 143, 154–62 (1983).

20. The point, together with others made in the text, points the way toward a criticism of the illuminating picture of legal reasoning in Ronald Dworkin, *Law's Empire* (Cambridge: Harvard University Press, 1986). Dworkin's account sees the judge as developing the "best constructive interpretation" of a practice, often by developing deeply theorized understandings of certain areas of law. But judges often find this task too difficult or hubristic. Like other people engaged in practical reason, they attempt instead to use low-level principles and default rules on which diverse people can converge. See *Legal Reasoning and Political Conflict*, chapter 2, for more detailed discussion.

21. See *The Methods of Ethics*, 7th ed. (New York: Dover Publications, 1966), pp. 96–104.

22. In Rawls's understanding of the search for reflective equilibrium, we consult "our considered convictions at all levels of generality; no one level, say that of abstract principle or that of particular judgments in particular cases, is viewed as foundational. They all may have an initial credibility." *Political Liberalism*, p. 8.

23. Joseph Raz, in *The Authority of Law: Essays on Law and Morality* (Oxford: Oxford University Press, 1979), defends analogical thinking as a response to the problem of "partial reform," that is, the risk that piecemeal reforms will fail to serve their own purposes, because public or private actors will adapt (as in the idea that the minimum wage decreases employment). In Raz' view, analogical thinking responds to this risk by ensuring that any "new rule is a conservative one, that it does not introduce new discordant and conflicting purposes or value into the law, that its purpose and the values it promotes are already served by existing rules" (p. 204). There is truth in this claim, but if the purpose or values are described in certain ways, the analogical process may lead in highly nonconservative directions, with no abuse to analogies themselves.

24. See Gerald N. Rosenberg, *The Hollow Hope: Can Courts Bring About Social Change*, (Chicago: University of Chicago Press, 1991).

25. Examples are offered in R. Shep Melnick, *Regulation and the Courts: The Case of the Clean Air Act*. (Washington: Brookings Institution, 1983), and Donald Horowitz, *The*

Courts and Social Policy (Washington: Brookings Institution, 1977). The point is described from the theoretical point of view in Lon Fuller, "The Forms and Limits of Adjudication," 92 *Harv. L. Rev.* 353 (1978), and Joseph Raz, "The Inner Logic of the Law," in *Ethics in the Public Domain*, p. 224.

26. Thus, Jefferson said that turbulence is "productive of good. It prevents the degeneracy of government, and nourishes a general attention to . . . public affairs. I hold . . . that a little rebellion now and then is a good thing." Letter to Madison (Jan. 30, 1798), reprinted in *The Portable Thomas Jefferson*, Merrill D. Peterson ed. (New York: Viking Press, 1975).

Part III

The Practice Reasoned About

8

RELATIONSHIPS AND RESPONSIBILITIES

Samuel Scheffler

How do we come to have responsibilities to some people that we do not have to others? In our everyday lives, many different kinds of considerations are invoked to explain these "special" responsibilities. Often we cite some kind of interaction that we have had with the person to whom we bear the responsibility. Perhaps we made this person a promise, or entered into an agreement with him. Or perhaps we feel indebted to him because of something he once did for us. Or, again, perhaps we once harmed him in some way, and as a result we feel a responsibility to make reparation to him. In all of these cases, there is either something we have done or something the "beneficiary" of the responsibility has done that is cited as the source of that responsibility.

Not all of our explanations take this form, however. Sometimes we account for special responsibilities not by citing any specific interaction between us and the beneficiary, but rather by citing the nature of our relationship to that person. We have special duties to a person, we may say, because she is our sister, or our friend, or our neighbor. Many different types of relationship are invoked in this way. Perhaps the person is not a relative but a colleague, not a friend but a teammate, not a neighbor but a client. Sometimes the relationship may consist only in the fact that we are both members of a certain kind of group. We may belong to the same community, for example, or be citizens of the same country, or be part of the same nation or people. In some of these cases, we may never have met or had any interaction with the person who is seen as the beneficiary of the responsibility. We may nevertheless be convinced that our shared group membership suffices to generate such a responsibility. Of course, claims of special responsibility can be controversial, especially in cases of this kind. While some people feel strongly that they have special responsibilities to the other members of their national or cultural group, for example, other people feel just as strongly that they do not. Nevertheless, it is a familiar fact that such ties are often seen as a source of special responsibilities. Indeed, we would be hard pressed to find any type of human relationship to which people have attached value or significance but which has never been seen as generating such responsibilities. It seems that whenever people value an interpersonal relationship they are apt to see it as a source of special duties or obligations.[1]

However, although it is clear that we do in fact cite our relationships to other people in explaining why we have special responsibilities to them, many philosophers have been reluctant to take these citations at face value. Instead, they have supposed that the responsibilities we perceive as arising out of special relationships actually arise out of discrete interactions that occur in the context of those relationships. Thus, for example, some special responsibilities, like the mutual responsibilities of spouses, may be said to arise out of promises or commitments that the participants have made to each other. Others, like the responsibilities of children to their parents, may be seen as arising form the provision of benefits to one party by the other. And in cases like those mentioned earlier, in which two people are both members of some group but have not themselves interacted in any way, it may be denied that the people do in fact have any special responsibilities to each other. As already noted, claims of special responsibility tend to be controversial in such cases anyway, and it may be thought an advantage of this position that it sees grounds for skepticism precisely in the cases that are most controversial.

Clearly, the view that duties arising out of special relationships can always be reduced to duties arising out of discrete interactions is compatible with the view that the relevant interactions, and hence the relevant duties, may be of fundamentally different kinds. Indeed, to some philosophers it seems clear that the relationships that have been seen as generating special responsibilities are so heterogeneous that the responsibilities in question cannot possibly have but a single ground. Nevertheless, one of the greatest pressures toward a reductionist position has come from those who believe that all genuine special responsibilities must be based on consent or on some other voluntary act. These voluntarists, as we may call them, are not hostile to the idea of special responsibilities as such. However, they reject the notion that one can find oneself with such responsibilities without having done anything at all to incur them. Different voluntarists disagree about the types of voluntary act that are capable of generating special responsibilities. Some insist that such responsibilities can only arise from explicit agreements or undertakings. Others believe that one can incur special responsibilities just by voluntarily entering into a relationship with someone, and that no explicit agreement to bear the responsibilities is required. Still others believe that one's acceptance of the benefits of participation in a relationship can generate responsibilities even if one's entry into the relationship was not itself voluntary. Obviously, then, voluntarists will sometimes disagree among themselves about the specific responsibilities of particular people. And different versions of voluntarism will be more or less revisionist with respect to our ordinary moral beliefs, depending on which types of voluntary act they deem capable of generating special responsibilities. For example, voluntarists who believe that special responsibilities can only be incurred through an explicit undertaking or the voluntary establishment of a relationship may deny that children have such responsibilities to their parents. But those who think that the voluntary acceptance of benefits can also generate special responsibilities may disagree, at least insofar as they think it makes sense to regard children as voluntarily accepting benefits from their parents. What all voluntarists do agree about, however, is that the mere fact that one stands in a certain relationship to another person cannot by itself give one a special responsibility to that person. In order to have such a responsibility, one must have performed some voluntary act that constitutes the ground of the responsibility.

Voluntarists are sensitive to the fact that special responsibilities can be costly and difficult to discharge, and thus quite burdensome for those who bear them. It would be unfair, they believe, if people could be saddled with such burdens against their wills, and so it would be unfair if special responsibilities could be ascribed to people who had done nothing voluntarily to incur them. In effect, then, voluntarists see a form of reductionism about special responsibilities as necessary if our assignments of such responsibilities are to be fair to those who bear them. Voluntarism is an influential view, and many people find the voluntarist objection to unreduced special responsibilities quite congenial. At the same time, however, there is another objection that may also be directed against such responsibilities. According to this objection, the problem with special responsibilities is not that they may be unfairly burdensome for those who bear them, but rather that they may confer unfair advantages on their bearers. And for the purposes of this objection, it does not matter whether the source of those responsibilities is understood voluntaristically or not.

Suppose that you have recently become my friend and that I have therefore acquired special responsibilities to you. Clearly, these responsibilities work to your advantage, inasmuch as I now have a duty to do things for you that I would not previously have been required to do. At the same time, there are at least two different ways in which my responsibilities to you work to the disadvantage of those people with whom I have no special relationship. First, in the absence of my responsibilities to you, I might have done certain things for them even though I had no duty to do so. Now, however, discharging my responsibilities to you must take priority over doing any of those things for them. Second, there may also be situations in which my responsibilities to you take priority over the responsibilities that I have to them simply as human beings. For example, there may be times when I must help you rather than helping them, if I cannot do both, even though I would have been required to help them but for the fact that you too need help. Thus, in both of these ways, my special responsibilities to you may work to the disadvantage of other people. In one respect, moreover, they may also work to my own disadvantage, since, as the voluntarist objection points out, such responsibilities can be quite burdensome. At the same time, however, my responsibilities to you may also confer some very important advantages on me. For, insofar as I am required to give your interests priority over the interests of other people, I am, in effect, called upon to act in ways that will contribute to the flourishing of our friendship rather than attending to the needs of other people. So my responsibilities to you may work to my net advantage as well as to yours, while working to the disadvantage of people with whom I have no special relationship. Furthermore, if you and I have become friends, then, presumably, not only have I acquired special responsibilities to you but you have acquired such responsibilities to me. And, just as my responsibilities to you may work both to your advantage and to mine, while working to the disadvantage of other people, so too your responsibilities to me may work both to my advantage and to yours, while working to the disadvantage of others.

Now the objection that I have in mind challenges this entire way of allocating benefits and burdens, on the ground that it provides you and me with unfair advantages while unfairly disadvantaging other people. Why exactly, this "distributive objection" asks, should our friendship give rise to a distribution of responsibility that is favorable to us and unfavorable to other people? After all, it may be said, the effect of such a distribution is to reward the very people who have already achieved a rewarding personal relationship, while penalizing those who have not. In addition to enjoying the benefits of our friendship itself, in other words, you and I receive increased claims to each other's assistance, while other people, who never received the original benefits, find that their claims to assistance from us have now become weaker.[2] The distributive objection urges that the fairness of this allocation must be judged against the background of the existing distribution of benefits and burdens of all kinds. Providing additional advantages to people who have already benefitted from participation in rewarding relationships will be unjustifiable, according to the distributive objection, whenever the provision of these advantages works to the detriment of people who are needier, whether they are needier because they are not themselves participants in rewarding relationships or because they are significantly worse off in other ways. And it makes no difference, so far as this objection is concerned, whether special responsibilities are thought of as voluntarily incurred or not. Either way, the distributive objection insists that unless the benefits and burdens of special responsibilities are integrated into an overall distribution that is fair, such responsibilities will amount to little more than what one writer has called a "pernicious"[3] form of "prejudice in favor of people who stand in some special relation to us."[4]

It may be protested that it is misleading to represent special responsibilities as providing additional rewards to people who have already secured the advantages of participation in a rewarding relationship. Part of what makes a relationship rewarding, it may be said, is that there are special responsibilities associated with it. So any rewards that special responsibilities may confer on the participants in such relationships are inseparable from the other rewards of participation. This reply raises a variety of issues that I have discussed elsewhere[5] but which cannot be dealt with adequately here. For present purposes, suffice it to say that the reply is unlikely, by itself, to persuade proponents of the distributive objection. They are likely to question whether special responsibilities—as opposed, say, to the de facto willingness of the participants to give special weight to each other's interests—are genuinely necessary for the achievement of a rewarding relationship. They are also likely to argue that, even if it is true that special responsibilities help to make rewarding relationships possible, this only confirms the fundamental point of the objection, which is that such responsibilities work to the advantage of the participants in rewarding relationships and to the disadvantage of nonparticipants. Thus, they are likely to conclude, it remains important that, so far as possible, these advantages and disadvantages should be integrated into an overall distribution of benefits and burdens that is fair.

As we have seen, the voluntarist objection asserts that the source of our special responsibilities must lie in our own voluntary acts. Otherwise, it claims, such responsibilities would be unfairly burdensome for those who bear them. Thus, according to this objection, fairness to the bearers of special responsibilities requires a version of reductionism with respect to such responsibilities. The distributive objection, on the other hand, challenges the fairness of special responsibilities whether or not their source is thought of as lying in the voluntary acts of those who bear them. And its claim is that such responsibilities, far from imposing unfair burdens on the people who bear them, may instead provide those people with unfair advantages. If a nonreductionist account of special responsibilities is to be convincing, it will need to address both of these objections.[6]

In this chapter, I will sketch the rudiments of a nonreductionist account. My discussion will remain schematic, inasmuch as I will be concerned with the abstract structure of a nonreductionist position rather than with a detailed accounting of the specific responsibilities that such a position would assign people. Nevertheless, I hope that my sketch may suggest a new way of understanding nonreductionist claims of special responsibility and that, in so doing, it may make nonreductionism seem less implausible than it is often thought to be. In any event, I believe that the type of position I will describe merits careful consideration. As is no doubt evident, questions about the status of special responsibilities bear directly on a number of the liveliest controversies in contemporary moral and political philosophy. For example, such question are central to the debate within moral philosophy between consequentailism and deontology. They are equally central to the debates within political philosophy between liberalism and communitarianism, and between nationalism and cosmopolitanism. Thus the way that we think about special responsibilities may have far-reaching implications, and it would be a mistake to dismiss nonreductionism without attempting to understand it sympathetically.

Nonreductionists are impressed by the fact that we often cite our relationships to people rather than particular interactions with them as the source of our special responsibilities. They believe that our perception of things is basically correct; the source of such responsibilities often does lie in the relationships themselves rather then in particular interactions between the participants. A nonreductionist might begin to elaborate this position as follows. Other people can make claims on me, and their needs can provide me with reasons for action, whether or not I have any special relationship to them. If a stranger is suffering and I am in a position to help, without undue cost to myself, then I may well have a reason to do so. This much is true simply in virtue of our common humanity. However, if I have a special, valued relationship with someone, and if the value I attach to the relationship is not purely instrumental in character—if, in other words, I do not value it solely as a means to some independently specified end—then I regard the person with whom I have the relationship as capable of making additional claims on me, beyond those that people in general can make. For to attach noninstrumental value to my relationship with a particular person just is, in part, to see that person as a source of special claims in virtue of the relationship between us. It is, in other words, to be disposed, in contexts which vary depending on the nature of the relationship, to see that person's needs, interests, and desires as, in themselves, providing me with presumptively decisive reasons for action, reasons that I would not have had in the absence of the relationship. By "presumptively decisive reasons" I mean reasons which, although they are capable in principle of being outweighed or overridden, nevertheless present themselves as considerations upon which I must act. If there are no circumstances in which I would see a person's needs or interests as giving me such reasons, then, according to the nonreductionist, it makes no sense to assert that I attach (noninstrumental) value to my relationship with that person. But this is tantamount to saying that I cannot value my relationships (noninstrumentally) without seeing them as sources of special responsibilities.[7]

If it is true that one cannot value one's relationship to another person (noninstrumentally) without seeing it, in effect, as a source of special responsibilities, then it hardly seems mysterious that such a wide and apparently heterogeneous assortment of relationships have been seen as giving rise to such responsibilities. Nor, given that different people value relationships of different kinds, does it seem mysterious that some claims of special responsibility remain highly controversial. For if one disapproves of a certain kind of relationship, or of the tendency to invest relationships of that kind with significance, then one is likely to greet claims of special responsibility arising out of such relationships with skepticism. Thus, to take three very different examples, although the members of street gangs, fraternities, and nations often attach considerable importance to their membership in those groups and although, in consequence, they often have a strong sense of responsibility to their fellow members, someone who disapproves of such groups, or of the tendency to invest them with significance, may be unwilling to accept these claims of responsibility. On the other hand, someone who values his own participation in a relationship of a certain kind is likely to ascribe special responsibilities to the other participants in such relationships, even when they themselves do not value those relationships or acknowledge responsibilities arising out of them. Thus, on the nonreductionist view, differences in the kinds of relationships that people value lead naturally to disagreements about the assignment of special responsibility.

The nonreductionist position as thus far described takes us only so far. It asserts that relationships and not merely interactions are among the sources of special responsibilities, and it claims that people who value their relationships invariably see them as giving rise to such responsibilities. As so far described, however, the position says nothing about the conditions under which relationships actually do give rise to special responsibilities. Now there is, of course, no reason to expect that all nonreductionists will give the same answer to this question, any more than there is reason to expect that all reductionists will identify the same types of interactions as the sources of special responsibilities. In this chapter, however, I wish to explore the specific suggestion that one's relationships to other people give rise to special responsibilities to those people when they are relationships that one has reason to value.[8] For ease of exposition, I will refer to this view simply as "nonreductionism," but we should remember that this is just an expository device, and that other versions of nonreductionism are possible.

Several features of the formulation I have given require comment and clarification. First, the term "value," as it occurs in that formulation and in subsequent discussion, should be taken to mean "value noninstrumentally," and the term "reason" should be taken to mean "net reason." In other words, if a person only has reason to value a relationship instrumentally, then the principle I have stated does not treat that relationship as a source of special responsibilities. And if a person has some reason to value a relationship but more reason not to, then again the principle does not treat it as generating such responsibilities. Furthermore, although the formulation I gave given does not presuppose any particular conception of the kinds of reasons that people can have for valuing their relationships, reasons that are *reflexively instrumental,* in the sense that they derive from the instrumental advantages of valuing a relationship noninstrumentally, are to be understood as excluded. In other words, if attaching noninstrumental value to a certain relationship would itself be an effective means of achieving some independently desirable goal, the principle I have stated does not treat that as a reason of the responsibility-generating kind.

Second, there is a perfectly good sense of "relationship" in which every human being stands in some relationship to every other human being. However, as far as the view that I am presenting is concerned, only socially salient connections among people count as "relations" or "relationships"—two terms that I use interchangeably. Thus, for example, if you happen to have the same number of letters in your last name as John Travolta does, that does not mean that you have a relationship with him. Nor does the fact that you admire Travolta suffice to establish the existence of a relationship in the relevant sense, for the fact that one person has a belief about or attitude toward another does not constitute a social tie between them. On the other hand, two members of a socially recognized group do have a relationship in the relevant sense, even if they have never met, and if they value their membership in that group they may also value their relations to the other members. Thus, the fact that you are a member of the John Travolta Fan Club means that you have a relation to each of the other club members, and if you value your membership you may also value those relations.

Third, valuing my relationship with another person, in the sense that matters for nonreductionism, means valuing the relation of each of us to the other. So if, for example, I value my status as the Brutal Tyrant's leading opponent but not his status as my despised adversary, then I do not value our relationship in the sense that the nonreductionist principle treats as relevant. Similar remarks apply, *mutatis mutandis,* to having reason to value a relationship.

Fourth, nonreductionism as I have formulated it is not committed to a fixed view either of the strength or of the content of special responsibilities. It is compatible with the view that such responsibilities can be outweighed by other considerations. It is also compatible with the view that the strength of one's responsibilities depends on the nature of the relationships that give rise to them, and on the degree of value that one has reason to attach to those relationships. As far as the content of the responsibilities is concerned, we may assume that this too depends on the nature of the relationships in question, but that, at the most abstract level, it always involves a duty to give priority of various kinds, in suitable contexts, to certain of the interests of those to whom the responsibilities are owed.

Fifth, the nonreductionist principle states a sufficient condition for special responsibilities, not a necessary condition. Thus the principle does not purport to identify the source of all such responsibilities. In particular, it does not deny that promises and other kinds of discrete interactions can also give rise to special responsibilities. It merely claims to identify conditions under which interpersonal relations give rise to responsibilities that need not be fully accounted for in reductionist terms.

Sixth, nonreductionism makes it possible to claim both that people sometime have special responsibilities that they think they lack, and that they sometimes lack special responsibilities that they think they have. For it is possible to think both that people can fail to value relationships that they have reason to value, and that they can succeed in valuing relationships that they have no reason to value. We may think, for example, that a neglectful father has reason to value his relations to the children he ignores, or that an abused wife lacks any reason to value her relation to the husband she cannot bring herself to leave. Similarly, we may feel that an ambitious young woman has good reasons to value her relationship with the devoted immigrant parents of whom she is ashamed, and little reason to value her relationship with the vain and self-absorbed classmate whose attention she prizes and whose approval she craves.[9]

Finally, however, our ability to sustain claims of this kind is clearly dependent on a conception of reasons, and, more specifically, on a conception of the conditions under which people may be said to have reasons to value their relations to others. The more closely a person's reasons are seen as linked to his existing desires and motivations, the less scope there will be for distinguishing between the relationships that he has reason to value and the relationships that he actually does value. On the other hand, the less closely reasons are thought of as tied to existing desires, the more room there will be to draw such distinctions. As I have indicated, nonreductionism does not itself put forward a conception of reasons. Its claim, rather, is that many judgments of special responsibility are dependent on the ascription to people of reasons for valuing their relations to others, so that any substantive conception of such responsibilities is hostage to some conception of reasons.[10]

Nonreductionism of the kind I have described makes possible the following simple defense of unreduced special responsibilities. We human beings are social creatures, and creatures with values. Among the things that we value are our relations with each other. But to value one's relationship with another person is to see it as a source of reasons for action of a distinctive kind. It is, in effect to see oneself as having special responsibilities to the person with whom one has the relationship. Thus, insofar as we have good reasons to value our interpersonal relations, we have good reasons to see ourselves as having special responsibilities. And, accordingly, skepticism about such responsibilities will be justified only if we are prepared to deny that we have good reasons to value our relationships.

It may seem that this argument is fallacious. For consider: even if I have reason to promise that I will meet you for lunch on Tuesday, and even though I would be obligated to meet you if I were so to promise, it does not follow that, here and now, I actually have such an obligation. On the contrary, I acquire the obligation only if I make the promise. Similarly, it may seem, even if I have reason to value my relationship with you, and even if I would acquire special responsibilities to you if I did value our relationship, it does not follow that, here and now, I actually have such responsibilities. On the contrary, I acquire the responsibilities only if I value the relationship. However, the nonreductionist will resist this analogy. In the promising case, I have reason to perform an act which, if performed, will generate an obligation. But the nonreductionist's claim about special responsibilities is different. The claim is not that, in having reason to value our relationship, I have reason to perform an act which, if performed, will generate responsibilities. The claim is rather that, to value our relationship *is*, in part, to see myself as having such responsibilities, so that if, here and now, I have reason to value our relationship, then what I have reason to do, here and now, is to see myself as having such responsibilities. In the promising case, the promise generates the obligation, and no obligation arises in the absence of the promise. But the existence of a relationship that one has reason to value is itself the source of special responsibilities, and those responsibilities arise whether or not the participants actually value the relationship. Or so the nonreductionist claims.

Even if the disanalogy with the promising case is conceded, it may nevertheless be said that the nonreductionist argument stops short of establishing that we really do have special responsibilities. As we have seen, the nonreductionist claims that, insofar as we have reason to value our interpersonal relationships, we also have reason to see ourselves as having such responsibilities. But, it may be said, even if we have reason to see ourselves as having such responsibilities, that is compatible with our not actually having them. This seems to me misleading, however. If the nonreductionist argument establishes that we have good reason to see ourselves as having special responsibilities, then that is how we should see ourselves. There is no substantive difference, in this context, between the conclusion that we do have special responsibilities and the conclusion that, all things considered, we have good reasons for thinking that we do.

Some may worry that the nonreductionist principle as I have formulated it focuses too much attention on the bearers of special responsibilities and too little on the beneficiaries. Sometimes, it may be said, the source of a special responsibility does not lie in the fact that the relationship is one that the bearer has reason to value, but rather in the vulnerability created by the beneficiary's trust in or dependence on the bearer. However, this suggestion is not incompatible with the principle I have articulated. For that principle purports to identify only a sufficient condition, and not a necessary condition, for a relationship to give rise to special responsibilities. Thus it no more precludes the possibility that relations of trust and vulnerability may also give rise to such responsibilities than the principle that one ought to keep one's promises precludes the possibility that there are other kinds of obligations as well.

How, then, might a nonreductionist respond to the voluntarist and distributive objections? The voluntarist objection, we may recall, points out that special responsibilities may constitute significant burdens for those who bear them, and asserts that it would be unfair if such responsibilities could be ascribed to individuals who had done nothing voluntarily to incur them. The first thing that nonreductionists may say in response to this objection is that, in addition to our special responsibilities, there are other moral norms that govern our treatment of people in general. These moral norms, they may point out, apply to us whether or not we have agreed to them. For example, one cannot justify one's infliction of harm on a person by saying that one never agreed not to harm people. There are, in other words, general moral responsibilities that can be ascribed to us without our having voluntarily incurred them. And although these general responsibilities, like special responsibilities, may be costly or burdensome, we do not ordinarily regard their imposition as unfair. So why, nonreductionists may ask, should special responsibilities be any different? If voluntarists do not require that general responsibilities be voluntarily incurred, how can they insist that special responsibilities must be? The voluntarist may reply that special responsibilities, unless voluntarily incurred, give other people undue control over one's life. If certain people can make claims on you without your having done anything to legitimate those claims, then, the voluntarist may argue, those people enjoy an unreasonable degree of authority over the way you live. However, since general moral norms also enable people to make claims on individuals who have done nothing to legitimate those claims, nonreductionists will again want to know why special responsibilities that have not been voluntarily incurred should be objectionable in a way that general responsibilities are not.

One reason for the voluntarist's concern about special responsibilities may be as follows. Our most significant social roles and relations determine, to a considerable extent, the ways that we are seen by others and the ways that we see ourselves. They help to determine what might be called our social identities. To the extent that we choose our roles and relations, and decide how much significance they shall have in our lives, we shape our own identities. But to the extent that these things are fixed independently of our choices, our identities are beyond our control. What disturbs the voluntarist about special responsibilities may be this: if our relations to other people can generate responsibilities to those people independently of our choices, then, to that extent, the significance of our social relations is not up to us to determine. And if the significance of such relations is not up to us to determine, then we may be locked into a social identity we did not choose. This suggests that special responsibilities may be troubling to the voluntarist, in a way that general responsibilities are not, because special responsibilities may seem to threaten our capacity for self-determination—our capacity to determine who, in social terms, we are. On this interpretation, it is not wrong to suggest that the voluntarist views special responsibilities, unless voluntarily incurred, as giving other people undue control over our lives. However, the problem is not simply that others may be able to make unwelcome claims on our time and resources. That much would be true even if we had only general responsibilities. The more fundamental problem is that other people may be able to shape our identities in ways that run counter to our wishes.

Seen in this light, the voluntarist's position has obvious appeal. The ability to have our social identities influenced by our choices is something about which most of us care deeply, and which seems to us an important prerequisite for the forms of human flourishing to which we aspire. We regard societies in which one's social identity is rigidly fixed, as a matter of law or social practice, by features on one's birth or breeding over which one has no control, as societies that are inhospitable to human freedom. This does not mean that we are committed to repudiating whatever communal or traditional affiliations may have been conferred upon us at birth. It only means that we want the salience in our lives of such affiliations to be influenced by our own wishes and decisions, rather than being determined by the dictates of the society at large. This is, of course, one reason why liberals insist that the legal status of citizens should be insensitive to facts about their race or religion or social class.

And yet, despite the value that we attach to having our social identities influenced by our choices, and despite the particular importance of protecting this value against political interference, it is clear that the capacity to determine one's identity has its limits. Each of us is born into a web of social relations, and our social world lays claim to us long before we can attain reflective distance from it or begin making choices about our place in it. We acquire personal relations and social affiliations of a formative kind before we are able to conceive of them as such or to contemplate altering them. Thus there is obviously no question, nor can the voluntarist seriously think that there is, of our being able actually to choose all of the relations in which we stand to other people. What the voluntarist can hope to claim is only that the significance of those relations is entirely up to us. However, this claim too is unsustainable. For better or worse, the influence on our personal histories of unchosen social relations—to parents and siblings, families and communities, nations and peoples—is not something that we determine by ourselves. Whether we like it or not, such relations help to define the contours of our lives, and influence the ways that we are seen both by ourselves and by others. Even those who sever or repudiate such ties—insofar as it is possible to do so—can never escape their influence or deprive them of all significance, for to have repudiated a personal tie is not the same as never having had it, and one does not nullify social bonds by rejecting them. One is, in other words, forever the person who has rejected or repudiated those bonds; one cannot make oneself into a person who lacked them from the outset. Thus, while some people travel enormous social distances in their lives, and while the possibility of so doing is something that we have every reason to cherish, the idea that the significance of our personal ties and social affiliations is wholly dependent on our wills—that we are the supreme gatekeepers of our own identities—can only be regarded as a fantasy. So if, as the nonreductionist believes, our relations to other people can generate responsibilities to them independently of our choices, then it is true that, in an important respect, the significance of our social relations is not fully under our control; but since the significance of those relations is in any case not fully under our control, this by itself does not rob us of any form of self-determination to which we may reasonably aspire.

In the end, then, the nonreductionist's response to the voluntarist objection is to insist that, although the significance of choice and consent in moral contexts in undeniable, nevertheless, the moral import of our relationships to other people does not derive solely from our own decisions. Nor, the nonreductionist may add, need we fear that this is tantamount to conceding the legitimacy of systems of caste or hierarchy, or that it leaves the individual at the mercy of oppressive social arrangements. For the relationships that generate responsibilities for an individual are those relationships that the individual has reason to value. No claims at all arise form relations that are degrading or demeaning, or which serve to undermine rather than to enhance human flourishing. In other words, the alternative to an exaggerated voluntarism is not an exaggerated communitarianism or historicism. In recognizing that the significance of our social relationships does not stem exclusively from our choices, we do not consign ourselves to a form of social bondage. In surrendering the fantasy that our own wills are the source of all our special responsibilities, we do not leave ourselves defenseless against the contingencies of the social world.

Yet even if these remarks constitute an effective response to the voluntarist objection, they may seem only to highlight the nonreductionist's vulnerability to the distributive objection. For, if relationships that are destructive of an individual's well-being do not, in general, give that individual special responsibilities, then presumably the relationships that do give him special responsibilities either enhance or at least do not erode his well-being. But, as we have seen, special responsibilities may themselves work to the advantage of the participants in special relationships, and to the disadvantage of nonparticipants. And, it may be asked, why should a relationship that enhances the well-being of the participants give rise to a distribution of moral responsibility that further advances their interests, while working against the interests of nonparticipants? How can the nonreductionist respond to the charge that, unless the benefits and burdens of special responsibilities are integrated into an overall distribution that is fair, such responsibilities will themselves provide unfair advantages to the participants in interpersonal relations, while unfairly penalizing nonparticipants?

The nonreductionist may begin by reiterating that, as long as people attach value to their interpersonal relations, they will inevitably see themselves as having special responsibilities. And as long as they have good reasons for attaching value to those relations, we must allow that they also have good reasons to see themselves as having such responsibilities. There may, of course, be room for general skepticism about people's reasons for valuing their interpersonal relations. But it seems unlikely that proponents of the distributive objection can afford to be skeptics of this sort. For the distributive objection is animated by a concern for fairness in the allocation of benefits and burdens, and if, as the skeptic asserts, people never have reason to value their social relations, then it is unclear why considerations of fairness should weigh with them at all. Rather than providing grounds for the rejection of special responsibilities in particular, general skepticism about our reasons for valuing personal relations seems potentially subversive of morality as a whole.

Provided that the distributive objection is not taken to support a wholesale repudiation of special responsibilities, however, nonreductionists may concede that it makes a legitimate point. There are important respects in which special responsibilities may work to the advantage of the participants in personal relationships, and to the disadvantage of other people. These facts seem undeniable once they are called to our attention. That we sometimes lose sight of them is due in large measure to the influence of voluntarism, which focuses exclusively on the respects in which special responsibilities can be burdensome for the people who bear them, and sees the task of legitimating such responsibilities solely as a matter of justifying those burdens. Once we face the facts to which the distributive objection calls attention, however, we must agree that there is another side to special responsibilities: that they may also provide significant advantages for the participants in interpersonal relations and significant disadvantages for nonparticipants. Insofar as the distributive objection insists only on the desirability of integrating these advantages and disadvantages into an overall distribution of benefits and burdens that is fair, nonreductionists have no reason to disagree.

Indeed, once the distributive objection is understood in this way, it may be seen as illustrating a more general point, with which nonreductionists also have no reason to disagree. The general point is that special responsibilities need to be set within the context of our overall moral outlook and constrained in suitable ways by other pertinent values. On a nonreductionist view, such constraints may, in principle, operate in at least three different ways. Some may affect the content of special responsibilities, by setting limits to the circumstances in which, and the extent to which, people are required to give priority to the interests of those to whom they have such responsibilities. Other constraints may affect the strength of special responsibilities, by supplying countervailing considerations that are capable of outweighing or overriding those responsibilities in various contexts. Still other constraints may affect people's reasons for valuing their relationships. Perhaps, for example, people have no (net) reason to value relationships which themselves offend against important moral values or principles, so that such relationships do not generate special responsibilities even if people do in fact value them.[11]

The upshot is that, although nonreductionism insists that unreduced special responsibilities must be part of any adequate moral scheme, it is not hostile to the idea that there are a variety of other moral values—including the values underlying the distributive objection—by which such responsibilities must be constrained and with which they must be integrated if they are to be fully satisfactory. For example, there is nothing to prevent the nonreductionist from agreeing that considerations of distributive fairness serve to limit both the strength and the content of people's special responsibilities. Of course, the mere fact that nonreductionism is open to such possibilities does not suffice to show that a single moral outlook will be capable of accommodating special responsibilities while fully satisfying the values underlying the distributive objection. In fact, I believe that there is a deep and persistent tension between these two features of our moral thought, and nothing in the nonreductionist position guarantees that we will be able simultaneously to accommodate both features to our own satisfaction.[12]

Although this is a serious problem, however, it is no more of a problem for nonreductionist accounts of special responsibilities than it is for reductionist accounts. In fact, it is a problem for any view that takes special responsibilities seriously, while remaining sensitive to the values underlying the distributive objection. Any such view, and indeed any view that recognizes a diversity of moral values and principles, needs to ask how far that diversity can be accommodated within a unified moral outlook. Too often it is simply taken for granted either that a unified outlook must in principle be available or that any tension at all among our values means that there is no possibility of jointly accommodating them. Neither assumption seems to me to be warranted. Instead, it seems to me a substantive question, the answer to which remains open, to what extent the diverse moral values that we recognize can be jointly accommodated within a unified scheme of thought and practice.

Pending an answer to that question, nonreductionism appears to have the following advantages as an account of special responsibilities. To begin with, it has the virtue of cohering better than do reductionist accounts with our actual practice, which is to cite relationships as well as interactions as sources of special responsibilities. It also has the advantage of being able to explain, in simple and straightforward terms, why it is that people have seen such a diverse and apparently heterogeneous assortment of relationships as giving rise to such responsibilities. Furthermore, nonreductionism makes it possible to agree that our ordinary practices of ascribing special responsibilities to the participants in significant relationships are broadly correct. Like those ordinary practices themselves, however, it also leaves room for the criticism of particular ascriptions of responsibility. Admittedly, the content of the nonreductionist principle depends on some conception of the kinds of reasons people have for valuing their relations to others. Thus, given this principle, disagreements about reasons will inevitably lead to disagreements about the circumstances under which special responsibilities should be ascribed to people. Even this may seem like an advantage, however. For there are many disagreements about the ascription of such responsibilities that do seem plausibly understood as reflecting a more fundamental disagreement about the reasons people have for valuing their relationships. To the extent that this is so, nonreductionism locates controversies about the ascription of special responsibilities in the right place, and provides an illuminating explanation of them. Finally, nonreductionism is sensitive to the concerns underlying the voluntarist and distributive objections, yet it provides reasons for insisting that neither objection supports the complete repudiation of unreduced special responsibilities.

Let me close by returning to a point that I made earlier. The nonreductionist position I have outlined, if it can be persuasively developed, may have implications for a number of important controversies in moral and political philosophy. Inasmuch as it offers a defense of special responsibilities that is non-consequentailist in character, for example, it points to a possible defense of at least some sorts of "agent-centered restrictions."[13] Similarly, I believe, it suggests some constraints that any adequate formulation of cosmopolitanism may need to respect. Detailed discussion of these implications, however, must await another occasion.

Notes

This essay was first published in *Philosophy and Public Affairs* 26(1997):189–209. It is a much-revised version of the paper that I delivered at the Eleventh Jerusalem Philosophical Encounter in December 1995. Versions of the paper were also presented to the NYU Colloquium in Law, Philosophy, and Political Theory; the Columbia Legal Theory Workshop; philosophy department colloquia at Arizona State, Stanford, the University of Miami, and the University of Michigan; and my fall 1995 graduate seminar at Berkeley. I am very grateful to all of these audiences for extremely helpful discussion. Special thanks also to Yael Tamir, who was my commentator in Jerusalem, and to Christopher Kutz, Jeff McMahan, Daniel Statman, Wai-hung Wong, and a reader for *Philosophy & Public Affairs* for providing me with valuable written comments.

1. In this paragraph and at other points in the next few pages, I draw on my discussions of special responsibilities in the following papers: "Individual Responsibility in a Global Age," *Social Philopophy and Policy* 12(1995):219–36; "Families, Nations, and Strangers," in *The Lindley Lecture* series (Lawrence: University of Kansas, 1995); "Liberalism, Nationalism, and Egalitarianism," in Robert McKim and Jeff McMahan eds., *The Morality of Nationalism* (New York: Oxford University Press, 1997).

2. If it is ultimately to be convincing, the distributive objection will need to provide a fuller accounting of the various advantages and disadvantages that special responsibilities may confer both on the participants in interpersonal relationships and on nonparticipants. I consider the implications of such an accounting in "The Conflict Between Justice and Responsibility," in L. Brilmayer and I. Shapiro eds., *NOMOS XLI: Global Justice* (New York University Press, 1999, pp. 86–106).

3. Robert Goodin, *Protecting the Vulnerable* (Chicago: University of Chicago Press, 1985) p. 1.

4. Ibid., p. 6.

5. In "Families, Nations, and Strangers," section 4.

6. I have discussed both objections at greater length in "Families, Nations, and Strangers" and in "Liberalism, Nationalism, and Egalitarianism." I have discussed the distributive objection most extensively in "The Conflict Between Justice and Responsibility."

7. The nonreductionist recognizes, of course, that it is possible for me to regard relationships in which I am not a participant as valuable. The nonreductionist's claim, however, is that valuing one's own relationship to another person is different, not because one is bound to see such a relationship as more valuable than other relationships of the same type, but rather because one is bound to see it as a source of reasons for action of a distinctive kind.

8. On some views, membership in a group may give one special responsibilities *to the group* that transcend any responsibilities one has to the individual members. The view I am exploring is agnostic on this question.

9. Of course, since the nonreductionist principle does articulate only a sufficient and not a necessary condition for special responsibilities, the fact that one has no reason to value one's relationship to a particular person does not by itself show that one has no special responsibilities whatsoever to that person—only that one has no responsibilities arising under the nonreductionist principle.

10. This means that it would be possible for a reductionist to argue that people's reasons for valuing their relations to others derive exclusively from discrete interactions that occur in the context of those relations. Even if this argument were accepted, however, it would remain the case that, according to the principle under consideration, the source of the relevant responsibilities lies in the relationships rather than the interactions. Furthermore, it may not be possible without loss of plausibility to translate reductionism about special responsibilities into reductionism about people's reasons for valuing their relationships. For some of the types of interaction that have been seen as generating such responsibilities do not seem plausibly construed as generating reasons for valuing relationships.

11. Might it be said, by someone sympathetic to the distributive objection, that relationships that run afoul of that objection violate this last type of constraint, and thus do not give rise to special responsibilities after all? This is unpersuasive because the distributive objection is not an objection to a class of relationships. In other words, it does not allege that certain relationships offend against important moral values. Instead, it claims only that considerations of distributive fairness prevent some relationships, which may be entirely unobjectionable in themselves, from giving rise to special responsibilities. But the constraint in question applies only to relationships that themselves offend against important moral values.

12. See, generally, Thomas Nagel, *Equality and Partiality* (New York: Oxford University Press, 1991).

13. See *The Rejection of Consequentialism* (Oxford: Clarendon Press, 1994 [rev. ed.]), esp. Chap. 4.

9
LOVE'S DOMINION

Yael Tamir

"I owe a lot to those I don't love"
Wislwa Szymborska, *People on a Bridge*,
translated by Adam Czerniawski

I. Introduction

Individuals face the world as children, parents, lovers, friends, fellow nationals, and it is from these contextualized points of view that they form their beliefs and preferences and evaluate their actions. Communitarians claim that these personal relationships and communal affiliations generate not only distinct perspectives but also responsibilities.[1] This claim troubles voluntarists, who argue that the sole ground of responsibilities is consent.

Several philosophers have recently criticized the voluntarist approach and advocated a nonreductionist point of view according to which not all responsibilities must be voluntarily assumed.[2] Relationships in which individuals find themselves due to history or fate, they argue, can also generate responsibilities. And yet, even those philosophers who defend nonreductionism are reluctant to endorse the view that all the different kinds of relationships—including immoral ones—can generate responsibilities. The alternative to voluntarism, they argue, is a nonreductionist approach which is "value-dependent."[3] According to this approach, only those relationships that pass a certain moral threshold can generate responsibilities. The idea that personal relationships, or social affiliations, can generate responsibilities irrespective of their moral nature should be rejected, as it is open to the following objection:

> A is a racist. She is traveling through the desert and comes across two starving people—another racist (B) and a black [person] (C). Both are in need of food and water: A only has enough for herself and one other. According to (P1-[the assumption that she has particular obligations to fellow members of her group]), she has a *moral obligation* to give to B since they belong to the same group. (P1) stipulates that A should act along racist lines, and if she does not do so this is a moral failing given her membership [in] a racist culture.[4]

This conclusion, Simon Caney argues, is implausible because there could be no moral reason to act along racist lines. We must then conclude that social bonds or personal relationships that are morally unacceptable cannot generate responsibilities. In *Law's Empire* Ronald Dworkin offers even more demanding moral standards; associative obligations emerge, he claims, only from membership in a group committed to the principle of equal concern and respect and not engaged in grave injustice.[5]

In "Relationships and Responsibilities" Samuel Scheffler joins advocates of a nonreductionist, value-dependent approach. Concentrating on personal relationships rather than on communal affiliations, he argues that responsibilities follow only from those relationships we have a reason to value; "no claims at all arise from relations that are degrading or demeaning, or which serve to undermine rather than to enhance human flourishing."[6] This approach, Scheffler claims, acknowledges the binding force of non-voluntary relationships in general while freeing individuals from the bonds of demeaning or evil ones.

> In other words, the alternative to an exaggerated voluntarism is not an exaggerated communitarianism or historicism. In recognizing that the significance of our social relationships does not stem exclusively from our choices, we do not consign ourselves to a form of social bondage. In surrendering the fantasy that our wills are the source of all our special responsibilities, we do not leave ourselves defenseless against the contingencies of the social world.[7]

This chapter shares the nonreductionist criticism of voluntarism yet argues against the "value-dependent" approach. Responsibilities, I argue, follow from all kinds of relationships, including those we have no reason to value.

In order to better understand the value-dependent approach and its criticism, I will place the debate within a larger context. The value-dependent approach is one manifestation of a larger attempt to draw national, communitarian, and liberal intuitions closer together, an attempt that motivates many of the current discussions in moral and political theory. One ought, however, resist the temptation to support an alliance between conflicting comprehensive views by advocating a moral theory that discounts the internal schisms individuals experience as a result of subscribing to these views. Efforts to construct a theory of liberal-communitarianism or liberal-nationalism are worthwhile if they teach us how to live with the tensions and contradictions embedded in these uneasy alliances. They are unwelcome if they produce a placid, though false, portrayal of human morality that eliminates internal tensions alltogether and leads one to overlook the immense personal difficulties ingrained in realizing a compromise between conflicting sets of values.

My objection to the value-dependent approach, then, is that it offers a too easy way of reconciling communitarian and liberal morality that eliminates all the possible tensions between them. The result is a theory that can neither explain the nature of human relationships and the responsibilities that follow from them nor account for the anxiety of those caught in a web of conflicting responsibilities.

II. Special and Personal Responsibilities

Before this claim can be defended, let me specify the kinds of relationships I am about to examine. To begin with, *relationship* or *relations* are vague terms covering a wide spectrum of human interactions—ranging from an occasional conversation with a stranger on a plane to a continuous love affair that lasts a lifetime. There is no reason to assume that such diverse interactions have something in common. I restrict my discussion to a limited set of cases that includes only those human interactions that are intense, intimate, and characterized by emotional affinity.[8]

To be more precise, the cases discussed here cover only relationships individuals have with those they care about for reasons not fully reducible either to role, gratitude, reciprocity, fairness, promises, or contracts, namely, to cases in which responsibilities are grounded in the affectional aspect of the relationship. The reason for this restriction is that affections produce a particular kind of responsibilities. I shall term those responsibilities grounded in either role, gratitude, fairness, promises, or contracts *special responsibilities* and those based on affection *personal responsibilities*.[9]

Even those who reject the claim that relationships generate personal responsibilities are likely to agree that individuals have special responsibilities grounded in either role, gratitude, contracts, or promises. In the case of special responsibilities, the personal aspect of the relationship could be the reason for a promise or a transaction, but it does not generate the responsibilities themselves. If I love a man and in the course of our relationship make promises to him, then these promises generate responsibilities that are independent of my love and continue to exist even when it fades away. Suppose that in the course of my relationship with D. I borrow his favorite disks, sign a contract to pay half of the rent of the apartment we share, and promise to visit his old mother while he is away. Even if I fall out of love, I ought to return the disks, respect the contract, and visit the old mother. The reason for doing so is not love but a set of voluntary transactions whose validity outlasts the relationship.

Unlike special responsibilities, personal ones are grounded in the relationship itself rather than in a transaction. Unfortunately, the philosophical literature has little to say about the nature of such responsibilities. While a defense of the existence of such responsibilities has been at the core of much of the recent feminist and communitarian writings, their scope and content are yet to be explored.[10] And yet, in this chapter I do not intend to elaborate on this issue; the purpose of my discussion is to ask a more fundamental question: are responsibilities an unalienable part of relationship or can a certain aspect of a relationship (its immoral nature) eliminate the responsibilities that follow from it.

Responsibilities grounded in relationships are composed of a combination of special and personal responsibilities. The relation between the two kinds is intricate:

affectionate relationships can stimulate actions that generate responsibilities, actions that generate responsibilities can foster affectionate relationships. Moreover, commonly there is a positive correlation between the strength of the relationship and scope of the special responsibilities they generate. The longer, more intimate, and more affectionate the relationship, the thicker and more comprehensive the range and scope of the responsibilities it is likely to generate. Consequently, not only the personal but also the special responsibilities generated by such a relationship are broader in range and thicker in substance.

Not only can affectionate relationships provide opportunities for the emergence of responsibilities generating actions and consequently of special responsibilities. The opposite is also true; affection, friendship, and love may be evoked by some sort of transactions. For example, I may be grateful to my neighbor for lending me her car when needed. As a result, I may invite her to lunch and find that we have a lot in common. We may then start to attend concerts and lectures together, introduce each other to members of our family, and become intimate friends. It is only then that I may develop toward her personal responsibilities that exceed the initial special responsibilities grounded in gratitude.

Obviously, not every relationship develops into a personal one. I can be said to have a personal relationship with my parents, and therefore have personal responsibilities to them, if I care about them not only because of my role as their daughter but also because I have developed emotional ties to them. Assume for a moment that I have been kidnapped as a child and did not see my parents for the last twenty years. One day I receive a letter announcing that they have been searching for me all these years, and now that they have found me, they wish to meet me and expect that I'll comfort and support them in their old age. My responsibility to meet their request cannot be grounded in my affections to them but only in my formal role as their child. Such role-dependent special responsibilities persist even if on meeting my parents I deeply dislike them. If, however, the meeting is the beginning of a wonderful friendship, I will acquire additional, personal responsibilities toward my parents, which would extend beyond my role-dependent responsibilities.

The following diagram illustrates the way special and personal responsibilities add up to construct responsibilities grounded in a relationship.

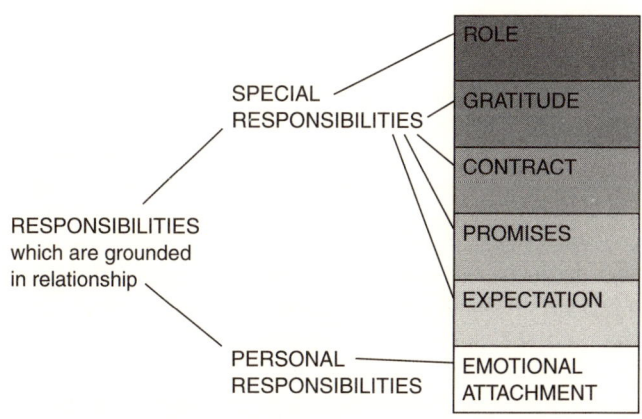

Love's Dominion

Obviously, each particular relationship need not generate all the possible kinds of responsibilities. Consequently, the range and content of particular responsibilities vary dramatically.

My purpose is neither to classify nor review the different kinds of particular responsibilities, though there is much more work to be done on this topic. Nor do I intend to discuss the nature of special responsibilities. As I have argued, they are not grounded in relationships, and they do not necessarily violate voluntarism. My only task is to explore the non-reductionist argument as it applies to personal responsibilities and argue that such responsibilities are an inherent aspect of personal relationships. Their emergence depends on the existence of a relationship and not on its moral (or immoral) nature.

Human relationships are unruly. Those who wish to domesticate them and make the responsibilities that follow from them dependent on moral judgments are destined to misunderstand the nature of relationships and the kinds of responsibilities that follow from them. Attempts to make responsibilities dependent on moral evaluations raise two sorts of questions: the first concerns the need to determine criteria of evaluation; the second concerns the need to define the way relationships and responsibilities relate to each other. In the coming sections I would claim that the value-dependent approach provides faulty answers to both questions: it fails to provide a standard for moral evaluation—a failure that for a value-dependent theory is detrimental—and it misrepresents the nature of the conjunction between relationships and responsibilities.

To clarify these claims, I shall analyze and criticize the most sophisticated and detailed expression of the nonreductionist, value-dependent argument as presented by Scheffler in "Relationships and Responsibilities." Scheffler's argument also has the virtue that it explores the issue of responsibilities tied to personal relations rather than to collective affiliations. It can thus appeal even to those who question the existence of national or communal responsibilities. If, however, I am able to refute Scheffler's approach, the argument will have bearings on the value-dependent approach as a whole—in both its individual and communal forms.

III. Reasons to Value

Like other scholars who adhere to a value-dependent, nonreductionist approach, Scheffler maintains that personal responsibilities are generated only by relationships that pass a certain moral threshold—or, to use his terminology, that "we have reason to value." Any approach that makes responsibilities dependent on a moral evaluation must offer, and defend, its evaluative criteria. Unfortunately, neither Scheffler nor the other defenders of the value-dependent approach fulfill this task. Their failure is by no means coincidental; it is grounded in a desire to force two different moral intuitions into one mold without losing their essence.

Like other defenders of the value-dependent approach, Scheffler wishes to make liberal morality his threshold without exposing himself to the criticism, raised by many communitarians, that he subscribes to a particularist moral approach that has no universal standing. He therefore chooses to remain silent on the nature of the moral theory he endorses, concentrating on a restricted number of disqualifying cases, assuming that a condemnation of these cases is shared by a large variety of moral outlooks. This move, as this section proves, is a questionable one

To begin with, the use of the term *value* by Scheffler is rather opaque; it obscures the fact that those relationships individuals assign value to are not necessarily the kinds of relationships they have a reason to value. This tension is downgraded in Scheffler's analysis. We would be hard pressed to find, he claims, "any type of human relationship to which people have attached value or significance but which has never been seen as generating such responsibilities. It appears that whenever people value an interpersonal relationship they are apt to see it as a source of special duties or obligations."[11] It thus seems as if the source of the responsibility is the fact that individuals actually value their relationship, rather than some external, objective evaluation. Yet making responsibilities dependent on the subjective evaluation of the relationship cannot answer the objection that motivated this discussion: the moral problem raised by this objection will not be eased by making the responsibilities dependent on what the individual—the racist in the above example—thinks of his relationship.

Nor will this objection be met by Scheffler's claim that "to value" should be taken to mean "to value noninstrumentally." That is, "if a person only has reason to value a relationship instrumentally, then the principle I have stated does not treat that relationship as a source of special responsibilities."[12] What does the term "only" stand for? My guess is that it is meant to exclude all self-serving reasons; for example, If I marry P only for his money, our relationship would be an instrumental one and would not count as a source of personal responsibilities, but if I marry him for love then it would count as non-instrumental and consequently as a source of responsibilities. But what if I am the kind of person who needs, or seeks, love more than money? Will the description of the relationships and the responsibilities that follow from them be reversed? And how do we determine what is instrumental and what is not? Under some description all intimate relationships have instrumental aspects; they allow us to develop our emotional life, expand our social skills, combat loneliness, find happiness, and so on. The term instrumental then is either too weak, as in one way or another all our relationships serve a personal goal, or too vague, as it cannot capture the variety and scope of these goals.[13]

It often seems that "instrumental" is reserved to those interests one disapproves of, interests that seem improper to mention, humiliating to those we are in a relationship with. But there is no universal standard of what a "proper interest" is. From some normative points of view, to say that I married P for money, property, or power will be to discredit the relationship and humiliate him; from another it is a way of consolidating the relationship and honoring P. The usage of "non-instrumental" depends then on a latent moral theory that is not laid out.

To avoid the need to offer such a theory, defenders of the value-dependent approach concentrate on features of the relationship that annul responsibilities rather than on features that generate responsibilities, assuming that there is a wider agreement on what is morally unacceptable than on what is morally valuable. But as the prevous example shows, an answer to the question of what is humiliating is neither trivial nor independent of a comprehensive moral view.[14] The value-dependent theory cannot escape the need to determine the nature of its moral criteria. Do these criteria reflect the moral theory a person holds, the social norms obtaining in one's society, or objective moral evaluation? We are left with no answer.

But even if we are able to clear these ambiguities and accept Scheffler's claim that a relationship generates responsibilities only if it has net (non-instrumental) value, it is still unclear what the exact meaning of this latter concept is. Like individuals, human conduct is not one-dimensional; virtue and vice merge in personalities as well as in relationships. Relationships among villains may have moral dimensions, as relationships among virtuous individuals may have demeaning aspects.

Some may wish to reserve the terms friendship or love only to those kinds of relationships which Aristotle defines as *perfect friendships*, relationships that develop only among those who are good and "wish well alike to each other qua good."[15] But even Aristotle recognized that there are friendships of a less perfect kind. These friendships may be based on contingencies and may therefore be less stable than perfect ones, but they qualify as friendships. "For the sake of pleasure and utility, then, even bad men may be friends of each other, or good men of bad, or one who is neither good or bad may be a friend to any sort of person."[16]

What is the status of such a relationship? Do we have a reason to value it? Can it generate personal responsibilities? Think for instance of the love between Bonnie and Clyde or the comradeship between members of a street gang or a Mafia chapter. As the bond of the relationship is a shared immoral purpose, do we have reason to value these relationships? Can they generate personal responsibilities? Does Bonnie have personal responsibilities to Clyde? Does a member of a street gang have a personal responsibilities to support a fellow gangster, to provide him with legal defense, or to help his family while he serves time in jail for crimes committed by the gang?

Research shows that individuals engaged in criminal activities think and act as if encumbered by personal responsibilities. When reporting on the Creeps and the Bloods, Los Angeles's most infamous gangs, Leon Bing notices that the same people who will torture outsiders to death "for no worse fault than being outsiders, can also look after wounded and paralyzed fellow gang members 'more lovingly' than many families do."[17] What is the value of this observation? Do gang members have personal responsibilities to act in this way, or are they wrong to assume that they should help and support each other because the immoral cause of their alliance cancels their personal responsibilities?

The parameters of the evaluation must then be clarified. Scheffler suggests that we should calculate the "net-value" of a relationship.[18] How should the net-value of a relationship be evaluated? Should we consider solely the nature of the interaction between those engaged in the relationship, should we also weigh their relationships with others, or should we evaluate both kinds of relationships and balance them out? How are we to evaluate the relationship between gang members who are mutually fair and supportive but harmful to outsiders? This is a case in which the internal dimension of the relationship contributes to human flourishing, whereas their external dimension thwarts it. And what about the opposite kind of case—a relationship between, say, a couple of nuns who dedicate their lives to help the needy, and yet whose relationship is marked by unfairness and mutual disrespect? In this case, a demeaning internal relationship develops in the context of activities that enhance the agents' dignity and moral growth. What is the net-value of this kind of relationship?

If net-value means that we should take into account the effects of a relationship on everyone who is directly and indirectly influenced by it, we would have to conclude that the gangsters' evil ways overshadow the virtue of their friendship, while the benefits of the nuns' activities overshadow the immoral aspect of their personal relationship. We will then have to claim that although gang members who care for each other have no mutual personal responsibilities, the nuns who deeply dislike each other do have such responsibilities. This conclusion concurs with our social interest that the nuns will be mutually supportive and in doing so will assure the continuity of their valuable project, while the gangsters will fight each other and the rift between them will reduce the damage of their actions. But these considerations, if taken into account, make the justifications of personal responsibilities contingent on the desirability of the outcomes of the relationship rather than on the nature of the relationship itself.

Outcomes could indeed give rise to responsibilities, but it would be misguided to claim that such responsibilities are personal ones. The nuns may have a reason to support each other if such support promotes their good cause. They have a reason to act in this way even if they loath each other, but it would be strange to claim that such responsibilities are generated by their relationships. Similarly, citizens may have reasons to support each other if such support is necessary for sustaining just institutions; these reasons are, however, different from those grounded in a feeling of belonging or national attachments.[19] In fact, even those who are not engaged in a relationship have a reason to support it if the outcomes of this relationship are morally desirable. The obligation to support the nuns' actions is then a general one as is the obligation to support just institutions, but such general obligations cannot be seen as a variant of personal responsibilities. To understand the nature of personal responsibilities, we must then concentrate on the nature of the relationship rather than its outcomes.

In what aspects of the relations are the responsibilities grounded? Scheffler does not address this question directly. Rather, he provides a list of negative conditions that, if present, negate the value of the relationship and suspend the responsibilities it generates. If a relationship is degrading or demeaning, he argues, if it undermines human flourishing rather than enhancing it, no responsibilities follow. We know, then, what will nullify personal responsibilities but have no clue as to what would generate them.

IV. Carrington's Plight

Before making an attempt to understand the origin of personal responsibilities, it is important to recall the motivation to analyze the moral status of personal responsibilities. The point of origin of the discussion is the widely held belief that individuals have responsibilities generated by their personal relationships or by their membership in particular communities. Defenders of the value-depended thesis start from an observation: relationships, especially those involving emotional affinities, generate responsibilities.[20] Nonreductionists, Scheffler admits, are

> impressed by the fact that we often cite our relationship to people rather than particular interactions with them as the source of our special responsibilities. They

believe that our perception of things is basically correct; the source of such responsibilities often does lie in the relationship themselves rather than in particular interactions between participants.[21]

And yet, adherents to a value-dependent theory of particular responsibilities cannot rely solely on the popular belief that relationships generate responsibilities: they must develop means of distinguishing between those relationships that generate responsibilities and those that do not. A convenient procedure is to begin by challenging cases that are inconsistent with common moral intuitions or seem flawed in some other way.

True to this procedure, Scheffler's argument concentrates on those relationships we have no reason to value, those that are demeaning or degrading. The most obvious kind of demeaning relationships are abusive ones. Such relationships are not infrequent. Consider the relationship between certain individuals of genius and their partners, lovers, and friends. Think of Katia and Thomas Mann. Think of Picasso, Marie-Therese, and Dora Maar. Consider the tragic relationship between Dora Carrington and Lytton Strachey. What sustains the attachment and devotion of the abused partner to the abusing one? This question has various answers: the desire to serve a genius thus indirectly supporting a noble cause, the need to feel needed, or to be dominated or guided. We do not know the mysteries of the human soul. Fortunately, not all happy families are alike; like unhappy ones, they do not resemble each other. The most troubled relationships furnish the substance of great tragedies; the most noble ones yield romantic poems and novels.

Many tragic relationships are one-sided. They often entail torment and humiliation for one of the partners (often the female one), but they are, at least in the eyes of the participants, valuable relationships. The abused partner may indeed acknowledge the asymmetry of the relationship, and even the damage it inflicts on her, and yet endorse the relationship and view it as a source of personal responsibilities. Consider Dora Carrington's description of her relations with Lytton Strachey: "I have had one of the most self-abasing loves," she says. Carrington needs no enlightenment. She sees through Strachey's egoism and maltreatment and yet goes on adoring him and devoting herself to him. What would it mean to argue that she has no personal responsibilities to the person whom she dearly loves?

One option is to question neither her feelings nor her behavior but the nature of her reasons for actions. Obviously, even if no responsibilities follow from her relationships with Strachey, she is free to act in a supererogatory way, voluntarily deciding to serve and support him. This behavior may be indistinguishable from that demanded by personal responsibilities; the difference lies solely in the kinds of reasons that support it. When one is found in a relationship one has a reason to value, the reason for action is: "I ought to do X." When one is found in an abusive relationship, the reason is "I want to do X." Consequently, while refraining from fulfilling one's responsibilities in the former case would lead to moral condemnation, in the latter case it would not. This description explains Carrington's behavior while reinforcing Scheffler's view, but it leaves the grounds for personal responsibilities unclear, as it suggests that personal responsibilities are not grounded in one's feelings. What then could their origin be?

Personal responsibilities do not emerge out of personal relationships; they are part and parcel of these relationships. There could then be no split between a relationship and the responsibilities that constitute it. To be in a particular kind of a relationship *is* to have responsibilities. [22] According to this description, as long as Carrington loves Strachey, she has personal responsibilities to him, regardless of the abusive nature of his behavior. Love is demanding. What would it mean to love a person if not to see oneself obliged to care for him; give priority to his interests and needs; compromise one's own well-being in order to advance his welfare, happiness, and prosperity; make time to spend together; lend an ear when necessary.

Note that the debate between the value-dependent and value-independent approach does not necessarily concern the way those who, like Carrington, love an abusive person. Those who support a value-dependent approach and those who support a value-independent approach may both agree that Carrington should abandon Strachey and disregard his needs. They may still disagree about the proper justification of this conclusion. Those who support a value-dependent approach claim that the abusive nature of the relationship expunges the responsibilities; those who hold a value-independent approach claim that as responsibilities are inseparable from love, then as long as Carrington loves Strachey, she has responsibilities to him, yet the abusive nature of his behavior produces additional reasons that override these responsibilities. According to the first approach, Carrington is free of all personal responsibilities; according to the second, she is bound by personal responsibilities but has overriding reasons not to be guided by them.

It is important to distinguish between these two claims as this distinction sheds light on the nature of personal responsibilities. If abuse can expunge the existence of personal responsibilities but not of love itself, a gap is created between the relationship (which persists) and the responsibilities (which expire). If, on the other hand, abuse produces overriding reasons that lead one to act against her personal responsibilities, then the fact that one should act in a certain way—abandon the loved one or ignore his needs and interests—cannot refute the claim that personal responsibilities are an inherent part of the relationship.

The two approaches differ not only in the justifications they offer but also in their understanding of human feelings. If abuse expunges personal responsibilities, then individuals should not be torn between these responsibilities and other reasons for action. If, however, abuse cannot cancel these responsibilities, then individuals who love an abusive person are pulled in opposing directions, painfully following one rather than the other. This can explain the agony individuals feel when they come to the (justified) conclusion that they have conflicting and overriding responsibilities that nullify their personal ones. Liberal morality often aspires to obliterate such tensions and offer a moral vision that embodies no justified pain, but in doing so it gives in to a shallow human psychology that misunderstands the nature of human relationships and the responsibilities that follow from them.

According to this view there must be a way to reduce, if not eliminate, internal schisms. One way of achieving this goal is by claiming that Carrington could not possibly love a person who treats her the way Strachey does. Yet love and friendship do not follow moral rules. Whether individuals find themselves attached to others or choose to develop such an attachment freely, the ground for the relationship is not (solely) a rational one. We would, in fact, find it strange, maybe even disingenuous, if a person would be able to give a clear and rational account of why she loves or befriends a person, referring only to objective moral criteria.

As Harry Frankfurt argues, we can love someone who is wicked or unworthy of our love:

> [D]oing that may be a misfortune; and it may be still further a misfortune to be fully aware that that is what one is doing. But such things happen. . . . At times, we speak of people or of other things as "unworthy" of our love. That something may be unworthy of love means that, notwithstanding the inherent value of loving, there are things that it would be better on balance not to love. . . . If my children should turn out to be ferociously wicked, I might come to feel that despite their possession of rational wills they are, all things considered, unworthy of my love. But I suspect that after recognizing the undesirability of loving then, I would continue to love them anyhow.[23]

Frankfurt is obviously right. Unfortunately for moral theory, and for us as moral agents, the objects of our love are not determined by moral considerations. Many human tragedies would have been spared if this WERE the case. But individuals do love those who are base and corrupt, who mistreat them and others, exploit their love, betray their friendship, and abuse their goodwill. When forced to confront the immoral, and sometimes cruel, nature of their loved ones, individuals are often unable to turn their backs, dissociate themselves, and ignore their emotions and the responsibilities that follow from them.

One may argue that this view is grounded in self-deception or false consciousness, as no one can really love an abusive person. Individuals could indeed misjudge their own feelings, suppress their emotions, or engage in self-deception. But could it be the case that *all* those who are found in a relationship they have no reason to value misjudge their feeling, that *all* of them delude themselves that they love an unworthy person? As much as we would like it to be the case, we have no reason to believe that individuals are more often misguided in evaluating those relationships they have no reason to value than in evaluating relations they have a reason to value. The reason for excluding relationships we have no reason to value as grounds for personal responsibilities cannot therefore be tied to the issue of self-deception or repression of one's true feelings.[24]

What then can nullify the ability of those relationships we have no reason to value to generate personal responsibilities, while affirming the power of all other relationships to generate such responsibilities? And how can such a nullification save us from the bonds of exaggerated communitarianism and historicism? Why shouldn't such an escape be offered to those caught in relationships they have a reason to value? After all, there is no reason to assume we would like to enter all the different kinds of relationships we do have a reason to value.[25] These questions are left unanswered by the value-dependent approach.

The value-independent approach presented here grounds responsibilities in the relationship themselves, claiming that the two are inseparable. If one cannot enter a wedge between the affectionate aspect of a relationship and the responsibilities that follow from it, can there be an escape from exaggerated historicism and communitarianism? According to the value-independent approach, such an escape depends not on the nature of relationships but on the ability of individuals to voluntarily enter and exit their relationships. I tend to think that individuals have a limited freedom to control their relationships and memberships. In this sense individuals are governed by powers they cannot control. These powers influence their identity, as well as their responsibilities. In this respect there is indeed no escape from historicism and communitarianism. This is not an idea liberal theorists find easy to endorse, but if there is one lesson to be taught from ordinary beliefs and sentiments, it is this one.

Yet, the fact that individuals have personal responsibilities does not, in itself, determine how they should act. Personal responsibilities must be balanced against other responsibilities and duties. This is why practical reasoning plays such an important role in human life. But practical reasoning has its limitations. It can assist individuals in the process of weighing and balancing conflicting responsibilities and reaching a decision about how they should act but it cannot—nor should it—alleviate the pain and anxiety such decisions embody.

Notes

This chapter is dedicated to D. P.; whose friendship I have many reasons to value. I am grateful to Edna Ullmann-Margalit, Menachem Lorverbaum, Susan Neiman, and Johnathan Lear for their helpful comments.

1. The problem with the communitarian claim is that it moves too easily between a descriptive claim that individuals believe they have responsibilities to the normative claim that individuals do have responsibilities. This move is justified only if responsibilities are constitutive of relationships rather than generated by them. I shall discuss these issues in greater details in section 3 of this chapter especially from page 26 onward.

2. S. Caney, "Individuals, Nations and Obligations," in S. Caney, D. George, and P. Jones (eds.), *National Rights, International Obligations*, Westview, 1996; R. Dworkin, *Law's Empire*, Fantana Press, 1986; G. Fletcher, *Loyalty*, Oxford University Press, 1994; S. Scheffler, "Relationship and Responsibility," *Philosophy and Public Affairs*, vol. 26, no. 3. 1997.

3. Caney, ibid., p. 127 Note that Caney endorses the communitarian assumption that if A and C were both black and B was white, A had a reason to prefer C. And in so doing A will not act in an immoral way.

4. Caney, ibid., p. 125.

5. Dworkin, ibid., pp. 204–205.

6. Scheffler, ibid., p. 205.

7. Scheffler, ibid., pp. 20–21.

8. There could be interesting border cases in which it is unclear whether a continuous intimate exchange could create a relationship; suppose that as an intelligence officer I am assigned to trail a particular person for years. I know everything about him and his family. My life is influenced by his life more than by the lives of my best friends. It is unclear whether such a relationship could generate responsibilities. Especially if the person I am assigned to trail is someone I have a reason to despise—for example, an ex–Nazi officer.

9. The notion of special responsibilities is similar to Hart's notion of special rights. See H.L.A. Hart, "Are There Any Natural Rights?" in J. Waldron (ed.), *Are There Any Natural Rights*, Oxford University Press, 1984, p. 84.

10. For example, see N. Noodings, *Caring*, California University Press, 1984; W. Kymlicka, *An Introduction to Political Philosophy*, chapters 6 and 7, Oxford University Press, 1995.

11. Scheffler, ibid., pp. 189–190.

12. Ibid.

13. I would like to thank Menchem Lorverbaum for discussing this issue with me.

14. I make a similar claim I a much more detailed way in Y. Tamir "The Land of the Free and the Fearful," *Constellations, vol. 3., no. 3, 1997.*

15. Aristotle, *Ethica Nicomachea,* book 7, 1156b, 5–25.

16. Aristotle, ibid., 1157, 15–25.

17. Cited in N. Kapur Badhwar (ed.), *Friendship: A Philosophical Reader,* Cornell University Press, 1995, p. 12. Note that the responsibilities gang members have to each other could be of both special and personal kinds.

18. Scheffler, ibid., p. 198.

19. For a more detailed argument regarding the nature of political obligations and national obligations, see Y. Tamir, *Liberal Nationalism,* Princeton University Press, 1993, chapter 4.

20. For example, Dworkin opens his approving discussion of associative obligation in *Law's Empire* with the following statement: "Most people *think* that they have associative obligations just by belonging to groups defined by social practice, which is not necessarily a matter of choice or consent" (p. 206). In the same spirit David Miller starts his defense of national obligations in *On Nationality* (Oxford: Clarendon Press, 1995) by advocating a philosophical approach that endorses ordinary beliefs "until strong arguments are produced for rejecting them. . . . In moral and political philosophy, in particular we build upon existing sentiments and judgments, correcting them only when they are inconsistent or plainly flawed in some other way."

21. Scheffler, ibid., pp. 195–196.

22. Needless to say, some external hindrances may prevent one from acting in ways demanded by her responsibilities.

23. H. Frankfurt, "Vellman on Love and Duty," a comment on Vellman's paper presented in the Eastern APA, 1998.

24. Note that this discussion is motivated by the descriptive claim that individuals see themselves as bound by responsibilities grounded in relationships. Such a claim can generate a normative claim that individuals are bound by responsibilities grounded in relationships only if the following two conditions are fulfilled: (1) responsibilities are constitutive of relationships and (2) individuals are able to give an accurate account of their relationships. Namely the move from the descriptive to normative claims, characteristic of the claims made by Scheffler, Dworkin, Caney, and others, can be justified on the basis of a value-independent approach but not on the basis of a value-dependent one.

25. Note that the value-dependent approach suggests not only that those relationships that do not pass a certain moral threshold fail to produce particular responsibilities but also that all valuable relations do. There is no escape from morally valuable relationships even if they are not voluntarily assumed. Nonreductionism offers then only a partial escape from historicism and communitarianism. Escape is grounded in the immoral qualities of the relationship rather than in the kind of attachments and feelings individuals have.

10

PRACTICAL REASON AND MORAL CERTAINTY

The Case of Discrimination

Janet Radcliffe Richards

I. Practical Reason and Moral Certainty

The trouble with practical reasoning is that although it is something everybody has to do all the time, doing it well is often appallingly *difficult*. It is difficult enough even when it concerns only the practicalities of how to achieve some already determined goal, and the problem lies in trying to work out how to reach that goal without disrupting too much else on the way. But when moral problems join the empirical ones, practical reasoning can seem impossible. It is all very well for philosophers to say that if you are a utilitarian you do this and if you are a Kantian you do that, but harassed doctors and politicians and directors of social services cannot get far on the basis of conditionals, and they cannot suspend all action until the fundamental truths of ethics have been finally settled. If moral philosophers are to be of any practical use, they must address the problems of making pressing decisions against a background of moral uncertainty and disagreement.

One enquiry of this kind is undertaken by Cass Sunstein earlier in this book, when he considers how much practical agreement is feasible against a background of theoretical disagreement. As it stands, his question is primarily about the extent to which people who hold different principles can reach practical agreement without compromising those principles, but it can also be understood as the question of the extent to which an individual, uncertain about how to resolve some problem of moral theory, can nevertheless be certain about how to act. In a way, the subject of this chapter is a mirror image of that. It approaches the problem of reaching practical certainty and agreement from the opposite direction, starting not with theoretical difficulties but with whatever fragments of moral truth we think we can be certain about. Its concern is the extent to which such certainties can be put to direct practical use, without the need for detours into complicated questions of normative theory. And although this is primarily a question for individuals trying to extend the usefulness of moral claims they regard as certain, the reasoning works in the same way between individuals whose theoretical disagreements are underlain by some core of agreement.

How such enquiries are approached depends on the kind of certainty in question. If, for instance, some aspect of a situation is accepted as *intrinsically bad*—as, for instance, in its involving suffering—that can be used to establish a direction of onus of proof. There is a presumption in favor of preventing or relieving the suffering. In any difficult or controversial case, of course, this presumption will immediately be met by the assertion of counterbalancing harms (as when it is claimed that legalized euthanasia would put people under pressure to ask for it) or opposing deontological principles (as when it is said that euthanasia is murder); and this may seem to restore the status quo ante, leaving the problem to turn, as usual, on questions of substantive moral principle and elusive fact. But matters may not always be as they seem. Surprisingly often, in areas of moral passion and controversy, close enough scrutiny of the details exposes familiar arguments as confections of twisted logic and wishful thinking; and when this happens, there may be no need to go into the merits of controversial moral principles or empirical claims. If the principles invoked do not support the conclusion they are supposed to support, for instance, it does not matter what their intrinsic merits are. The blocking argument fails anyway, and practical judgment must revert to the default of preventing the harm in question.[1] Arguments of this kind can often turn popular moral wisdom upside down, and because they work at the level of familiar argument rather than esoteric theory, they may even do so in ways persuasive to the purveyors of that popular wisdom.

Here I want to consider a related but different kind of case, in which moral certainty or agreement attaches not to the intrinsic goodness or badness of some element of a state of affairs, but to the rightness or wrongness of actions and policies. Where this occurs, the question arises of the extent to which that certainty can be be directly and legitimately extended to other similar, but less clear, situations.

It is not worth saying much about this in abstract. Apart from the fact that abstract discussions of method are dull, and hard to follow without illustrations, the problems of practical reason are too varied in kind to allow for much progress without constant reference to the problems themselves. Until a range of these has been disentangled, it will probably not be possible to see whether there are patterns that can be generalized into theory. What follows, therefore, is a particular case study: the application of this approach to the problem of discrimination. This tips the balance of the chapter more towards discrimination than towards the wider thesis about practical reason and moral certainty, but the case will, I hope, illustrate the approach in a way that demonstrates its general value.

II. Pinning Down Discrimination

One advantage of working at this ground level of moral argument is that this is where the most familiar arguments about discrimination are found in practice. The idea of discrimination, in its political, pejorative, sense, is rooted in a range of paradigm cases of actions and policies that seem obviously wrong, in being unjust to the group discriminated against; and when a label comes complete with pejorative connotations, people will always try to stretch it to cover their own cases. This is much simpler than trying to work out a full-blown theory of justice and then show its implications for your particular case. If disadvantageous treatment on grounds of race or sex is discrimination and unjust, then so, it will be asserted, must be disadvantageous treatment on grounds of age, or sexual orientation, or disability, or culture, or obesity, or ugliness; if actually excluding women from various areas of life and work is discrimination, then so must be making it harder for them to get into those areas, or not changing the rules to make it easier, or not changing the whole working environment to make it more congenial to women, or not providing free child care. And so the ripples spread, until a stage is reached when people who readily acknowledged the injustice of the paradigm cases may find themselves feeling that things have become seriously out of hand, but having no idea when or how the slip started.

It is not surprising that this happens. The real-life extension of discrimination claims seems to work on the assumption that if your case resembles one of the paradigms, or resembles one of the cases that resembles one of the paradigms, you can legitimately call it discrimination and take its injustice for granted. But unless you have first established what it is about the paradigm cases that justifies these connotations of injustice, and made sure that the word is attached to new situations only if they resemble them in the relevant respects, the usual process of extension amounts to a chain of fallacies of equivocation, and not surprisingly has counterintuitive consequences.

The method being investigated here amounts to a controlled version of the familiar process. The problem is to work out *what it is* about the paradigm cases that gives them their intuitive force and certainty, so that when the word and its retinue of connotations are attached to new situations, we can be sure that the point of resemblance is the right one. That will both show how far the legitimate extensions can stretch and block the proliferation of the spurious.

What is needed, then, to provide both an illustration of the problem and a basis for trying to solve it, is one of these paradigm cases: something that nearly everyone who uses "discrimination" as implying moral wrong would count as a clear instance, in the full-blooded sense of constituting an injustice to the disadvantaged group. Such clear instances are rather hard to find these days, since they are of course the first to fall before antidiscrimination legislation, but there is no disadvantage for this purpose in excavating history. Consider, then, the situation supposed to have occurred at one of the London Transport (LT) bus garages in 1969, when the male drivers were rising in protest about recent moves to allow women to join their ranks, on the grounds, they said, that women were (inter alia) just not strong enough to drive buses.[2] They eventually conceded that the women could drive the little, single-decker buses, but not the big ones, which were obviously men's work. And for a while they succeeded in persuading LT to exclude women from bus driving.

If this account is accurate (and nothing turns on whether it is or not), the situation does seem to have been a paradigm case of discrimination. But if so, what made it so? If what LT and the drivers did was wrong, and in a way reasonably described as discrimination against women, *what was the standard* their policy failed to meet? The problem calls for a series of thought experiments to isolate different *aspects* of this situation, to find out which of them seems to exemplify the kind of wrongness we intuitively regard as discrimination. If we can do that, we can see when the same judgment can properly be made of other situations.

II.A. The Moral Issue and the Word

The bus drivers' policy obviously did discriminate between the sexes, in the simple sense that it involved treating them differently. It put them on different sides of a line, dividing people who were ruled out at the start from those who were allowed to pass on to the detailed selection process. But this needs to be mentioned only for the sake of completeness, because this kind of discrimination—simply drawing distinctions—is obviously a non-starter as a criterion for discrimination in the strong sense that implies injustice to the group on one side of the treatment-dividing line. *Any* view of how to act must imply indefinitely many requirements of treating different things, and different people, differently. Discrimination in this sense therefore cannot constitute a ground for complaint by anyone's standards and may usefully be described as *neutral*.

A more promising possibility lies in the related fact that the drivers' policy did not merely discriminate *between* the two groups, but did so in a way that was *less good* for one than the other, in placing it on the less advantageous side of the treatment divide. There are two ways in which people can be treated at any stage in a process of selection: they can be ruled out, or they can be offered the opportunity to pass on to the next stage. Bus driving may not be the summum bonum, but it is better to have the option open than closed[3], and since this policy ruled women out at the start, it takes little linguistic innovation to say that they were discriminated *against*.

This is obviously a more plausible candidate than neutral discrimination as a basis for complaint, but in fact it fares no better. If this were the criterion for discrimination in the strong sense that implies injustice, everyone eliminated at every stage of the selection process, for any reason, would be unjustly treated. Anyone rejected because of incorrigibly defective vision, or proneness to epileptic seizures, or perpetual drunkenness, or temperamental inclination to treat anything on wheels as a racing vehicle, would by this criterion be just as much discriminated against as were women. Even choosing the best person would, by this standard, count as discriminating against everybody else. Any principle of selection at all would, by this criterion, discriminate against everyone whose characteristics placed them on the undesirable side of the specified dividing line. If this kind of discrimination is wrong in itself, so is nearly all selection of any kind for any purpose, and not many people would want to stretch their idea of discrimination as far as that. Furthermore, even if anyone did want to make such a surprising claim, it could still not form basis of the accusation that the drivers were discrimination against women. The complaint that women, in particular, are discriminated against—unfairly disadvantaged in the selection process—arises only against the background of there being a selection process in the first place. So we still need to establish what it is about the drivers' treatment of women that makes it seem that they were discriminating against women in the strong sense that implies injustice, and not just in what might be called the *weak* sense, of placing them on the disadvantageous side of a dividing line.

This weak use of the term is important to notice, because in it lies the root of a good deal of the fallacious stretching of the paradigm cases of discrimination. Perhaps nobody would claim, when it was put in that way, that all disadvantageous differentiation between two groups must be wrong; and indeed we implicitly recognize this when we say that some discrimination is *unjustified*, or that we must not discriminate *unnecessarily* against some group, and in doing so imply that discrimination need not be unjustified or unnecessary. But "discrimination" is also often used on its own, to imply something *essentially* unjust, as when the complaint about the drivers' policy is expressed simply as its discriminating against women. If the weak kind of discrimination against a group, which is easily established but needs further argument to demonstrate its wrongness, is conflated with the strong kind of discrimination (still to be identified) that *constitutes* some kind of wrong, the opportunity for political conjuring is obviously endless. And, as a small amount of observation will show, it is an opportunity widely exploited in practice.

II.B. *Wrongful Discrimination*

As implied in the last paragraph, however, the fact that weak discrimination is not wrong in itself does not preclude the possibility that it is wrong in any particular case. It means only that since it cannot be wrong *because* it is weak discrimination, any wrongness must lie in its contravening some other moral principle. Perhaps, then, the paradigm cases of strong discrimination just are cases of weak discrimination that fail by the standards of some other moral principle that most people take to be self-evident.

This begins to seem plausible, and in the case of the buses there does indeed seem to be a suitable candidate standard. The disadvantageous exclusion of women was wrong, it will be said, because sex is *irrelevant* to the driving of buses. Buses should be driven by the people best able to do the job. In other words, this (weak) discrimination against women is wrong because the standard that ought to be applied is the classic liberal ideal of *careers open to talents* (to use the traditional term), according to which all jobs ought to be open to competition and given to the people who can do them best.

This principle is widely taken for granted; and it is noteworthy that the drivers implicitly accepted it too, since in saying women were too weak to drive buses they were claiming, in effect, that sex was *not* irrelevant to doing the job well. However, their justification failed. Quite apart from the fact that women are not too weak to drive buses, as has since appeared and as a minimal amount of investigation would have established at the time, the conclusion that women should be formally excluded from bus driving cannot be derived from the principle that the best people should drive the buses. If LT wanted competent bus drivers, it must have had tests to weed out substandard men among its applicants, and if all women really had been too weak to drive buses, they would all have failed those tests. This means that the woman-excluding rule had no point unless it was assumed that women *were* likely to be able to drive buses, and must be excluded even if they could. Far from being justified by the principle of careers open to talents, the woman-excluding rule had no function except as a potential *overrider* of it. And this means that the principle of careers open to talents does provide a standard by which the drivers' (weak) discrimination against women comes out as unjustified.

What has emerged so far, then, is an account of *unjustified discrimination* against women by the drivers, where the discrimination is in itself morally neutral but must be regarded as wrong in this case by anyone who accepts the principle of careers open to talents. And it is easy to assume that this demonstrates the meaning of "discrimination" in the strong sense that implies injustice: that the paradigm cases of discrimination in the strong, morally loaded sense, just are cases of weak discrimination that fall short of some other moral standard accepted as self-evident by whoever is making the complaint. There are, however, serious problems about this conflation.

In the first place, it still does not seem to accord with familiar intuitions about the use of the term. We typically have the idea that discrimination is a special *kind of wrong*, needing special policies to stop it. But this idea is not justified by the account just given. When (weak) discrimination is wrong, on this account, its wrongness derives from the contravention of some other moral principle (in this case, we are supposing, the principle of careers open to talents). But in that case there is no moral difference between *discrimination* that fails by those standards and anything else that does—including, even, *failure* to discriminate. If London Transport had decided to allocate its driverships by lucky dip, there would have been no distinction of treatment between applicants, and therefore no weak discrimination at all, but the people who did less well under this system than they would have done if there had been proper driving tests would have been just as wrongly treated *by the standard of careers open to talents* as were the excluded women.But if what is wrong with weak discrimination that fails by that standard is morally identical with anything else that does, it seems implausible that it should be identical with strong discrimination, which seems to be a distinctive *kind* of wrong.

And when this is pursued further, the difference becomes more marked. Wrongful weak discrimination—where "wrongful" means wrong by whatever positive standards are accepted by the critic—turns out to be neither necessary nor suffient for our intuitive idea of discrimination in the strong sense.

Suppose, for instance, the drivers and LT had come under the influence of some union leader who had taken it into his head that it was inherently appropriate to allocate driverships on the basis of ability to memorize tracts of telephone directories. Such a remarkable policy would, in the weak sense, discriminate against everyone who could not do this, but it would be very odd to express an objection to the policy as a complaint that LT was discriminating against people without that kind of memory. We would be much more likely to say simply that its criterion for driver selection was ridiculous. If so, a complaint about weak discrimination that is wrong by the standards of the critic is not an adequate intuitive basis for an accusation of (strong) discrimination. It is not *sufficient* for strong discrimination.

And now imagine the same situation, but with the added proviso that no women would be accepted, no matter how well they managed the telephone directory test. In such a situation we should not hesitate to say that women were being discriminated against, but we could not express that by saying that this was because anyone disadvantaged by the non-application of careers open to talents was discriminated against, since that would apply just as much to the men who failed the test as well as to good drivers among women. It is clear that the women would have another complaint, plausibly called discrimination, that the men did not have, as well as the one both sexes shared. And if so, weak discrimination that fails by the standards of career open to talents—or whatever other standard the critic accepts—is not *necessary*, either, for strong discrimination.

II.C. Strong Discrimination

It seems, then, that an accusation of (strong) discrimination must be regarded as something other than weak discrimination regarded as wrong by the standards of the critic, for which it is neither necessary nor sufficient. What, then, could it possibly be?

Consider again the second of the telephone-directory memorizing cases, in which London Transport does seem to be discriminating against women by excluding them, even though what it is doing cannot be explained as weak discrimination that fails by the standards of the principle of careers open to talents. The construction of this case, in which *nobody* is treated properly by that standard, suggests what is wrong with the additional exclusion of women in particular. This seems discriminatory not because it cannot be justified the general standards accepted by the *critic*, but because it cannot be justified even in terms of the general (directory memorizing) standards professed by the *recommenders and perpetrators of the policy* themselves. They seem to be disadvantaging women not merely without the *right* justification, whatever that is, but without *any* justification. The exclusion of women seems to be arbitrary and an end in itself; a not-further-explainable benefit to men at the expense of women.

If this is right, it means that a distinction needs to be drawn between two quite different kinds of standard by which the treatment of a group may give rise to a complaint. First, the treatment can fail to accord with the standards of whatever principles the critic thinks should be applied, and in that case, anyone to whom that principle is not applied will be regarded as wrongly treated, and anyone subject under those circumstances to weak discrimination—put on the disadvantageous side of a treatment dividing line—will be *wrongly discriminated against*. Second, the treatment may arbitrarily disadvantage one group, in the sense of being unjustifiable in terms of any generalizable principles accepted by the people doing the treating, who must therefore be disadvantaging the group as an end in itself. And this second seems just what we intuitively think of as discrimination in the strong sense: discrimination that actually constitutes a particular kind of wrong, as opposed to discrimination that is neutral in itself but of which particular instances may be wrong by other standards.

Now consider again the real drivers, as opposed to the ones with the telephone directory test. They were certainly practicing weak discrimination against women, in putting them on the disadvantageous side of a treatment dividing line, and a critic who accepted the principle of careers open to talents would say that this discrimination was wrong. But it can now be seen that they were practicing what on this account comes out as (strong) discrimination *as well*. They were disadvantaging women without *any* justification, even an unacceptable one of their own. It happens that in this case, where the principles of the critic and the principles professed by the drivers coincide, the complaints coalesce: if the drivers stopped the wrongful weak discrimination, they would, ipso facto, stop the strong discrimination, and vice versa. But that does not make the complaints the same. All it does is account for the elusiveness of the distinction.

III. Discrimination as Arbitrary Disadvantaging

III.A. A Distinct Kind of Wrong

This account does look as though it may be on the right track. A principle along these lines seems to catch some of our strongest intuitions about discrimination. It accords with the sense that discrimination involves a particular kind of wrong, rather than something neutral that might or might not be wrong by other standards, and justifies the ordinary language distinction between "discriminated against" and "wrongly discriminated against." It also explains why the two are easily conflated, since they often coincide in paradigm cases of discrimination.

It also accounts for the intuition that discrimination involves arbitrariness of treatment, and is essentially connected with irrelevance, without running into the problem that what is arbitrary or irrelevant by one standard may not be by another. Discrimination defined this way is disadvantageous treatment irrelevant by the standards of any general principles its perpetrators accept.

Discrimination so defined is also something that most people are likely to regard as obviously and uncontroversially wrong (important for the purpose of this investigation, which is concerned with the extension of moral certainty), as is indicated by the way people nearly always try to justify disadvantageous treatment in terms of general principles. The drivers could have said they wanted to keep the work for men because women's interests simply mattered less, but instead they fudged a justification that appealed to the need for well-driven buses. There is also a good theoretical underpinning for this reluctance, since it amounts to a wish to (be seen to) avoid infringing principles of positional indifference and the equal consideration of interests, which are widely accepted as fundamental to any morality.

Nevertheless, in spite of all consonance with familiar intuitions, this account of discrimination is extremely curious in other respects. Most conspicuously, *it makes (strong) discrimination relative*. The principle of non-discrimination does set real constraints—you must not disadvantage people in ways not justified by your own general principles—and therefore does provide a standard by which someone can be judged to be acting unjustly or recommending what is unjust. *But it does not rule out any particular kinds of action or policy as such.* A policy not justifiable in terms of one set of principles might well be justifiable in terms of another, and therefore discriminatory when perpetrated or recommended by one person, but not another.

This means that even if the *drivers* can be shown to be discriminating, and their policy *as perpetrated by them* discriminatory, we cannot, by this criterion, say it of the policy of excluding women as such.[4] The bus drivers might have held a general principle from which the exclusion of women did follow; and then, even though you might criticize this principle—and so conclude that their (weak) discrimination against women was wrong—you could not on this account complain that women were discriminated against, in the strong sense. This seems decidedly out of line with what we ordinarily think about discrimination. We usually think people are entitled to say that they are discriminated against just in virtue of being treated in particular ways, quite irrespective of the moral standards of whoever is doing the treating.

Furthermore, it may also seem to show that if this is what discrimination really is, the idea is useless. Suppose, as a result of this kind of analysis, you are able to identify some particular case, such as that of the drivers, as involving strong discrimination. What purpose is served by your doing that? If you yourself accept the principle of careers open to talents, you do not need to identify the drivers' policy as involving strong discrimination in order to criticize it, since the principle of careers open to talents itself identifies their policy as wrong. If, on the other hand, you happened to accept some other general principle, in terms of which the exclusion of women was justified, then even though the drivers were themselves guilty of strong discrimination, you would still think their *policy* right and would not oppose it. And if you had no clear standards of judgment at all, and no idea what LT's policy should be, your having identified the bus drivers as discriminators would not help you to decide.

So, although there is a criterion for (strong) discrimination that seems to fit our intuitions in many ways and offers a hook on which the drivers and many others may get caught and exposed as discriminators, it is not yet clear that it is a hook worth catching anyone on. For practical purposes, the idea of discrimination may seem entirely superseded by the substantive matter of which positive principles should be adopted.

And if that is so, it also follows that the line of enquiry being pursued in this chapter has led nowhere. The whole idea was to make practical moral progress without taking on the difficulties of seeking out general normative principles. But if the moral certainty so far identified applies only to judgments that *particular moral agents* are guilty of discrimination, and what we need to know is whether their *policies* are defensible or not, this account of discrimination begins to seem of little practical use.

Needless to say, however, my choosing this case to illustrate the effectiveness of this approach to practical reason shows that I hope to be able to reach a different conclusion.

III.B. Actions and Agents

To make a judgment about the woman-excluding *policy* espoused by drivers and LT, there is no avoiding appeal to substantive moral principles; and it was the difficulty of finding satisfactory substantial principles, let alone reaching agreement about them, that motivated this attempt to see how much moral certainty could be achieved by more direct methods.

Suppose, however, you did succeed in establishing a set of normative standards that satisfied you, and which would, when conjoined with appropriate empirical information, put you in a position to say how everybody ought to be treated by everybody. This would still be only a first step for the purposes of practical ethics. The ultimate purpose of practical moral enquiry is to bring about improvement, and for that it is not enough for *you* to have found satisfactory princples and be in a position to judge any action or policy that arises. You must want *other people* to accept these principles as well. No policy of social improvement can get far unless you can persuade other moral agents to adopt the attitudes you regard as right. And this already brings matters a step nearer to the account given here of discrimination as a distinctive kind of wrong, since this analysis shows accusations of discrimination to be agent-directed complaints.

On the other hand, this is not yet enough to rescue the antidiscrimination principle from the appearance of superfluity. For surely, it may be argued, if you want everyone to be treated properly (by the standards of whatever principles you have reached), then what you need to do is to persuade other people to adopt those principles. Until people hold the right principles, a campaign against discrimination would be pointless, because all it could achieve would be the impartial application of principles you disapproved of. Conversely, if you can persuade people to adopt the right principles, they will automatically endorse the right actions and policies, and a separate antidiscrimination principle will have nothing to do. If the bus drivers had been true believers in careers open to talents, they would not have excluded women in the first place.

But that way of putting the matter begins to reveal the crack in the argument. If people are failing to act according to a principle you think should be followed, and you want to remedy this state of affairs, it is not enough to know simply *that* they are falling short of the ideal: you need to know *why*. You need to know what is getting between them and what they ought to be doing, and there are all kinds of possibilities. They may, perhaps, be inadequately convinced of the truth of your theory and need persuasion, or they may misunderstand it and need further instruction. But there are innumerable other reasons why people may fail to act in the way required by a particular set of moral standards (such as careers open to talents), and many of these have nothing to do with failing by that set of standards in particular, but are rather of a kind that would result in their falling short of virtue by *any* standards. They may be lazy, or morally unserious, or serious only on Sundays, or ignorant, or stupid, or careless with facts, or morally fickle, or hopeless at logic, or generally feckless, or easily led, or weak willed, or any of innumerable other things that might come between them and the proper implementing of *whatever* principles they (in some sense sincerely) accepted.

Complaints of this sort, in being generic, are quite irreducible to complaints about falling short of the standards of any particular theory. And to whatever extent it is shortcomings like these that are coming between your standards and their fulfillment, there is no point in repeating your principles in a louder voice or instituting indoctrination courses. You need to identify the impediment and work directly to eliminate it, *as well as* engage in whatever kind of missionary work is needed to make people accept the particular principles you take to be right.

The relevance of this point is, of course, that complaints about discrimination, on the account offered here, come into this generic category. Discrimination has been identified as a matter of disadvantaging a group not *because* of general principles held by the agent in question, whatever those are, but *in spite* of them. Discrimination on this account works as an *overrider* of generalizable principles. In spite of apparently accepting that the best people should drive buses (since they tried to make out that women were to be excluded because of incompetence through weakness), the drivers had in effect a *separate,* superimposed principle about keeping women out of this traditionally male area, whose effect on the quality of bus driving could only have been to make it worse.

When moral shortcomings are of such quite general kinds, unconnected with a failure to implement any particular normative principles, there is equally no a priori reason to think they would be corrected by a change of principles. And, in fact, there is a good deal of evidence to think that they usually are not. The arbitrary disadvantaging of various groups has persisted through radical changes of moral attitude on many occasions. The founding fathers of the United States put forward new views of liberty, apparently without noticing that those views were incompatible with keeping women out of government and making slaves of Africans; and similar things happened in other countries with respect to women (at least) when socialism took over from capitalism. New moral sensibilities that accompany such revolutions may sometimes result in a rethinking of other attitudes, but if so, that is incidental. It cannot be relied on.

So the identification of discrimination as a distinct kind of wrong is not superfluous. It is not needed for deciding whether particular actions and policies are right (whether women should be excluded from bus driving): for that, the appropriate kind of positive standard is needed. But awareness of discrimination as a separate problem *is* essential if what is at issue is the wider question of how to set about righting social wrongs. To whatever extent discrimination is what is wrong with some situation, only separate identification and attack can offer a systematic way of putting it to rights.

IV. Conclusion

That is not the end of the matter. Discrimination itself needs to be subdivided, because a disposition to discriminate in this sense can have indefinitely many different roots and appear in innumerable forms. But what has been said is enough for the purposes of the project outlined at the outset, of seeing how to extend fragments of moral certainty and agreement against a background of vast uncertainty and disagreement.

Wherever accusations of discrimination may arise, there are bound to be doubts and controversies about the standards that should be used to assess individual actions and public policies. Even in the context of the very limited issue considered here, of employment and the apparently clear and uncontentious principle of careers open to talents, matters become intractably complicated as soon as details are drawn out of the impressionistic generalities. But if this analysis is right, there is, corresponding to most of our intuitions about discrimination, a quite different matter that can be pursued independently of any conclusions about the kinds of positive principles we should use as the basis for social life. *Whatever* principles we think we should adopt, we do not want them overridden to the arbitrary disadvantage of one group, since that is both unjust in itself *and* a failure to implement the principles at issue. If people have preconceptions, prejudices, and ingrained ideas about the positions of particular groups, and these have a life of their own, overriding whatever general principles are accepted for other purposes while often spuriously rationalized in terms of them, those preconceptions need tackling in their own right.

This separateness of complaints about discrimination from complaints dependent on specific normative standards is relevant to the general problem addressed by this chapter in two ways. First, if the intuitive moral certainty that attaches to the paradigm cases of discrimination is not derived from specific normative standards, that augurs well for the possibility of extending the certainty beyond the root cases. You identify discrimination not by looking at disadvantageous treatment and deciding whether it can be justified in terms of your own normative standards, but by establishing whether its perpetrators have attitudes that potentially lead to the overriding of whatever generalizable principles they otherwise accept. This is, of course, by no means easy. These discriminatory habits of mind need to be identified, and as they can take indefinitely many forms, and are often unrecognized by the people who have them, they have to be tracked down in obscure places, such as arguments fudged to make entailments out of contradictions (as when the drivers tried to derive women's exclusion from a claim about their weakness). Then counter-strategies need to be devised and implemented, a matter whose difficulty needs no comment. Nevertheless, to a large extent this work raises no *moral* problems. It is fully supported by the minimal principle of impartiality or equal consideration of interests, and can be pursued by anyone who is certain at least of that.

And second, there is the converse of the claim made in the last section, that since discrimination was separate from failure to comply with specific normative standards, it had to be tackled separately. What is also true is that it *can* be tackled separately. Because the problem has nothing to do with which general principles should be accepted, an attack on discriminatory attitudes can be set up as an independent project. We can try to identify and eliminate whatever beliefs and attitudes people have that result in their failing to apply to some groups the principles they apply, or think they should apply, to others.

Furthermore, this possibility—that people who are uncertain about the details of which positive normative standards to accept may nevertheless take on with confidence a project of opposing discrimination—also implies the possibility of agreement among otherwise divided people. People can unite in undermining the preconceptions that would prevent the proper implementation of *any* principles, even when they disagree about what those principles should be. Even if you disapprove of the prevailing principles in your society, you can rationally work to have them impartially implemented, because to do so is not a matter of giving positive support to those principles, but of removing preconceptions and habits of mind would otherwise undermine the implementation of any general principles at all, including your own. This is why there can and should be a united core of feminism (for instance), in spite of the wide disparity of politcial theories held by different feminists.

It would be ideal to end with a more general conclusion about ways to extend fragments of moral certainty and agreement for practical purposes, but, if such is to be found, I presume it will come only from the discovery of patterns in particular cases. For now all I am claiming is that this case provides an illustration of what I suggested at the outset: the worthwhileness of seeing how much can be done by keeping close to the ground, rather than in trying to scale the heights of normative theory with a view to descending later. It is a kind of moral enquiry that offers immediate practical implications, and it also has the considerable incidental advantage that it continues the discussion of practical ethics at the level where it usually takes place, and where its point is often clear to the philosophically uninitiated. It also offers the possibility of real philosophical advance, in revealing aspects of problems that might otherwise not have appeared. This account of discrimination could not have emerged from familiar discussions of the just allocation of benefits.

How much more can be be achieved by methods of this general kind remains to be seen. My own view is that their potential is great.

Notes

1. I have developed arguments of this form elsewhere, e.g., in *The Sceptical Feminist: A Philosophical Enquiry* (RKP 1980; Penguin 1982 and 1994), ch. 8, on abortion; "Euthanasia," in *Nature Medicine*, July 1995 (pp. 618–620); and "Nephrarious Goings On: Kidney Sales and Moral Arguments," *Journal of Medicine and Philosophy*, vol. 21, no. 4, August 1996, pp. 375—416.

2. Sheila Rowbotham, *Woman's Consciousness, Man's World*, (Pelican, 1973), p. 95.

3. At least, this is implied by anyone who wants to claim that the policy discriminates against women, because discrimination is a matter of unfair *disadvantage*. People may disagree about what constitutes a disadvantage, and arguments against claims of discrimination often involve denials that some alleged disadvantage is a disadvantage at all: "I wish *I* could just be at home all day, and have someone else go out and earn the money." Such arguments are about what things are valuable, and I shall not discuss them. My concern here is only with questions about the distribution of *whatever* is valuable: whether *if* this or that is a good thing, it is fair that this or that group should be deprived of it.

4. That is, except in limiting cases where no possible set of principles could justify it, or (equally useful in practice) the only candidates are principles that nobody would be willing to admit to accepting. There are probably many such cases.

11

THE EMBATTLED PUBLIC SPHERE
Hannah Arendt, Jürgen Habermas, and Beyond

Seyla Benhabib

In 1927 the American journalist Walter Lippmann published *The Phantom Public*.[1] Written against the background of growing despair and disillusionment about the viability of representative democracies in Europe and North America, this work decries the "ideal of sovereign and omnicompetent citizens" as a fiction at best and a phantom at worst. Lippmann's elitist and pessimistic assessment of the fiction of collective deliberations engaged in by informed citizens elicited a spirited response from John Dewey in *The Public and Its Problems*.[2] Granting that the experience of industrial and urban modern societies undermined "the genuine community life" out of which American democracy had developed, Dewey admitted: "The public seems to be lost. . . . If a public exists, it is surely as uncertain about its whereabouts as philosophers since Hume have been about the residence and make-up of the self."[3]

Indeed, theories of the public sphere, from Walter Lippmann to Hannah Arendt, from John Dewey to Jürgen Habermas, appear to be afflicted by a nostalgic trope: once there was a public sphere of action and deliberation, participation and collective decision making; today there no longer is one, or if a public sphere still exists, it is so distorted, weakened, and corrupted as to be a pale recollection of what once was. Whether one chooses the Athenian *polis* as a paradigm or looks at the experience of republican city-states in the Italian Renaissance, whether one locates the authentic public in the coming together of private persons of the Enlightenment to use their "private reason to discuss public matters" (Habermas), or whether one idealizes the New England town meetings, there is always a curious "what was then and what no longer is" quality to these theories. The public is a phantom that will not go away: even after the many funeral rites and orations it has been subjected to, it comes back to haunt conscience and memory.[4]

The idea of the sovereign people, deliberating collectively about matters of common concern to all, is a *regulative ideal* of the democratic form of government, and disquiet about the public sphere is at bottom anxiety about the viability of democracy in modern, complex, multicultural, and increasingly globalized polities. The regulative principle of democracy requires the idea of an autonomous public sphere, as the medium through which self-governance through the deliberation of a collectivity can take place. Between this regulative ideal of democracy and the increasingly desubstantialized carriers of the anonymous public conversation of mass societies, a hiatus exists; this hiatus transforms the regulative ideal of democracy into a *constitutive fiction*, and this fiction causes continuous anxiety. There are no easy sociological and institutional solutions to the transformations of the public sphere brought about, not only by the rise of the new technologies of communication, such as the electronic media and the new information technologies,[5] but by advancing processes of global interdependence in financial and labor markets, the global flow of peoples, information, and capital. What a political philosopher can contribute to these issues is a normative clarification of the concept of the public sphere and its centrality for democratic theory and practice. After all, not all forms of democratic theory are concerned with this concept: democratic theories based on interest-group pluralisms do not accord a place of honor to the public sphere. In the pluralist tradition, the public sphere is viewed as a not terribly significant institutional correlate of the rights of freedom of speech, assembly, and organization.

By contrast, two traditions of political thought accord the public sphere a central place: the republican virtue tradition, as resuscitated by Hannah Arendt in the twentieth century, and the Kantian liberal tradition, beginning with Kant's own well-known reflections on the "public use of reason," and continued by John Rawls and Jürgen Habermas. It is the dialogue between these two traditions that interests me. My thesis is that neither of these positions is adequate today to allow the full complexity of the public sphere to come to the fore in contemporary democratic theory and practice: Hannah Arendt's model is flawed, because more often than not, it seems to fly in the face of the realities of the modern world and because she never clearly establishes the link between the public space of politics and democratic modes of legitimacy. The liberal legitimacy models proposed by Rawls and Habermas have their problems as well: in the Rawlsian model, the public sphere shrinks to a normative concept of "public reason"; the give and take, antagonism, conflict and agon of democratic politics is removed from the public sphere even before it has a chance to articulate itself. In Jürgen Habermas's model, the agon of politics is indeed present in the public sphere, but Habermas does not face the problem that an agonistic public sphere will not allow the kind of "consensual reaching agreement on practical norms" that his discourse theory of legitimacy privileges.

Indeed, in thinking about the "public sphere," we are caught between the pull of strong assumptions of normative unity and consensus on the one hand, and the push of multicultural, multivocal, polyphonous dialogues and conversations on the other. Is there a way out of this dilemma? In my concluding considerations, I will bring together the normative and the sociological problems and suggest a reconceptualization of the public sphere for the "electro-iconographic societies" of late capitalism.

I. Hannah Arendt and the Recovery of Public Space under Conditions of Modernity

Hannah Arendt is the central political thinker of this century whose work has reminded us with great poignancy of the "lost treasures" of our tradition of political thought, and specifically of the "loss" of public space, of *der oeffentliche Raum*, under conditions of modernity. Arendt's major theoretical work, *The Human Condition*,[6] is usually, and not unjustifiably, treated as an antimodernist political work. By the "rise of the social" in this work, Arendt means the institutional differentiation of modern societies into the narrowly political realm on the one hand—the state and its apparatus—and the realms of the economy and the family on the other. As a result of these transformations, economic processes that had hitherto been confined to the "shadowy realm of the household" break away from their confines and become public matters. The same historical process that brought forth the modern constitutional state also brings forth "society," that realm of social interaction that interposes itself between the household on the one hand and the political state on the other. A century ago, Hegel had described this process as the development in the midst of ethical life of a "system of needs," of a domain of economic activity governed by commodity exchange and the pursuit of economic self-interest. Arendt sees in this process the occluding of the political by the "social" and the transformation of the public space of politics into a pseudospace of interaction in which individuals no longer "act" but "merely behave" as economic producers, consumers, and urban city dwellers.

This relentlessly negative account of the "rise of the social," and of the decline of the public realm has been identified as the core of Arendt's political "antimodernism." Yet it is greatly misleading to read Arendt primarily as a nostalgic thinker. She devoted as much space to analyzing the dilemmas and prospects of politics in this century as she did to the decline of the public sphere under conditions of modernity.[7] Indeed, if one locates Arendt's concept of the "public space" in the context of her theory of totalitarianism, it acquires a rather different focus than the one dominant in *The Human Condition*. The terms agonistic and associational can capture this contrast.[8]

According to the "agonistic" model, the public realm represents the space of appearances in which moral and political greatness, heroism and preeminence in deeds and words are revealed, displayed, and shared with others. This is a competitive space, in which one competes for recognition, precedence, and acclaim; ultimately it is the space in which one seeks a guarantee against the futility and passage of all things human: "For the *polis* was for the Greeks, as the *res publica* was for the Romans, first of all their guarantee against the futility of individual life, the space protected against its futility and reserved for the relative permanence, if not immortality, of mortals."[9]

By contrast, the "associational view" of public space suggests that such a space emerges whenever and wherever, in Arendt's words, "men act together in concert."

In this model, public space is the space "where freedom can appear." It is not a space necessarily in a topographical or institutional sense: a town hall or a city square where people do not "act in concert" is not a public space in this Arendtian sense. But a private dining room in which people gather together to hear a Samizdat or in which dissidents meet with foreigners can become a public space, just as a forest or a field can also become a public space if it is the object and the location of an "action in concert," of a demonstration to stop the construction of a highway or a military base, for example. These diverse topographical spaces become public in that they become the "sites" of power—both the space in which power unfolds and the space in which power appears and is sighted.

The distinction between the agonal and the associational models corresponds roughly to the differences in the Greek versus the modern experience of politics.[10] The agonal space of the polis was made possible by a morally homogeneous and politically exclusive community, egalitarian toward its members, antagonistic and hierarchical toward those whom it perceived as others—not only foreigners, but women, slaves, and servants as well. By contrast, for the moderns the public space is essentially porous; neither access to it nor its agenda of debate can be predefined by criteria of moral and political homogeneity. With the entry of every new group into the public space of politics since the American and the French, and in our century, the Russian revolution, the scope of the public gets extended. The emancipation of workers made property relations into a public-political issue; the emancipation of women has meant that the family and the "domestic-intimate" sphere become political issues; the attainment of rights by non-white and non-Christian post- and neo-colonial peoples has put cultural questions of collective representations of self and others on the agenda. Not only is it the "lost treasure" of revolutions, in the Arendtian sense, that eventually all can participate in them but equally, when freedom emerges from action in concert, there can be no agenda to predefine the topic of public conversation.

When Arendt names the public space, "the space of appearances" within which action and speech unfold, she has primarily in mind a model of face-to-face human interactions. Not only does this view privilege direct human interaction, it also presupposes a fair degree of ethical and value homogeneity and convergence around a shared ethos. For how otherwise would action "manifest" its meaning to others? How, without a fair degree of cohesion around interpretative repertoires, would a group of humans be able to recognize the "whatness" of an action and the "whoness" of the doer? Cohesion does not mean unanimity but a certain amount of convergence in interpretation. I would like to name this the *holistic* function of public space. Public space, according to this view, is a space in which a collectivity becomes present to itself and recognizes itself through a shared interpretive repertoire. I will suggest that this dimension of the public sphere corresponds to what Habermas calls 'ethical discourses' and what John Rawls names 'comprehensive doctrines'. Issues of collective and individual identity; the value orientations of a group in the light of which it views its past, present, and future, and patterns of cultural signification and understanding through which individuals interpret their needs and construct visions of the good life would become topics of discussion, as well as the projects of social action, through such ethical discourses and comprehensive doctrines.

In addition to its holistic one, the public sphere has an *epistemic* function. This dimension is particularly salient in Arendt's thesis that the process of public-political struggle must transform narrow self-interest into a more broadly shared public or common interest. This dimension of the public sphere comes to the fore increasingly in Arendt's later, and more Kantian rather than Aristotelian, writings.[11] According to this view, which, following Kant, Arendt describes as the standpoint of the enlarged mentality—*die erweiterte Denkungsart*—what constitutes the authentic political attitude is the capacity and willingness to give reasons in public, to entertain others' point of view, to transform the dictates of self-interest into a common public goal. Arendt put it beautifully in her commentary on Kant's theory of judgment:

> [T]he power of judgement rests on a potential agreement with others, and the thinking process which is active in judging something is not, like the thought process of pure reasoning, a dialogue between me and myself, but finds itself always and primarily, even if I am quite alone in making up my mind, in an anticipated communication with others with whom I know I must finally come to some agreement.[12]

This is the epistemic function of the public space, and such "anticipated communication with others" transcends the boundaries of the face-to-face society. We may say that this Arendtian reading of Kant also forms, *in nuce*, the kernel of Habermas's dialogic or discursive theory of legitimacy in the public sphere.

II. Habermas and the Modernist Transformation of the Public Sphere

In 1962 Jürgen Habermas published *The Structural Transformation of the Public Sphere*.[13] Although the very first pages of this work reveal the centrality of Habermas's dialogue with Arendt,[14] the complexity of their interchange and the magnitude of his intellectual debt to her have not been given their due. After *The Human Condition*, Habermas's *The Structural Transformation of the Public Sphere* was the work emphatically to call to our attention the centrality of this concept for modern, and not merely ancient, politics. In the move from the Arendtian concept of the "public space" to the Habermasian concept of the "public sphere," certain crucial transformations took place: whereas Arendt sees a *decline* of the public sphere under conditions of modernity, Habermas notes the emergence of a new form of *publicity* in the Enlightenment, that is, the coming together of private individuals to reason about public matters.[15] The bourgeois reading public of the early Enlightenment, which constitutes *in nuce* the critical-political public of the late eighteenth and early nineteenth centuries, exercises its reason about public matters by discussing a third voice, the voice of the absent author.

Whereas the Arendtian conception of the public is bound to topographical and spatial metaphors, like "space of appearance," "the city and its walls," Habermas focuses on the transformations brought about in the identity of the public with the rise of the printed media.[16] There is a shift from the model of an *ocular* to an *auditory* public; the public is no longer thought of as a group of humans seeing each other, as in the case of the united *demos*. Rather, the public is increasingly formed through impersonal means of communication, such as the printing press, newsletters, novels, literary and scientific journals.

Finally, whereas in Arendt's political philosophy the public space is the space within the confines of which a community of equals act and speak together, for Habermas, the public sphere is not just, or even principally, an arena of *action* but an impersonal medium of *communication, information,* and *opinion-formation.* The terminological shift in German allows us to capture this point more readily: whereas Arendt writes of *der oeffentliche Raum,* Habermas uses the term *die Oeffentlichkeit,* translated into English variously as the "public sphere," "publicity," and "public opinion." The public becomes increasingly desubstantialized or decorporealized in this process.

Through Habermas's systematic transformations of the Arendtian concept of the public sphere, it becomes possible for us to establish the link between the public sphere and democratic legitimacy.[17] In the following, building upon the "discourse theory of ethics,"[18] I would like to develop the outlines of a theory of democratic legitimacy. This conceptual elaboration will allow me to substantiate the claim that the ideal of the deliberative public is both a *regulative ideal* and *constitutive fiction* of the democratic form of government.

III. Democratic Legitimacy and the Public Sphere

Democracy, in my view, is best understood as a model for organizing the collective and public exercise of power in the major institutions of a society on the basis of the principle that decisions affecting the well-being of a collectivity can be viewed as the outcome of a procedure of free and reasoned deliberation among individuals considered as moral and political equals.[19] Certainly any definition of essentially contested concepts such as democracy, freedom, and justice is never a mere definition; the definition itself already articulates the normative theory that justifies the term. Such is the case with the previous definition. My understanding of democracy privileges a deliberative model over other kinds of normative considerations. This is not to imply that economic welfare, institutional efficiency, and cultural stability would not be relevant in judging the adequacy of a normative definition of democracy. Economic welfare claims and collective identity needs must also be satisfied for democracies to function over time. However, the normative basis of democracy as a form of organizing our collective life is neither the fulfillment of economic welfare nor the realization of a stable sense of collective identity. For just as the attainment of certain levels of economic welfare may be compatible with authoritarian political rule, so too antidemocratic regimes may be more successful in assuring a sense of collective identity than democratic ones.

According to the deliberative model of democracy, it is a necessary but insufficient condition for attaining legitimacy in the collective decision-making processes of a polity that the institutions of this polity are so arranged that what is considered in the common interest of all results from processes of collective deliberation conducted rationally and fairly among free and equal individuals.[20] The more collective decision-making processes approximate this model, the more the presumption of their legitimacy increases. Why?

The basis of legitimacy in democratic institutions is to be traced back to the presumption that the instances that claim obligatory power for themselves do so because their decisions represent an impartial standpoint said to be equally in the interests of all. This presumption can only be fulfilled if such decisions are in principle open to appropriate public processes of deliberation by free and equal citizens.

The "discourse model of ethics" formulates the most *general principles* and *moral intuitions* behind the validity claims of a deliberative model of democracy.[21] The procedural specifics of those special argumentation situations called "practical discourses" are not automatically transferable to a macro-institutional level, nor is it necessary that they should be so transferable. A theory of democracy, as opposed to a general moral theory, would have to be concerned with the question of institutional specifications and practical feasibility. Nonetheless, the procedural constraints of the discourse model can act as test cases for critically evaluating criteria of membership, rules for agenda setting, and for the structuring of public discussions within and among institutions.

The critical dimension of the deliberative democracy model is particularly salient if we keep in mind the following: influential currents in contemporary political theory, under the guidance of economic models of reasoning in particular, proceed from a methodological fiction. This is the fiction of an individual with an ordered set of coherent preferences. This fiction does not have much relevance in the political world. On complex social and political issues, more often than not, individuals may have views and wishes but no ordered set of preferences, since the latter would imply that they would be enlightened not only about the preferences but about the consequences and relative merits of each of their preferred choices in advance. It is actually the deliberative process itself that is likely to produce such an outcome by leading the individual to further critical reflection on his already held views and opinions; it is incoherent to assume that individuals can start a process of public deliberation with a level of conceptual clarity about their choices and preferences that actually can result only from a successful process of deliberation. Likewise, the formation of coherent preferences cannot precede deliberation; it can only succeed it. Very often individuals' wishes, as well as views and opinions, conflict with one another. In the course of deliberation and the exchange of views with others, individuals become more aware of such conflicts and feel compelled to undertake a coherent ordering.

More significantly, the very procedure of articulating a view in public imposes a certain reflexivity on individual preferences and opinions. When presenting her point of view and position to others, an individual must support them by articulating "good reasons" in a public context to her co-deliberators. This process of *articulating good reasons in public* forces the individual to think of what would count as a good reason for all others involved. One is thus forced to think from the standpoint of all involved whose agreement one is "wooing." Nobody can convince others in public of her point of view without being able to state why what appears good, plausible, just, and expedient to her can also be considered so from the standpoint of all involved. Reasoning from the standpoint of all involved not only forces a certain coherence upon one's own views, it also forces one to adopt a standpoint of the "enlarged mentality."[22]

Any proceduralist and deliberative model of democracy is prima facie open to the argument that no modern society can organize its affairs along the fiction of a mass assembly carrying out its deliberations collectively in public. Here, more than an issue of size is at stake. The argument that there may be an invisible limit to the size of a deliberative body, which, when crossed, affects the nature of the reasoning process is undoubtedly true. Nonetheless, the reason why a deliberative and proceduralist model of democracy need not operate with the fiction of a general deliberative assembly is that the procedural specifications of this model privilege a plurality of modes of association in which all affected can have the right to articulate their point of view. These can range from political parties, to citizens' initiatives, to social movements, to voluntary associations, to consciousness-raising groups, and the like. It is through the interlocking web of these multiple forms of associations, networks, and organisations that an anonymous "public conversation" results. It is central to the model of deliberative democracy that it privileges such a public sphere of mutually interlocking and overlapping networks and associations of deliberation, contestation, and argumentation. The fiction of a general deliberative assembly in which the united people expressed their will belongs to the early history of democratic theory. Today our guiding model has to be that of a medium of loosely associated, multiple foci of opinion-formation and dissemination that affect each other in free and spontaneous processes of communication.[23]

IV. The Rawlsian Concept of Public Reason

The Rawlsian model of "public reason" and the deliberative model of democracy share certain fundamental premises.[24] Both theories view the legitimation of political power and the examination of the justice of institutions to be a public process, open to all citizens. The idea that the justice of institutions be "in the public's eye," so to speak, for the public to scrutinize, to examine, and to reflect upon is fundamental.[25] In three significant ways, the Rawlsian idea of public reason differs from the model of public deliberation proposed before. Some of these differences are of a sociological nature; others indicate significant philosophical divergences.

First, unlike the deliberative model, which insists on the openness of the agenda of public debate, Rawls restricts the exercise of public reason to deliberation about a specific subject matter. These are issues involving "constitutional essentials" and questions of basic justice.[26] Rawls's model of public reason proceeds from a *restricted agenda*.

Second, for Rawls public reason is best viewed not as a *process* of reasoning among citizens but as a regulative *principle* imposing limits upon how individuals, institutions, and agencies ought to reason about public matters. The limits of public reason are set by a "political conception of liberalism."[27]

Third, for Rawls the social spaces within which public reason is exercised are also restricted. The limits of public reason do not apply to personal deliberations and reflections about political questions or "to the reasoning about them by members of associations such as churches and universities, all of which is a vital part of the background culture."[28] The reasoning of corporate bodies and associations is "public" with respect to their members, "but nonpublic with respect to political society and to citizens generally. Nonpublic reasons comprise the many reasons of civil society and belong to what I have called the 'background culture', in contrast to the public political culture."[29] The public sphere, for Rawls then, is located not in civil society but in the state and its organizations, including first and foremost the legal sphere and its institutions.

Yet Rawls himself cannot sustain the distinction between "civil society" and the restricted conception of the public in two respects: first, in a constitutional democracy many, if not all, associations and organizations are also "public" bodies, for to become incorporated and recognized as a corporate body, they have to comply with the same constitutional essentials and the rule of law as do all other more obviously public institutions. Take the case of country clubs in the United States that discriminate against blacks, Jews, Hispanics, and so on. To be recognized as a legally incorporated entity under the due process of the law, such country clubs in recent years have had to change their charters. The constitutional-democratic state and the institutions of civil society are therefore not as sharply separable as some of Rawls's formulations suggest. All clubs, associations, and organizations within civil society have charters that can be subject to public as well as legal scrutiny.

Second, institutions, individuals, and movements in civil society attempt to influence the public-political process and in doing so cross the boundaries between public and more private-civil associations. For Rawls, this is the case with citizens who engage in political advocacy in the public forum and with members of political parties, candidates, and individuals supporting them.[30] But to say that when in civil society these individuals and associations are governed by one kind of reason, a non-public one, but that they have to respect the limits of public reason as soon as they enter the political arena, is erroneous, for civil society is also public. Civil society and its associations are not public in the sense of always allowing universal access to all, but they are public in the sense of being part of that anonymous public conversation in a democracy. A deliberative model of democracy is much more interested than Rawls in "background cultural conditions," precisely because politics and political reason are always seen to emerge out of a cultural and social context. Public reason can certainly distance itself from this context and evaluate it critically, but it can never completely render transparent all the background presuppositions that give rise to it. This is the kernel of truth in post-modernist critiques of Kantian rationalism: namely, that reason is always situated in a context that it can never render completely comprehensible to discursive analysis.

In these three respects, the Rawlsian model diverges from the deliberative model: the deliberative model does not restrict the agenda of public conversation; in fact, it encourages discourse about the lines separating the public from the private;[31] second, the deliberative model locates the public sphere in civil society[32] and is much more interested in the ways in which political processes and the "background culture" interact. Finally, while the Rawlsian model focuses upon "final and coercive political power," the deliberative model focuses on non-coercive and non-final processes of opinion formation in an unrestricted public sphere.[33]

Thus, it is not surprising that for Rawls the prime exemplar of the exercise of public reason is not the anonymous public but very often is and "ought to be" the Supreme Court: "public reason is well suited to be the court's reason in exercising its role as the highest judicial interpreter but not as the final interpreter of the higher law; and second, that the supreme court is the branch of government that serves as the exemplar of public reason."[34]

In recent discussions Rawls's concept of public reason has come under increasing scrutiny and criticism for presupposing an impossible separation of public reason from private convictions. Not only Tom McCarthy, writing from within a Habermasian framework,[35] but also Samuel Sheffler, who is much more sympathetic to Rawls's basic project, share this criticism.[36] To appreciate the force of these criticisms, consider briefly the abortion controversy that has raged in the United States since the 1973 Supreme Court ruling in *Roe v. Wade*. If those who defend the right to life, and believe that the fetus is a moral being that must be protected by the full force of the law, were to disassociate these "private" beliefs, as they exercise them in civil society and in other political associations, from the public arena, there would be no abortion controversy. Likewise, if those who believed in the centrality of the woman's right to choose whether to carry a pregnancy to term would limit this to the sphere of private morality alone, from their point of view they would have already conceded that argument to their opponents.[37] Most controversial moral, ethical, and political questions of our time—from abortion to pornography, from immigration rights to the implications of new medical technologies—would not even be on the agenda of public debate if those who participated in these struggles subscribed to Rawls's conception of "public reason." This conception of public reason is empirically flawed and sociologically limited for analyzing the public sphere of our societies.

Yet a more sympathetic reading of the Rawlsian view is possible: if one were to take public reason to refer to the logic of justification regarding constitutional essentials that *ought* to be put forward in a liberal-democratic society, then Rawls's claim has a certain plausibility: we do not want the highest courts of law in the land, and other significant decision-making instances, to appeal to abstruse scientific and theological doctrines when justifying public norms and principles, nor do we want them to bring in contested value questions and other comprehensive moral doctrines, which cannot possibly be shared by all in a pluralistic moral universe. Such doctrines and views, values and principles will nonetheless play a role in individual and collective deliberation processes. But Rawls is concerned that they do not find their way into the law books and legal doctrines of the land. Perhaps we would do better then to rename Rawls's view of public reason a doctrine of "public justification" and admit that it has little to do with the political speech and deliberation of ordinary citizens in the public market place.

Yet Rawls clearly has more than this in mind when he writes that the exercise of public reason imposes a "duty of civility" that the idea of democratic citizenship entails.[38] Whenever we are tempted to get sectarian and appeal to our deepest value convictions, we must ask ourselves, in Rawls's words: "How would our argument strike us, presented in the form of a supreme court opinion?"[39] Rawls certainly has a very idealized view of the reason exercised by the U.S. Supreme Court itself. A look at some recent decisions of the Court, like the *Bowers v. Hardwick* case, in which the Court sustained a Georgia statute that made engaging in acts of sodomy a criminally punishable offense, would show that the Court does not always exercise "public reason."[40]

Nonetheless, there is something both right and attractive in Rawls's demand that we, as citizens burdened with the duty of civility, should be ready to ask ourselves this question. It is not too far-fetched to discern in this Rawlsian requirement a political and institutionalist interpretation of the famous Kantian principle:

namely, that as moral beings we should only act upon those principles that we would want to be universalizable for all. Rawls is asking us to think of ourselves as legislators in a kingdom of ends. The core intuition of this Kantian position, which I share, is that all normative justification—moral, political, and legal—must present reasons that we would be ready to claim equally valid and fair for all involved. And around this point there is considerable convergence among all three theorists considered in this chapter. Arendt takes Kant's formulations on aesthetic judgment in the *Third Critique* and makes them the center of her theory of political judgment, namely, to woo the consent of everyone else with whom I know I must come to some agreement. Likewise, for Habermas discourse ethics is a reformulation of the Kantian universalizability principle. In discourse ethics, "[t]he basis of legitimacy becomes what all could will not as noumenal selves but as participants in practical discourse, whose adoption of the moral point of view enables them to transcend not only interest-oriented perspectives but also value-based perspectives."[41]

Thus, for all three theorists, the value of publicity would correspond to what I named its "epistemic" dimension: the normative requirement that for a principle, a law, a course of action to be deemed publicly acceptable, it must appear so from the standpoint of all involved. Participation in the public realm imposes the obligation to reverse perspectives and to be ready to think and reason from the standpoint of concerned others. This epistemic dimension was already implicit in the Kantian moral principle to act in such a way that the maxim of one's actions could be a universal law for all.

Herein lies, however, the aporia of the public sphere: the very concept of a public sphere forces us to think from the standpoint of all involved, whether we do this through enlarging our mentality as Arendt asks us to do, or through reasoning as Supreme Court justices would, as Rawls requires, or through reversing perspectives in practical dialogue, as Habermas urges. Yet, even after we engage in such processes of actual or virtual reasoning and dialogue, it is unlikely that we will have eliminated our differences, our clash of values and beliefs, the disparity among our deeply held convictions. Perhaps the very concept of the public sphere reeks of rationalist idealism: it seems to presuppose transparent selves who can know themselves and each other. At this point we can see that post-modernist skeptics, like Jean-François Lyotard, who question any method of universalizability; interest-group liberals who think that politics essentially is about bargaining on goods, some commensurable and some not; and advocates of "the politics of phenomenological positionality" will join hands.[42]

If the technological, sociological, and economic transformations of global capitalism appear to generate communication without deliberation, these philosophical considerations suggest another aporia: the illusion of being able to reach agreement in a world of incommensurable values, or "warring gods," to use Max Weber's phrase. Let me offer a defense of public sphere theories despite these aporias and difficulties.

V. Conclusion

I want to begin by noting that the concept of the public sphere is a regulative principle as well as constitutive fiction of democracy. It is a regulative principle because it articulates an ideal of deliberation and justification in the light of which we, as citizens, formulate our positions, dialogue with others, try to convince them of our point of view. Surely, the alternative to such practices of justification and public reasoning are many. Violence is inherent in the political; it lurks at the limits of the sayable and the communicable. To force others to accept our point of view rather than wooing them to see the good reasons behind it is a permanent temptation.

Equally, not violence but bargaining over incommensurables is possible. Here, one should distinguish between theories of the political that see this domain to be but an extension of the general logic of instrumental and market rationality dominant in the social realm—certain rational choice models for example—and other theories of the political, such as Donald Moon's and, increasingly, Tom McCarthy's, which recognize the need "to agree to disagree" about incommensurables.[43] A deliberative theory of democracy which is also a proceduralist theory of argumentation and conflict resolution incorporates the principle that disagreements at the first level can nonetheless concur about procedures at the second level, about rules of discourse and other institutional specifics that govern first-level disagreements and modes of living with them.

Whether such a separation between first- and second-order rules is possible to maintain philosophically as well as institutionally is a burning issue. Many of the debates raging today in multicultural democracies about group rights—and in particular, what Will Kymlicka has called group differentiated citizenship rights[44] turn around the viability and possibility of such a separation between first- and second-order rules of coexistence on the one hand and the articulation of cultural difference on the other.

As significant as such institutional agreements to disagree may be in the functioning of multicultural democracies, I would contend that they do not offer the solution to the pull and push of unity and multiplicity inherent in the concept of the public sphere. For in a democracy the public sphere is also a sphere of critique, contestation, and challenge. While such "modus vivendi" agreements, or what Cass Sunstein calls incompletely theorized agreements, are vital for the day-to-day functioning of democracies,[45] they may also be deeply oppressive and hierarchical and may hide power compromises rather than being the sites of genuine agreements. The public sphere is the domain in which such "pseudo-agreements" and compromises are critically examined, challenged, and called into question. It is also the sphere within which the lines of compromise separating the "public" and the "private" are debated. I do not at all question the necessity to draw a line between the private and the public spheres in all complex democratic societies, nor do I challenge the necessity to constitutionally anchor privacy rights in a fashion more sound than is currently the case in the U.S. Constitution, for example.[46] However, as a feminist democratic theorist I am also deeply suspicious of past and current practices of drawing these lines and about the legal and institutional compromises that have been reached around women's and children's rights. The task of the critical public sphere is to challenge the secret logic of power, hierarchy, and domination behind such modus vivendi agreements.

The institutional complexity of modern societies requires a differentiated model of public discourse and public justification. So far, deliberative democratic theories emerging out of the Habermasian discourse model, including my own previous work, have not been sufficiently attentive to the multiplicity of institutional configurations within the public sphere.[47] I would still agree with Habermas that the model of a deliberative public must occupy a "place d'hônneur" within such a theory precisely because it is the paradoxical ideal and fiction of democracy. Nonetheless, as my discussion of Rawls's concept of "public reason" has suggested, we should distinguish between legislative and adjudicative public spheres and their corresponding logics, between deliberative and decision-making public bodies and their corresponding constraints. Not only is the contemporary public sphere an anonymous conversation of interpenetrating discourses and debates, it is also a sphere in which different rules of appropriate and inappropriate speech and diverse logics of constraint meet and often clash with each other.

The citizens of complex democracies have an enormous work of institutional translation to do. They have to be able to see that what is appropriate to say in the heat of a public debate in the marketplace may not be appropriate if and when enunciated as the position of the Supreme Court of the land. The citizens of contemporary democracies have to negotiate the multiplicity of incommensurable institutional perspectives. Walter Lippmann was right to be pessimistic about all that is expected of democratic citizens: reflexivity about one's own value positions; the capacity to distance oneself from one's convictions and entertain them from the perspective of others; the ability to live with religious, ethical, and aesthetic incommensurables; the equanimity to accept the multiplicity of values and the clash of the gods in a disenchanted universe—these are the cognitive and moral qualities that a democratic public sphere requires from its citizens, undoubtedly a task at which individuals and nations will often fail.

So far I have focused on the legislative and deliberative, that is, the narrowly political public sphere. In our societies the lines separating the political from the cultural and from the religious, scientific, and aesthetic public realms are porous. In the life world of the civil societies of complex, multicultural democracies, a film can become the instigator and the occasion for a complex dialogue on political membership, media representation, and structures of everyday prejudice—take the contributions of the director Spike Lee, for example, to the debate about race and, in particular, black-white relations in the United States.

The recent prominence of cultural politics and identity-based political movements all over the world suggests that the decentering as well as democratization of the public sphere in the last three decades has brought with it many new and different voices. The decentered public sphere has become the site where hitherto excluded and marginalized groups—women all over the world, non-Christian and non-white ex-, post-, and neo-colonial peoples, gays and lesbians—use the new means and channels of communication to carry out their cultural and political struggles. The electronic media in particular are becoming the "site" in which value wars are waged, identities fashioned, needs renegotiated, images of the good life circulated. Nancy Fraser has coined the felicitous phrase the "subaltern publics" to describe these new developments.[48]

The ever increasing fluidity of lines between culture and politics brings with it great hope as well as danger. On the one hand, the cultivation of qualities of mind and character of democratic citizenship will partially take place through immersion in these new multiple subaltern publics. On the other hand, I am skeptical about what I shall call the iconographic medium of the electronic means of representation. There is a tendency in the electronic media toward the presentation of the individual as a type, as an icon of a position, of a movement, of an idea, of a perspective. Increasingly, the complexity and ambivalence of all individual lives, the opacity and mystery of our inner beings are hollowed out as we are reduced to simplistic social, cultural, and political positions, easily recognizable by a public of viewers that is itself equally flattened and hollowed out. The public becomes the phantom applause and laughter that accompany American sit-coms, a reminder that this line was funny, that here we were supposed to laugh, cry, or sigh.

What is of concern in this trend toward the iconographic public is not the decline of aesthetic value alone. Rather, it is worrisome that the qualities of mind that all public sphere theorists emphasize—let me briefly refer to them with Kant's phrase "the enlarged mentality"—may not be served by these developments. The iconographic public sphere flattens out the complexity and the co-constitution of self and other perspectives. It freezes in space and time, whether in one's moral imagination or one's mode of argumentation, the incessant negotiations of understanding and misunderstanding, interpretation and reinterpretation that the communicative practices of the everyday life world involve.

To recognize and to come to grips with the implications of its own diversity, a democratic people needs to reenact its identity in the public sphere. As with individuals, so with collectivities, threats of being different that are not diffused turn into resentment toward others. The free public sphere in a democratic polity must allow equal access to all groups within civil society to re-present themselves in public. In entering the public, every new social, cultural, or political group presents its point of view to others, or it re-presents itself to others, in the sense of refashioning itself as a presence in the public. This process of self-representation and articulation in public is still the only means through which the *civic imagination* can be cultivated. The process of articulating good reasons in public forces one to think from the standpoint of all others to whom one is trying to make one's point of view plausible and cogent, and to whom one is trying to tell one's own story. The ability of individuals and groups to take the standpoint of others into account, to be able to reverse perspectives and see the world from their point of view, is a crucial virtue of moral and aesthetic imagination in a civic polity. Certainly this ability becomes most necessary, as well as most fragile, under conditions of incommensurability and social opacity. The public sphere is like the pupil in the eye of the body politic; when its vision is murky, cloudy, or hindered, the sense of direction of the polity is also impaired.

Notes

This essay has previously appeared in *Theoria: A Journal of Social and Political Theory* Dec. 1997), no. 90, pp. 1–25.

1. Walter Lippmann, *The Phantom Public*, with a new introduction by W. M. McClay, New Brunswick, N.J.: Transaction Publishers, 1993.

2. John Dewey, *The Public and Its Problems*, Chicago: Swallow Press, 1954. (First published in 1927.)

3. Dewey, *The Public*, pp. 117–118.

4. Yet this continuing nostalgia and irritation about the public—has it ever existed? can it be revived?—is accompanied by a burst of contemporary research about the topic

in the humanities and social sciences. Female participation in the salons of the European Enlightenment, as well as the end put by the French Revolution to women's political activism, has been extensively studied in recent years (Deborah Hertz, Joan Landes, Dana Goodman); the formation of multiple publics, defined along class, gender, and national lines, has been scrutinized in the European as well as American contexts (Oskar Negt and Alexander Kluge, Geoffrey Ely, Daniel Gordon, David Bell, Mary Ryan, Linda Kerber). Since the transformations of 1989 in East-Central Europe, and the former Soviet Union, the formation of an independent public sphere has assumed a major place in the project of reconstructing democracy in these societies as well (Arato & Cohen). Perhaps what distinguishes the more recent scholarship and theorizing in this area from the work of Lippmann and Dewey, Arendt and Habermas, is the less nostalgic but increasingly more *historicist* approaches to the plethora of phenomena referred to by the terms public, public sphere, and public space. In much of this recent work, the "normative" dimension of the public is no longer at the center. What has replaced the earlier preoccupations with the normative decline of the public is instead a multiplicity of empirical analyses showing the variety, diversity, and often incommensurability of the experiences with the public of differing groups, divided along class, gender, race, national, and occupational lines. Our knowledge of the richness and variety of the public experiences of different groups has expanded, while the normative relevance of the concept within a theory of democracy has receded.

5. See C. Wright Mills, *The Power Elite*, New York: Oxford University Press, 1956. Mills's distinction between "public" and "mass" is based on his theory of social control. It is doubtful in the days of the Internet, radio talk shows, cable TV, ham radio operators, and other innumerable forms of access to means of communication by diverse groups that Mills's social control theory of the masses would hold water. In the contemporary situation, the carriers of this anonymous public conversation have become so diffuse, inchoate, and varied that even the contrast between the "public" and "mass" is too flat to capture the changing nature of the public in the age of the information revolution.

6. Hannah Arendt, *The Human Condition*, 8th edition, Chicago: University of Chicago Press, 1973, pp. 46ff. (First published in 1958.)

7. A more detailed account of Arendt's theory of modernity is presented in my book *The Reluctant Modernism of Hannah Arendt*, Thousand Oaks, California: Sage Publications, 1996.

8. I have presented a more detailed discussion of these issues in "The Pariah and Her Shadow," *Political Theory*, vol. 23, no. 1, February 1995, pp. 5–24; reprinted in *Feminist Interpretations of Hannah Arendt*, by Bonnie Honig, University Park, Penn.: Pennsylvania State University Press, 1995, pp. 83–105.

9. Arendt, *Human Condition*, p. 56.

10. See also my earlier essay "Models of Public Space. Hannah Arendt, The Liberal Tradition, and Jüergen Habermas," in *Situating the Self: Gender, Community and Postmodernism in Contemporary Ethics*, New York: Routledge, 1992, pp. 89–121.

11. See in particular, Arendt, *Lectures on Kant's Political Philosophy* (ed. and with an interpretive essay by Ronald Beiner), Chicago: University of Chicago Press, 1982; but also, *Between Past and Future: Six Exercises in Political Thought*, New York: Meridian Books, 1961, and *Crises of the Republic*, New York: Harcourt, Brace & Jovanovich, 1969.

12. Arendt, "Crisis in Culture," in *Between Past and Future*, pp. 220–221.

13. Jürgen Habermas, *Strukturwandel der Oeffentlichkeit*, Darmstadt und Neuwied: Hermann Luchterhand, 1962 (transl. into English by Thomas Burger, with the assistance of Frederick Lawrence), *The Structural Transformation of the Public Sphere: An Inquiry into a Category of Bourgeois Society*, Cambridge, Mass.: MIT Press, 1991.

14. Habermas, *Structural Transformation*, pp. 4ff.

15. Habermas, *Structural Transformation*, pp. 28ff.

16. Habermas, *Structural Transformation*, pp. 36ff.

17. See Habermas's statement "Public debate was supposed to transform *voluntas* into a *ratio* that in the public competition of private arguments came into being as the consensus about what was necessary in the interest of all" (in *Structural Transformation*, p. 83).

18. See S. Benhabib, *Situating the Self: Gender, Community and Postmodernism in Contemporary Ethics*, New York: Routledge, 1992.

19. Parts of this section have appeared before as Benhabib, "Deliberative Rationality and Models of Democratic Legitimacy," in *Constellations—An International Journal of Critical and Social Theory*, ed. by Andrew Arato & Seyla Benhabib, vol. 1, no. 1, April 1994, pp. 26–53; a revised and expanded version can be found in *Democracy and Difference: Contesting the Boundaries of the Political*, ed. by Seyla Benhabib, Princeton, N.J.: Princeton University Press, 1996.

20. My formulation is wholly akin to that proposed by Joshua Cohen, "Deliberation and Democratic Legitimacy," in *The Good Polity—Normative Analysis of the State*, ed. by Alan Hamlin and Philip Pettit, London: Basil Blackwell, 1989, pp. 17–34; see also Josh Cohen, "Procedure and Substance in Deliberative Democracy," in *Democracy and Difference*.

21. This argument presupposes the general line of interpretation set forth in *Situating the Self* in chapters 1, 2, and 3 in particular and documents my effort to apply the principles of discourse ethics to political-institutional life. Independently of the project of discourse ethics but in fascinating affinity to it, in recent years there has been a revival of deliberative models of democracy among political theorists and legal philosophers. See in particular Frank T. Michelman, "Law's Republic," *Yale Law Journal*, vol. 93, 1984, pp. 1013ff; Cass R. Sunstein, "Beyond the Republican Revival," *Yale Law Journal*, vol. 97, 1988, p. 1539.

22. Hannah Arendt, "Crisis in Culture," in *Between Past and Future*, pp. 220–221.

23. For a recent statement of the transformation of the concept of the public sphere from a centralized to a decentered model, see Jürgen Habermas, "Ist der Herzschlag der Revolution zum Stillstand gekommen? Volkssouveräenitaet als Verfahren. Ein normativer Begriff der Oeffentlichkeit?" in *Die Ideen von 1789*, ed. by Forum fur Philosophie Bad Homburg, Frankfurt: Suhrkamp, 1989, pp. 7ff.

24. In addition to John Rawls's *Political Liberalism*, New York: Columbia University Press, 1993, see also the manuscript "On the Idea of Free Public Reason" (lecture delivered at the "Liberalism and the Moral Life" Conference at CUNY in April 1988); and the article "The Idea of an Overlapping Consensus," *Oxford Journal of Legal Studies*, vol. 7, no. 1, 1987, for a development of Rawls's views on the matter. A great deal more needs to be said about the contrast of these two projects than I can undertake in this section, but see also Thomas McCarthy, "Kantian Constructivism and Reconstructivism: Rawls and Habermas in Dialogue," *Ethics*, vol. 105, no. 1, October 1994, pp. 44–64.

25. Rawls, *Political Liberalism*, p. 214.

26. See Rawls, *Political Liberalism*, pp. 223 ff. In his comments on an earlier version of this argument delivered in the Political Theory Colloquium of the Department of Government at Harvard University (spring 1994), Stephen Macedo construed these remarks to mean that I was attributing to Rawls some kind of infringement or limitation upon First Amendment rights of free speech and expression. This is a misunderstanding of the phrase "restricted agenda." Obviously, Rawls's theory does not restrict the exercise of the most extensive basic liberty of free speech compatible with the like liberty of all; the lexical ordering of the two principles of justice means that the principle of basic rights and liberties cannot be simply abrogated. My phrase "restricted agenda" refers to what Rawls's conception of public reason considers as being the *proper domain* or *subject matter* of public reason. This is less a question of free speech rights and limitations of them than a question of one's social theory of civil society and democratic politics.

27. Rawls, *Political Liberalism*, p. 227.

28. Rawls, *Political Liberalism*, p. 215.
29. Rawls, *Political Liberalism*, p. 220.
30. Rawls, *Political Liberalism*, p. 215.
31. See Benhabib, "Models of the Public Sphere," in *Situating the Self*, pp. 89–121.
32. For a broad statement of the theoretical and political significance of the project of civil society to contemporary democracy, see Jean Cohen and Andrew Arato, *Civil Society and Political Theory*, Cambridge, Mass.: MIT Press, 1992.
33. The question of coercion would have to be dealt with in the context of the institutionalization of deliberative processes. It is within this framework as well that issues of closure, decision-making prerogatives, and jurisdictions would have to be articulated.
34. Rawls, *Political Liberalism*, p. 231. Rawls draws the distinction between the Court as the "highest" judicial interpreter of the Constitution as opposed to being the "final" interpreter of the higher law, because, following Bruce Ackerman, he wants to retain a principle of popular sovereignty, respecting the will of "We the People."
35. Thomas McCarthy, "Kantian Constructivism and Reconstructivism: Rawls and Habermas in Dialogue," *Ethics*, vol. 105, no. 1, October 1994, p. 52.
36. Samuel Sheffler, "The Appeal of Political Liberalism," in *Ethics*, vol. 105, no. 1, October 1994, p. 16.
37. In a footnote to his discussion of "The Idea of Public Reason," Rawls upholds a version of the *Roe v. Wade* decision that leaves the decision concerning whether or not to carry a pregnancy to term in the first trimester up to the woman and her physician. He maintains that "at this early stage of pregnancy the political value of the equality of women is overriding, and this right is required to give it substance and force" (*Political Liberalism*, p. 243). Note, however, that in resting the right of abortion in the first trimester upon the premise of the "equality of women," Rawls himself departs from the judgment of the Supreme Court, which based this right upon "privacy" rather than equality. See *Roe et al. v. Wade*, decided January 22 through March 21, 1973, in United States Reports, vol. 410; see in particular section 8 of Justice Blackmun's decision. Whether one bases the right of a woman to abortion on a conception of her equal citizenship rights or on the right to privacy of all persons under the U.S. Constitution is no minor matter of doctrinal or judicial interpretation. These issues too are part of the public debate and discourse about abortion rights. The point illustrates Rawls's erroneous assumption that "there are many nonpublic reasons and but one public reason" (*Political Liberalism*, p. 220).
38. Rawls, *Political Liberalism*, pp. 253–254.
39. Rawls, *Political Liberalism*, p. 254.
40. *Bowers v. Hardwick et al.*, June 30, 1986, United States Reports, vol. 478.
41. Thomas McCarthy, "Practical Discourse: On the Relation of Morality to Politics," in *Ideals and Illusions: On Reconstruction and Deconstruction in Contemporary Critical Theory*, Cambridge, Mass.: MIT Press, 1991, p. 182.
42. Indeed, theorists of incommensurability, like Jean-François Lyotard, and phenomenological positionality, like Iris Young, all emphasize the impossibility and ultimately undesirability of reversing perspectives, of there being "symmetry" in moral perspectives. Their argument is that such normative exhortations are not a plea to respect "alterity," the irreducible otherness of the others, but rather a gesture of imperialistic universalism that reduces otherness to likeness and incommensurability to fungibility (see J-F. Lyotard, *The Differend: Phrases in Dispute* (transl. by Georges Van Den Abbeele), Minneapolis: University of Minnesota Press, 1989; and Iris Young, "Communication and the Other: Beyond Deliberative Democracy," in *Democracy and Difference: Contesting the Boundaries of the Political*, ed. by Seyla Benhabib, pp. 120–137; Iris Young, "Asymmetrical Reciprocity: On Moral Respect, Wonder, and Enlarged Thought," in *Constellations: An International Journal of Critical and Democratic Theory*, ed. by Andrew Arato and Seyla Benhabib, vol. 3, no. 3, January 1997, pp. 340–364). I have dealt with some aspects of

Iris Young's important criticisms in Benhabib, "Toward a Deliberative Model of Democratic Legitimacy," in *Democracy and Difference*, pp. 81–84.

43. See J. Donald Moon, *Constructing Community: Moral Pluralism and Tragic Conflicts*, Princeton, N.J.: Princeton University Press, 1993; T. A. McCarthy, note 37 and "Practical Discourse: On the Relation of Morality and Politics," in *Ideals and Illusions*. For critical perspectives on the concept of self-interest in politics, see *Beyond Self-Interest*, ed. by Jane J. Mansbridge, Chicago: University of Chicago Press, 1990.

44. See William Kymlicka, *Multicultural Citizenship*, Oxford: Clarendon Press, 1995, and "Three Forms of Group-Differentiated Citizenship in Canada," in *Democracy and Difference*, ed. by Seyla Benhabib, pp. 153–171.

45. Cass R. Sunstein, "Incompletely Theorized Agreements," in *Harvard Law Review*, vol. 108, no. 7, May 1995, pp. 1733–1772.

46. For a powerful defense of privacy rights, see Jean Cohen, "Redescribing Privacy: Identity, Difference, and the Abortion Controversy," *Columbia Journal of Gender and Law*, vol. 3, no. 1, 1992, pp. 43–117.

47. In my earlier article "Toward a Deliberative Model of Democratic Legitimacy" (in *Democracy and Difference*, ed. by Benhabib, pp. 67–95), I signaled the questions that would arise through irreconcilable value and moral differences (p. 93, fn. 41) but did not really explicate how the deliberative democracy framework could accommodate such issues. My current work on "Democracy and Identity: In Search of the Civic Polity," *Philosophy and Social Criticism*, vol. 24, no. 2/3 (1998), pp. 85–100, focuses on these issues from the perspective of citizenship rights and normative incorporation in regimes of cultural differences.

48. Nancy Fraser, "Rethinking the Public Sphere: A Contribution to the Critique of Actually Existing Democracy," in *Habermas and the Public Sphere*, ed. by Craig Calhoun, Cambridge: MIT Press, 1991, pp. 109–142.

12

MORALLY SPEAKING

Gerald Dworkin

> In 1977, when Havel was arrested, he sent the public prosecutor a request for his release which he formulated "in a way that at the time seemed extremely tactical and cunning: while saying nothing I did not believe or that was untrue, I simply 'overlooked' the fact that truth lies not only in what is said, but also in who says it, and to whom, why, how, and under what circumstances it is expressed."
>
> For a priest, boundaries aren't important. They mean nothing, in fact less than nothing: it's a kind of duty that they be ignored. A priest can say anything as long as it's the truth. He never has to worry if it's his place to say it: every place is his place, since he has no place of his own. . . . If he sees it as the truth he has to say it.
>
> Mary Gordon
> *The Rest of Life*, p. 41

This chapter is a study in the pragmatics of moral discourse. It concerns who can say what to whom. It will, therefore, focus on moral reasoning as dialogue. First-person moral reasoning may also best be thought of as a dialogue of the person with herself, but at least initially I shall be focusing on reasoning that takes place between at least two persons.

Traditional theorists of language have made a tri-partite distinction of aspects of language: syntax, semantics, and pragmatics. The syntax of the language involves its grammatical structure, how its parts go together. The semantics of the language involve how it hooks onto the world, how its parts get a meaning. The pragmatics of the language concern how people use a language to accomplish certain effects, or what people must presuppose, or assume, in order to make sense of what other people say. Almost all recent moral philosophy has focused on the syntax or the semantics of moral discourse. Discussions of moral realism, or prescriptivism, or projectivism, or naturalism, have concentrated on the syntax (are moral statements disguised imperatives?) or semantics (do they have truth value?). My methodological hypothesis is that examining the pragmatic aspects of moral discourse may throw light on various moral phenomena that remain unilluminated by the exclusive concentration on syntax and semantics.

I.

Let me set the stage by presenting a number of different cases in which, intuitively, it looks as if something has gone wrong in the making of various moral statements.

- A. Two burglars are breaking into a house. One says to the other, "You are doing something immoral and illegal."
- B. A judge says to a defendant: "I know you are probably innocent of this crime, but you deserve to be punished for other crimes you committed but were never charged with so I am going to punish you anyway."
- C. I say to someone suffering from spina bifida: "It would have been better (the world would have been a better place) if you had never been born."
- D. I do not accept p as unjust. You do. I complain to you that an unjust standard p is being applied to me. In fact, p is actually unjust.
- E. A says about B, "He has led a very difficult life and should not be held responsible for the bad things he does."
  A says of himself, "I have led a very difficult life and should not be held responsible for the bad things I have done."
- F. A protester against capital punishment says about a convicted murderer, "He ought not to be executed. He has a right to life."
  The murderer, protesting against his execution, says "I have a right to life."
- G. Someone is drowning a short distance from the shore. A turns to his companion B and says: "Somebody ought to rescue that person."
- H. After a life of debauchery, A has reformed. Seeing B drinking too much, he harshly criticizes B for failing to live a life of sobriety.
- I. A supporter of the Israeli state argues that only Jews have a right to criticize the policy of that state toward Palestinians. Others, who would make the very same criticisms, ought to refrain from doing so, and ought not to be heeded if they do.
- J. The talented say to the untalented, "You ought to give us a larger share of wealth, because if you do so we will work harder and you will be better off."[1]

These are, intentionally, very different types of situations. However, they all have at least the following in common. Each statement is true, or warranted, or whatever substitutes for epistemic approval in one's meta-ethical theory. Each statement is itself a moral assessment or directly relevant to a moral assessment. And there is something inappropriate about the making of the statement in the particular context.

There is something about the person who makes the statement, or the person to whom it is being made, or the circumstances in which it is made, that results in some, as Austin would put it, infelicity.

By seeing just where and why something has gone wrong, I hope to find out something interesting about our moral discourse—something that we would not discover if we concentrated simply on the "logic" of moral statements. The task of classifying the different ways in which things can go wrong is itself a very large project. In this chapter I want to concentrate on one, very large category, that of making a criticism of another along a dimension on which one is also at fault. I shall call this "hypocrisy," although that term covers a much broader range of acts.

II.

In the Sermon on the Mount, Jesus asks, "How can you say to your brother, 'Let me take the speck out of your eye' when all the time there is that plank in your own?"[2] Note that the issue is precisely what one can *say*, not what is the case. For it may very well be that there is a speck in the eye of the brother.

And it is important that the notion is one of what one "can" say—as opposed to what one "ought" to say. We are not dealing with the idea, familiar from consequentialists, that certain utterances, while they may be true, ought not to be uttered because their utterance will lead to worse consequences. It may be that the brother, perceiving his brother's plank, will be less likely to change his behavior as a result of the criticism; that is, it will be counter-productive. But that is not the point of Christ's statement.

The charge is that the speaker is "not in a position to" lodge a certain moral criticism against another, in spite of the fact that the criticism is accurate and correct. There are a number of possible ways in which a speaker might not be entitled to his criticism, but I want to concentrate on hypocritical criticism.

An important point to note is that the infelicity may be weakened or reduced or canceled depending on what the criticizer believes about himself and how the conversation goes on. Consider, for example, the case of the two burglars breaking into the house. Suppose the second burglar says, "But you are doing the very same thing I am. How can you criticize me?" Here are various possible continuations:

1. Yes, I know. But I am too old to change my ways. There is still a chance for a youngster like you.
2. Yes, but I need to do this. My wife has to have an operation.
3. Yes, I know. But I have been trying to reform. I even arranged to be out of town today so I couldn't be here, but my ride fell through.
4. But, you asked for my opinion.

A more accurate way of formulating the issue, then, is that there is an initial inappropriateness that calls for some kind of further clarification to remove. My question is what accounts for the initial situation.

One objection might be that the speaker is not in a position to assess the criticism as accurate. So, for example, a woman might resent a man's criticism of some act of sexism because she feels that he really doesn't know what it feels like to be the target of such acts. But this doesn't seem to be what has gone wrong in our example. It is not as if the plank in my eye blinds me to the presence of the speck in my brother's. In fact, it could be argued that having the same fault makes one sensitive to its presence in others. This is relevant if what was involved was just a matter of a discovery being announced. But in the cases we are concerned with, a criticism is being voiced. The defect has something to do with when one is in a position to make a criticism of another.

It is not at all clear what the presuppositions in question are. Is it that in order to be in a position to level a criticism, in this case of the presence of a fault or defect of character, one must not oneself possess the fault or defect? This seems far too strong.

Is it, perhaps, that only if our fault is less prominent or strong we may criticize its presence in others—as is suggested by the metaphor of speck and plank? This runs counter to the fact that it would not be hypocritical for one to criticize a fault in others that was less significant than a fault one had, as long as it was a different fault. It is not a matter of one's relative purity, so that what is inappropriate is the less pure criticizing the more pure. What seems crucial is that the fault one is criticizing is the very same fault one has.

Does it make a difference whether one is aware one has the same fault? Is it merely possessing the fault, or is it the belief that one has the fault, which makes it inappropriate to criticize others? Suppose someone believed they had the trait but in fact were mistaken about this. The same charge of hypocrisy would hold. So belief is sufficient for the charge.

When we say that someone is "in no position to" make a certain claim, is this always relative to his belief about his position or, so to speak, to his actual location? Perhaps this issue should not be resolved at this point, but we should let the discussion about why we have any such restriction settle it. When we understand the point of having such conditions, we may be able to see whether such conditions are subjective or objective.

Let us assume that at least roughly the idea is that one is not entitled to make a moral criticism of another person with respect to some faulty character trait, or the failure to act correctly, when one possesses the same trait to roughly the same degree, or one has acted, or is prepared to act, in a similar fashion. Let us call this the requirement. Why should moral discourse have this feature? What point or purpose is secured by requiring that the person launching a criticism not be guilty of the same fault?

In general, two kinds of explanation would make sense of such a requirement. One shows that some end served by making moral criticisms would be served by the requirement. The other shows that some constitutive feature of moral criticism is served by the requirement.

Why do we assess as wrong, criticize, or blame the traits and actions of other people? The answer to this is actually rather complicated. It will not do to simply say, "in order to get them to change." When, for example, the person being criticized is dead, or we have reason to believe is so corrupt that he will not change, or the assessment is made to a person other than the person being criticized, we cannot be trying, at least directly, to change the person being criticized. We may be simply trying to get the record straight. We may be expressing our resentment at the way we have been treated. We may be trying to show something about ourselves, perhaps that we recognize what is going on. We may be trying to manifest solidarity with others. Or we may be trying to influence others to change.

However, as I said at the beginning, I am concentrating on the dialogue between the person criticizing and the person being criticized. In most such cases we have, at least as one of our aims, a desire to have the person make some change in behavior, or dispositions, or character traits. How would such aims be facilitated by the presence of the requirement?

In the central cases, we are dealing with someone whom we regard as a member of the moral community. He may be defective in some ways, but he is not someone who is immune to moral criticism. Just as the Kantian procedure—asking whether the maxim of one's action can be made universal law—is best thought of as being used by a person who seeks to guide her actions by the right, rather than a skeptic or a person trying to justify an immoral act. So we ought to think of practical criticism as a practice in which both parties are seeking to do what is right and to foster desirable character traits.

What we want in a critic is someone who is a reliable detector of the normative. We want to build into our practice of criticism features that increase the likelihood that criticisms will be accurate, fair, and reasonable. The requirement says that one is only entitled to make criticisms when one does not suffer from the defect in question. From the standpoint of reliability, does the requirement make sense?

Let us call those who possess the same trait they criticize the "guilty" and those who do not the "innocent." Is there any reason to think the innocent are more reliable detectors of the normatively valid than the guilty? It seems to me that the matter is rather complicated, and it is not at all obvious that this is so. At the extremes, that is, the saintly and the wicked, one might think it plausible. But in the messy middle, where we are all located and where most moral criticism takes place, it is not at all clear. My own experience is that I am most keenly aware of the faults in others that I myself suffer. I am much more likely to be completely unaware of traits that I do not share, sometimes because I cannot even imagine that I, and therefore others, might have them.

It is useful to make the comparison with cognitive criticism. Suppose I criticize you for not going over your calculations and checking for arithmetical mistakes. This happens to be something that I fail to do on a regular basis as well. Does the fact that I have the same cognitive defect make me a less reliable detector of the trait in others? Do we have the same intuition that I am not in a position to make the correction? In both cases, my inclination is to say no. There seems to be something different about the moral case, and the difference does not seem to lie in the direction of reliability. If this is true, it is particularly interesting because it would mean that some feature at work is special to morality as a sub-set of the normative. The cognitive criticism is also normative. It seeks to change how you should behave, to make your performance better. It holds you to a norm or standard. Yet the notion of hypocritical criticism seems less relevant.

My suggestion is that we look for a feature tied to moral dispositions but not (at least necessarily) linked to reliability. I take my cue here from a passage by Bernard

Williams who speaks of "the ethically important disposition that consists in a desire to be respected by people whom, in turn, one respects. In particular, they may have a motivation to avoid the disapproval of other people—for instance, their blame."[3]

The idea here is that the sanctions of morality—censure, ostracism, blame, disapproval, disgust—operate effectively only when they resonate with the person being sanctioned. The target of criticism feels that she is being distanced from a person, or a moral community, that she sees as legitimate and worthy. It is not sufficient that the criticism be correct or accurate. It must come from a source whose criticism I care about. It is because the criticism causes me to lose status in the eyes of the person who makes the criticism that it moves me.

Now we have an explanation for the requirement. When the person who calls attention to my character fault suffers from the very same fault, this puts him on a par with me—with respect to this fault at least. If I lose respect in his eyes because of the presence of this fault, he must lose respect in my eyes as well. But this means that I do not care as much whether he disapproves of my conduct. And this means that the criticism cannot be as effective as it normally would have been.[4]

Here is another way of looking at this point. It has often been noted that moral criticism operates somewhat as legal sanctions do to affect behavior. Criticism is a way of giving someone a "hard time." But it is not just any old way of giving that person a hard time. For example, with respect to legal sanctions, the attitude behind them can be expressed directly as "we are going to give you a hard time because we don't like the way you are behaving and are trying to deter you from continuing." I don't have to see the dislike as "legitimate" in order to recognize that I will be better off if I change my behavior.

But with moral criticism (leaving aside for the moment questions of what can be done to me by the criticizer and her friends) the attitude expressed before cuts no ice. The "hard time" at issue is just the fact that you disapprove of my behavior. Unless this resonates with me, unless I care about your judgments of me, it provides me no motive for change. In a world of rational egoists, the only force of criticism is its predictive value as to what further things might be done to me—for example, ostracism. But in our world, a world of moralized agents, we value being valued by those we value.

Another way of putting the same point, again similar to something that Williams says about blame, is that moral criticism is part of an effort to recognize and recruit agents into a common moral community. For such a practice to be effective, the critic must be recognized as a member of that community in good standing. By manifesting the very trait that she criticizes in me, she undercuts her membership. To avoid such self-defeat, she must produce one of the ways of going on that I mentioned earlier. By doing so, she recognizes she shares the defect and that this is consistent with her criticism.

I have been using the example of hypocritical criticism as a case study of moral pragmatics.[5] What I hope to have shown is that investigating the pragmatic features of moral discourse can increase our understanding of moral phenomena. In particular, investigating in a systematic fashion the idea of "being in a position" to make various moral judgments will be an important tool for distinguishing the "moral" from the larger class of normative judgments within which it resides.[6]

Notes

1. This example comes from G. A. Cohen's Tanner lectures. My thinking about these issues stems from reading those lectures in manuscript. Cohen is the first (and only) person to my knowledge who has commented on the phenomenon in question.

2. Matthew 7.3–5.

3. "Internal Reasons and the Obscurity of Blame," in *Making Sense of Humanity* (Cambridge, 1995) p. 41.

4. Yuval Eylon points out that a similar situation exists with respect to praise. A compliment from a generous person about one's own generosity means more than a similar compliment from an ungenerous one. My account, when extended to praise, seems to work in this case as well.

5. Among other areas that need exploration is clarification of what is involved in accepting a standard of conduct for oneself. One would want to distinguish between internalizing such a standard, i.e., conforming one's behavior to it, approving the standard, i.e., judging that it is good to be so disposed, and being bound by the standard, i.e., having the appropriate feelings if one (or others) does not live up to it.

6. I want to thank Yuval Eylon for his constructive and helpful comments at the conference. I also want to thank Charles Chastain for being skeptical about the phenomenon in question.